CHINA HANDS

CHINA HANDS

The Globe and Mail in Peking

Charles Taylor, Editor

McClelland and Stewart Limited

Photo Credits: All photographs *The Globe and Mail* except as follows: Allen Abel: pages 339 bottom, 341, 351; John Burns: pages 2, 12, 155 bottom, 168 top, 185 top; Bryan Johnson: pages 282, 297 top, 325 top and bottom, 329; Elizabeth MacCallum: pages 244, 265 top and bottom; Colin McCullough: page 111; Ross H. Munro: pages 205, 225; Frederick Nossal: pages 24, 28, 32; David Oancia: pages 78 top, 79, 86, 87 top and bottom, 101; Stanley Oziewicz: pages 305 top and bottom, 310, 311 top, 317, 321, 324, 339 top; Lorie Sculthorp: page 311 bottom; Charles Taylor: pages 51, 65; Norman Webster: pages 127, 129, 132, 133 bottom, 145 bottom, 146, 147.

The Canadian Publishers
McClelland and Stewart Limited
25 Hollinger Road, Toronto M4B 3G2

Canadian Cataloguing in Publication Data

Main entry under title:
China hands

Selections by journalists who manned the Globe and Mail Peking bureau from 1959–1984, originally published in The Globe and Mail.
ISBN 0–7710–8436–6

1. China — Foreign opinion, Canadian. 2. China — Social life and customs — 1949–   3. Foreign correspondents — Canada — Biography. 4. Foreign correspondents — China — Biography. I. Taylor, Charles, 1935–   II. The Globe and Mail.

DS779.23.C48   1984   951.05   C84–099240–8

Printed and bound in Canada

CONTENTS

PREFACE

This is the story of 25 years in the life of the Chinese People's Republic, as seen by 11 *Globe and Mail* correspondents who were based in Peking between 1959 and 1984. In China's long history, a quarter century is only an eye-blink: given the durability of some previous dynasties, the Communists must still be regarded as relative newcomers. Yet few periods have brought such dramatic and often profound changes in the day-to-day existence of ordinary Chinese, in the structure of their society and in China's relations with the outside world.

When the late Frederick Nossal arrived in Peking in the autumn of 1959 (to open the first Western newspaper bureau since the Communist victory a decade earlier), he joined a mere handful of foreign residents and soon came to share their overwhelming sense of isolation from the Chinese all around them. Peking still paid deference to Moscow as the leader of the Communist world, and its hostility to the West was strident and apparently implacable. The Chinese economy was staggering from Mao Tsetung's drastic programs to regiment the peasants and to stir industry into a "Great Leap Forward". At the same time, city dwellers in particular were subjected to relentless political campaigns.

There would be enormous changes during the subsequent quarter century. In 1984, Allen Abel was reporting from a capital that was filled with Western businessmen and tourists. In the post-Mao era, the new leaders were actively pursuing their "opening to the West", along with moderate economic policies that had always been abhorrent to the Maoists.

Between Nossal and Abel, the other *Globe* correspondents reported on the rift with Moscow, "Ping-Pong diplomacy" and the historic visit of President Richard Nixon. They also covered the violent turmoil of the Cultural Revolution, the deaths of Mao and Chou Enlai, the overthrow of the Gang of Four, the brief-lived Democracy Movement and the in-again, out-again fortunes of Deng Xiaoping. On trips that ranged from Manchuria in the far northeast to Tibet in the remote southwest, they explored communes and factories, markets and housing estates, schools and theatres. From these trips — and from interviews, official newspapers and unofficial contacts — they pieced together a picture of political and economic upheaval, of disastrous failures and dramatic achievements. Above all, they outlined the transition of an ancient civilization into a modern power, and the effect of this struggle on the Chinese masses.

This selection of stories and photographs emphasizes the first-hand observations of the 11 correspondents. It attempts to convey the look and feel of Chinese cities and the Chinese countryside during a quarter century of turbulent change. Although each of the correspondents wrote lengthy articles of political and economic analysis, these have been largely sacrificed in favor of more vivid stories based on direct experience — whether it be Ross Munro describing the great riot in Tienanmen Square, John Burns discovering the ice-fishers in the Valley of the Ming Tombs or John Fraser addressing a vast crowd of democracy activists. Throughout the period there was no shortage of pundits who pontificated on China from afar or on the basis of brief visits. But *The Globe and Mail* maintained a bureau on the spot and staffed it with inquisitive observers. This, then, is a reporters' book.

The stories in this book describe events and changes that were often baffling at the time. In retrospect, certain patterns emerge.

When the Chinese Communists celebrated their tenth anniversary in 1959, Nikita Khrushchev was their principal guest, and their speeches were filled with harsh invective against the West and clamorous support for revolutionary movements in the developing world. Soon, however, it became evident that a serious rift was emerging between the Chinese and their Soviet allies. At first these differences were expressed in theoretical polemics; later the ideological dispute was transformed into a basic struggle for power and influence between two great nation-states, even to the point of armed conflict along their common border. As the breach

with Moscow widened, Peking moved to repair its relations with the West and especially the United States. With the end of the Vietnam War, and the downfall of the Gang of Four, the "opening to the West" was accelerated in a bid to obtain not only diplomatic support but also the technology that could make China a modern industrial power.

In domestic affairs, the pattern is more complex. By 1959, with the failure of the Great Leap Forward, the Chinese leadership had tacitly repudiated Mao's revolutionary romanticism: as we now know, Mao had lost much of his effective power. In the early 1960s, relatively moderate policies were introduced by the head of state, Liu Shaoqi, and Premier Chou Enlai. Biding his time, Mao prepared a counter-attack with the help of allies in the military hierarchy and among radical leaders in Shanghai. Launched in the spring of 1966, the Great Proletarian Cultural Revolution was Mao's last desperate attempt to topple his opponents and to reverse their "revisionist" policies. With millions of teenage Red Guards running amok across the nation, thousands of key administrators and educators were victimized. As violent clashes broke out in nearly every major city, the country teetered on the brink of anarchy and the People's Liberation Army was given extraordinary powers to restore a semblance of order. Through the early 1970s, moderate leaders such as Deng Xiaoping made a partial comeback and there was a new emphasis on uniting the contending factions and rebuilding the shattered Communist party. But the death of Chou Enlai in 1976 removed the chief architect of compromise. Protected by the ailing Mao, his wife Jiang Qing and her Shanghai cohorts regained the initiative for the radicals. That autumn, however, Mao's own death was followed by a speedy and dramatic reversal: his widow and her allies (the Gang of Four) were arrested and their policies were repudiated.

China was now nominally ruled by Mao's hand-picked successor as Party Chairman, the little-known Hua Guofeng. But real power seemed to rest with the wily survivor Deng Xiaoping and his network of allies in the party, government and military hierarchies. While Mao was still honored as the great leader of the Chinese revolution, his favorite policies were once again ignored. Instead, the new leaders introduced a wide range of reforms including economic incentives to both peasants and workers. Finally, in 1981, the Mao era came to an end, with the trial and sentencing of the Gang of Four, the demotion of Hua Guofeng, and his replacement as Party Chairman by a close colleague of Deng Xiaoping.

For more than two decades, the Chinese people had endured a bewildering series of reversals and upheavals. In part it was always a power struggle, but it also involved a basic debate over how best to adapt Communist doctrines to Chinese realities. In the mid-1980s, Deng and his allies were gambling that the Chinese were tired of endless political campaigns and that economic incentives would prove more effective in mobilizing their talents and energies. But Deng had quashed the Democracy Movement — which called for sweeping political reforms — and China remained a ruthless totalitarian state with millions of disillusioned and disaffected youth. As the decade continued to unfold, it was safe to predict only that China had entered a new and dramatic era.

Another theme that runs through this book is the treatment of foreigners — and especially foreign correspondents — by the Chinese authorities and the Chinese people. Here again the pattern is complex, especially in the field of travel. Every *Globe* correspondent made strenuous efforts to see as much of China as he could, on the obvious grounds that life in any capital gives a distorted picture of the whole nation, especially one so large and diverse. After the isolation suffered by Frederick Nossal, Charles Taylor was given unusual freedom to travel widely in the early 1960s, although several key provinces remained out of bounds. With the advent of the Cultural Revolution, however, foreigners were virtually confined to Peking: both David Oancia and Colin McCullough rarely left the capital. By the early 1970s, there was a steady relaxation: first Norman Webster, and then John Burns and Ross Munro were permitted to travel ever farther afield. Then, after the downfall of the Gang of Four, John Fraser reached such previously forbidden areas as Sichuan and Tibet. After him, Bryan Johnson, Stanley Oziewicz and Allen Abel had frequent opportunities to travel. As a result, this selection includes not only such obvious datelines as Peking, Canton and Shanghai, but also Loyang, Sian, Kunming, Nanking, Changchun, Silinhot, Wuhan, Tangshan, Chungking, Lhasa, Kaifeng, Haikou and Dazhai.

Whether in Peking or on the road, every *Globe* correspondent contended with suspicious officials who were motivated by both traditional Chinese xenophobia and modern Communist techniques of secrecy, and who seemed determined to engulf the correspondent with vacuous propaganda while denying him hard information and spontaneous contacts with ordinary Chinese. These difficulties have often been described — not least in the columns of *The Globe and Mail* — and they have led some skeptical observers to conclude that it is impossible for foreigners to write anything serious about China, since all they see is a shadow play produced for them by the Chinese authorities. This may well be the case when the foreign resident or visitor is a sympathizer or a sycophant who *wants* to see only the shadow play. Most emphatically, it is not the case when the foreigner is a trained reporter with an awkward passion for the facts. On this point, readers can reach their own conclusions on the basis of the stories in this book.

Except for a brief period during the Cultural Revolution, the dispatches of foreign correspondents in China have never been censored. But skeptics also suggest that the residents must censor themselves for fear of instant expulsion. No *Globe* correspondent ever operated in this manner. The proof is in the record: two of the 11 *were* expelled, and the others endured "serious warnings" and other signs of official disfavor. One was physically abused by the Red Guards and another was labelled an "international spy" by the Public Security Bureau. Yet none ever restrained his curiosity or his criticism. Again, readers of this book can judge for themselves.

In January, 1979, the Chinese government adopted the spelling known as "Pinyin" for all its publications in any romanized language. Until then, *The Globe and Mail* and other Western newspapers had used the more familiar Wade-Giles system for the names of persons and places. In common with other newspapers and news agencies, *The Globe and Mail* also switched to the Pinyin system. In this book, we have followed the actual usage of the period — for example, Teng Hsiao-ping before 1979, and Deng Xiaoping afterwards. For further details see page 254.

Charles Taylor

Frederick Nossal with Ho, a refugee in Hong Kong. Ho escaped from China.

CHAPTER ONE: 1959—1962

FREDERICK NOSSAL

In the autumn of 1959, China's Communist rulers were celebrating their first decade in power with a display of pride and confidence. Arriving in Peking in the midst of the anniversary festivities, Frederick Nossal found thousands of Chinese marching along the wide boulevards and wrote in his initial dispatch: "National sentiment is so intense that any Westerner not used to mass demonstrations is taken completely by surprise." Nossal, 31, already had an international reputation as a journalist. Born in Vienna, he had worked for newspapers and news agencies in Britain, Canada and Australia. Most recently, while on the staff of the *Melbourne Herald,* he had served as *The Globe and Mail*'s representative on a variety of assignments in Australia and the Far East. There were only two other Western journalists based in Peking at the time, the correspondents of Reuters and Agence France-Presse. Although his visa was for two months, it was assumed that Nossal was opening a permanent bureau (the first to be established by a Western newspaper in the Chinese Communist capital), and that his wife and four children would be joining him.

With the festivities over, Nossal began to explore a capital in which foreigners were a distinct rarity. Trudging through Peking for hours one day, he saw not a single European face. Western residents — most of them diplomats and their families — were cut off from contacts with ordinary Chinese; in the newspapers and at official banquets, they were exposed to strident anti-Western diatribes. Beneath the pride and the bluster, however, Nossal soon found signs of major setbacks in the Chinese drive to lift their nation out of dire poverty. It was now grudgingly admitted that the Great Leap Forward had run into unexpected difficulties. In particular, the campaign to make iron and steel on the newly established communes had resulted in lower agricultural production. Also on the communes, the authorities had been forced to modify the original harsh regimentation: peasants were again allowed to till their tiny private plots and to retain a few animals for their private use. To restore the economic balance, Peking was giving priority to agriculture.

Above all, the Chinese leaders were telling their people that they must toil even harder. In another early dispatch, Nossal described work as China's new religion. On the streets of Peking, he watched workmen tear down an ancient city wall — higher than a three-storey building, about 50 feet thick, filled with tens of thousands of tons of earth, and several miles in length. Instead of using mechanical shovels, bulldozers and trucks, the Chinese were clawing at the wall with picks and shovels, and lugging away the debris in small hand trolleys and in little carts pulled by shaggy donkeys. A few days later, Nossal saw an even more dramatic demonstration of the new religion.

PEKING — The men laughed as they built their mountain, and ran wildly with their loads of earth and stone as if taking part in some weird and endless novelty race.

They sprinted with their barrows, joking with each other. Some slithered across the soft earth and tumbled to the ground as they emptied their loads.

The men making the mountain about 40 miles from Peking were some of the dam-builders of China. Today I saw tens of thousands of them — trudging, toiling, lifting, laughing.

For 24 hours a day and seven days a week these men (there were only a few women and children around) are building the Miyun Reservoir, the largest water-storage project in North China. At the height of the work-drive to get the reservoir under way 200,000 men worked on the various dams.

With winter approaching fast, much has to be done on the land and at the moment, I was told, only 60,000 dam-builders are on this job. Only 60,000 !

From a distance, they looked like an army going into battle — a blue-clad army with their red banners leading them toward the enemy.

In this region, the enemy is the river water, which each year has rushed down from the mountains to flood farms in the Tungchou, Shunyi, Chihsien, Wuching and Paotie counties. The Chao and Pai rivers are being tamed so they can no longer wash away villages, livestock and sometimes people.

To catch the flood peak that occurs each summer the army of workers is linking various hills in the mountains north of Peking with dams.

But these are not the smooth concrete structures being built in the West. They are actually man-made mountains.

One of the chiefs of the Miyun Reservoir project, Yen Chen Feng, explained that there will be two big dams and nine smaller ones. In two or three years the smaller hills will disappear beneath a huge lake covering well over 100 square miles.

But the most fascinating part of his story was how the dams were begun. When work was started in September last year the men carried the earth and stone in baskets. Then they got quaint barrows with two bicycle wheels on each side. That made it a little easier.

As the dams grew, lines and pulleys were rigged, and the filling was hauled up by rope. Today, with about 90 feet on the two main dams still to go, both manpower and machines are being used.

The earth and stone is brought by rail to the bottom of the dams. Thousands unload the freight cars, take the filling to conveyor belts, which carry it to the top of the dam.

And there the men with the bicycle barrows take over.

The stones and earth clatter against the wood of the barrows, they rush to empty them, run back for more.

"Why do they run?" I asked one of the officials.

"Time is precious," he said. "They want to finish the reservoirs before next summer to stop the floods. Already this year they had the dams high enough to save many thousands of acres from flooding."

Then he himself mentioned forced labor. The Chinese are very touchy on this question.

"You can call it forced labor if you like," the official said to me, "but the floods and nothing else is forcing these men to work as they are."

He pointed to the spot where the dam was highest, where the men seemed to be running faster than elsewhere.

"Those men are from the regions that will benefit most," he said. "Previously the river carried away their food and their homes. They are glad to work here."

The terms "forced labor" and "slave labor" have different meanings in different countries; they conjure up various pictures in men's minds.

But here, on this river-damming project, it was a case of hard labor, as far as I could tell. There were no soldiers with rifles, no barbed wire. It was certainly not a forced-labor camp in that sense.

It was more like an army camp. I saw the men (the Chinese call them "volunteers") arriving by train — long lines of them, carrying their bedding and their few personal belongings on their back.

They marched behind one another toward their new homes, low mud huts with straw matting covering doors and windows.

That night or the following morning they would go to the dams. They would see engraved in the mountainside, in red Chinese characters 10 and 20 feet high, the messages which told them whose idea the Miyun Reservoir was. "Long live the People's Republic of China", say the messages, which are clearly visible even from the far end of the main dams, which are about 1,000 yards in length. "Long live the Party's general line". "Long live our beloved Chairman Mao Tse-tung".

And then, to the blare of martial music and with the red banners flying, they will go to work. Each day each man will add earth and stone, and next year the artificial mountains he has helped to make will stem back more than 4,000,000,000 cubic yards of water.

As I watched the countless thousands of people, barrow-pushers a few yards away and tiny massed figures in the distance, working as if a demon were inside them, the official standing next to me said:

"This is the force that is building China!"

All through China — the third largest country in the world after Russia and Canada (9,600,000 square kilometres) — people are working in the same way. The pace may not be as fast. But the same motive applies: you must work to build up China!

For some Western politicians to say that China is failing in her efforts is ludicrous. By propaganda, by pleading and by persuasion, the Communist Party has harnessed a labor force so large that one's imagination boggles at its potential.

Like other Western observers in Peking, Nossal gave the Chinese Communists full credit for remarkable achievements in both agricultural production and capital construction. Despite the setbacks of the Great Leap Forward, it was obvious that the living standard of most Chinese was slowly improving, and that social and economic exploitation had been severely curbed. At the same time, Nossal became increasingly distressed at the price the Chinese were paying for such progress. Everywhere he went in the capital, he found that the Chinese spent much of their time at political meetings at which they were sternly encouraged to criticize each other and themselves and to learn the latest slogans. "Through political education," he wrote, "the Communist Party is turning the Chinese people into a race of human parrots. If the present trend continues, everyone in the land will soon talk and think alike."

Much of the propaganda was based on constant reminders of how China had been humbled and despoiled for decades by the Western powers and their alleged agent, the Kuomintang regime of Generalissimo Chiang Kai-shek. Tiny children heard this lesson daily in their kindergartens; older Chinese were constantly reminded of it in their newspapers, over the radio and even in the theatre.

PEKING — In Chinese opera, hands are all-important. The actors' hands must have grace and beauty and should be able to express all kinds of emotions.

This is the story of a young girl called Hsu Hsuh-hui — a story about her hands. She is only 18 and hails from the south of China, from Yunnan Province.

In the Assembly Hall of the National People's Congress the crowd was clapping in unison. The evening of music, dancing and opera was drawing to a close. . . .

As the audience applauded, several dozen Communist leaders and outstanding workers climbed on to the stage to congratulate the cast. They shook hands with the actors and singers, the dancers and acrobats.

And right in the centre of the group was Hsu Hsuh-hui in a

In the deserts of Singkiang, Inner Mongolia, Kansu province and many other parts of China, peasants are fighting a brown sea of sand by building canals and planting tough grasses.

This little Peking store, under its makeshift roof, hasn't much to sell. The customers haven't much to buy.

jacket of bright green. She had been asked to come on the stage too.

But she had not applauded like the others, and she could not shake hands. For she had no hands. The sleeves of her bright green jacket hung loosely over where her hands had been.

A whisper ran through the great hall. For nobody could miss her. Among the severely dressed Communists, Hsu Hsuh-hui's bright green jacket stood out. She was in the middle of the line, she stood near Chu Teh, the popular chairman of the standing committee of the National People's Congress. And she had no hands.

"Her hands were cut off by bandits," the Chinese next to me explained. "They robbed the bank and when she wouldn't let go the safe they wanted, they chopped off her hands at the wrists. They were Kuomintang agents who crossed the border from Burma into Yunnan Province."

This, I felt, needed checking. Another Chinese told me he was not sure whether the bandits did cross from Burma, but they were definitely Kuomintang agents. That was certain, I was assured.

And so they had brought Hsu Hsuh-hui on to the stage. She had sat watching the acrobats stand on their hands, watching the lilting hands of the dancers, watching the fluttering, trembling hands of the king and queen as the tragic opera drew to a close. What must she have thought — the girl with no hands?

On the way home I thought about this strange Chinese Communism which never allows its followers to forget. The Chinese take their revolution even into the theatre.

Fired by memories of past humiliations, the Chinese leaders were looking beyond their borders with defiance. Despite Khrushchev's plea for peaceful co-existence, they were showing few signs of compromise in their simmering border dispute with India while their demand for the return of Taiwan, where the defeated Chiang Kai-shek still held sway, remained as strident as ever. On Easter Sunday, 1960, Nossal attended a mass rally dominated by anti-Western invective.

PEKING — It is Easter Sunday in Peking. In the jam-packed National People's Congress Hall 10,000 Chinese clap wildly as speaker after speaker hurls insults at the Western powers.

Kuo Mo-jo, one of China's most frequent speechmakers, shouts angrily about colonialism, imperialism, military blocs and guided missiles.

Kuo, chairman of the Chinese People's Committee for World Peace, roars out warnings about Washington's war preparations.

For a handful of Westerners in Peking, it is a strange Easter Sunday.

Kuo attacks half the world in his speech — the United States, Britain, France, Belgium and South Africa.

He blasts Bonn and Tokyo for being friends with Washington. The occasion for this latest verbal assault on the West was the fifth anniversary of the Bandung conference, which 29 Afro-Asian countries held in Indonesia in 1955.

"The day is not far off when the great African peoples will all become masters again of the African continent," Kuo said.

"A complete and thorough collapse of the imperial colonial system in Africa is becoming more and more imminent," Kuo added. Though "British imperialists and French and Belgian colonialists" got rough treatment from Kuo, he saved his harshest words for the United States.

He threw Peking's entire foreign-policy book at Washington, accusing the United States of subversive activities against Arab states, arming West Germany, fostering Japanese militarism, launching the Matador guided missile in South Korea, obstructing the unification of Vietnam, plotting to expand the civil war in Laos and occupying Taiwan.

During the two-and-a-half-hour rally in the massive hall, Communist trade-union youth leaders from Algeria, Uganda, Zanzibar, French Africa, Iraq and Japan made ringing speeches attacking colonial powers and also asking China to help them "throw out imperialists".

The huge hall was lit by a thousand strong bulbs and a sea of faces listened eagerly as speakers painted word pictures of the Western powers being chased out of every non-European country on the globe.

Through special earphones, the big audience could hear the chatter of voices as the speeches were translated into English, Russian, French and Chinese.

Behind the speakers, all of whom sat on the stage facing the audience, was a large painting of two clenched fists — one yellow and one brown — each holding a golden torch with a bright red flame. Underneath it, Chinese characters said, "To the solidarity of Asian and African peoples."

It is a sad Easter Sunday in Peking because so many of the accusations shouted against the West today were not only unkind but utterly false.

Totally forgotten, as always, were the many boons the West brought to uncivilized lands.

And yet, despite manufactured emotionalism among thousands of very young persons thronging the hall, despite the hackneyed Communist phrases repeated time and again with dreadful monotony, it was a most interesting occasion.

For on this Easter Sunday in Peking the world wind of change — whirlwind of nationalism rushing across the continents of Africa and Asia — was in the air.

Increasingly, Peking's belligerence was at odds with Moscow's moderation. In February, the Chinese had marked the tenth anniversary of the Sino-Soviet friendship treaty with speeches and editorials that lavished praise on the Russians and trumpeted the "great alliance" between the two Communist giants. In May, however, a major and lengthy article in the theoretical journal *Red Flag* implicitly warned the Russians not to be tricked by overtures of friendship from the West. Calling for world revolution, the article maintained that even if the "imperialists" launched a nuclear war, this would not mean the annihilation of mankind. In a sentence that would long remain notorious, the anonymous author added: "On the debris of a dead imperialism, the victorious people would create with extreme rapidity a civilization thousands of times higher than the capitalist system and a truly beautiful future for themselves." As Nossal concluded: "The most tragic thing about the latest Chinese Communist pronouncement on the state of the world is that it represents without a doubt a mighty blow against the principle of peaceful co-existence as it is understood in the West." The Chinese article appeared on the eve of the Paris summit between Khrushchev and President Dwight D. Eisenhower. When the Soviet leader broke off the summit over the U-2 incident, involving the shooting down of Francis Gary Powers' spy

A line of refugees is interviewed by Hong Kong police before entry into the Crown Colony.

aircraft, the Chinese massed three million people for demonstrations in the capital during which Eisenhower was described as a blood-stained monster.

On the home front, the Chinese leaders were continuing to mobilize their people in a desperate effort to make China into a nation with sufficient power to back up their angry pronouncements. Part of this drive involved a massive campaign to wipe out illiteracy. On a trip to the industrial cities of Manchuria, Nossal found workers in every factory sitting before blackboards and learning how to read and write. Across the whole countryside, he wrote, more than a hundred million peasants were attending similar classes. Praising the education drive as one of the more admirable aspects of the Peking regime, Nossal was also critical of one of its main goals: "From a Western viewpoint, the tragedy of all Chinese education today is that it is not merely education for the sake of spreading knowledge as we know it. Its main purpose is to build and cultivate what the rulers of Peking call 'the new Communist man'."

At the same time, Peking was telling its people to work ever harder. Also in the spring of 1960, the National People's Congress (China's parliament) heard the Chinese leaders call for increased efforts to raise food production on the communes. Similar exhortations were delivered constantly to factory workers and bureaucrats, leading Nossal to wonder whether the Chinese could long stand such unrelenting pressure.

PEKING — In China people sleep anywhere — on buses, in the street, at political rallies and even when discussing business. In the land of toil sleep comes easily.

When I arrived in China last October, the sight of workmen sleeping in long rows on the footpath outside Canton railway station amazed me.

Today I showed not the faintest surprise when one of three men who came to my hotel room to talk business kept falling asleep on the sofa.

He sat between his two comrades, and no amount of prodding could keep him awake.

His big eyes, when they were open in a vague, empty fashion, stared ahead into nothingness; then they would close slowly, and his head would loll.

The young Communist on his right would punch him quietly but sharply on the arm, while the man on the left kept knocking his knee with quick jabs.

The unfortunate Chinese, an expert on foreign cars, had been working too hard. He himself kept wiggling his knees, shaking his head and rolling his eyes in a desperate attempt to wake himself up.

Watching people sleeping peacefully beneath blaring loudspeakers and even during Peking opera performances when the Chinese musical accompaniment seemed loud enough to keep the tiredest workers awake, I have felt deep pity for the toiling people of China.

But more often I have admired them — for the sleepers are the exception rather than the rule. Especially the young generation has immense energy.

Complete leisure as the Westerner knows it is very rare in China.

The endless cycle of life in China today consists of working, studying, eating and sleeping. When the day's labors and collective meals are at an end, there are still the studies, which virtually all Chinese are supposed to do.

It is certainly the first time in the world's history that a vast nation such as China has been driven so hard. This is naturally putting a very great physical and mental strain on the Chinese people, but at the same time it is obvious that they are pulling through these present tough times, and are, in fact, putting up with all the weariness, the discipline, the food rationing in the hope that either they or their children will one day see the results of their fantastic collective labors.

Only history will tell whether or not the Communists have awakened the Chinese giant too rudely, whether in their impatience to move forward and upward on the global-power chart they will alienate the people from the aggressive and absolute Communism now being held up by Peking as an example to the world. . . .

On those occasions when I have seen the weary workers, the worn-out women, the peasants dead beat with physical fatigue, I have wondered whether the Peking regime can maintain its strict methods without giving the Chinese more and better food. But then, on the roads and in the fields, in the cities and in the countryside, you meet the strong, healthy children, you watch the massed labor gangs working constantly and willingly.

On a trip to the southern metropolis of Canton, Nossal sensed a much more relaxed atmosphere that made him wonder whether Peking could ever achieve its goal of strict political conformity.

CANTON — This gateway to China is a poor, bedraggled, dirty, yet delightful city. Its charm is its honesty and the obvious fact that it won't conform to the absolute Communism as taught in Peking.

The Westerner living in Peking moves generally in the finer quarters of the Chinese nation's capital, in the districts where large new buildings are springing up like mushrooms. But the forced pace of construction in Peking makes it into a manufactured city. Some areas lack character because of their newness.

Not so with Canton. This city is filled with life and color and character.

Like most of China's millions, the Cantonese are poor. And they are not ashamed of it. They live in their tiny, dark rooms — thin-faced old women, their ragged grandchildren and the hard-working parents — very much as they did before the Communists took over.

They live on the Pearl River in barges and junks and sampans, and many obviously won't or can't send their children to the Communist schools and kindergartens that are so common in North China.

Perhaps there aren't enough kindergartens. Even on weekdays you see thousands of tiny children roaming the streets. They can hardly be called clean, but they look happy and bright-eyed. No carefully tutored sing-song greetings here.

Peking is probably almost as poor but there the poverty is more hidden, and parents are often chastised if they let their little ones roll in the dust. Everything about Peking is too pure, too puritanical.

The poor but proud people of Canton seem determined to maintain their own way of life.

They back the Communist regime but they refuse to conform in the same way as their highly disciplined countrymen in the north. Canton must be one of the most nonconformist of Communist cities.

Teams of Chinese workers dig a wide trench by hand.

It is a happy-go-lucky, ragtag commercial town that the Communists are trying desperately to turn into an industrial city. It is doubtful whether they are succeeding.

The only conformity, for example, I saw in Canton was in the long queues outside community dining rooms and food shops.

It was very evident that the 2,200,000 residents of Canton were not as well dressed as the citizens of Peking or, for that matter, most of the people I saw in the large industrial cities of Manchuria. But there was no tension in their eyes. They moved freely and easily through the streets. They were very relaxed.

Climate is a vital factor. While it is still bitter winter in Peking, Canton is as warm as London on a midsummer day.

Surely it is not chance that the two great capitals of Communism — Moscow and Peking — both have long and freezing winters, and are fundamentally cold-weather cities. The Chinese Communists picked Peking as their national capital in preference to Shanghai or Nanking for a special reason.

They preferred Peking because they knew from experience, and from the lessons of history, that utter discipline is enforced more easily in cold climates. Under the chill blue skies of Peking it is easier to train rigid and faithful Communists than in warmer climates.

In the cold north, obedience to Communist principles means not only food, but also warm clothing and a roof over their heads. But in Canton, many sleep under roofs of straw and if they feel hot they may bed down in some spot by the Pearl River. Nor do they need as much food as the northern Chinese. Thin cotton trousers and a jacket are sufficient clothing most of the year.

For these reasons the people of Canton are less responsive to the regimentation that characterizes the present form of Chinese Communism. It is clear after walking along the narrow, teeming streets, through watching the faces of the passing parade from a pedicab, by driving through a city made up largely of three- and four-storeyed buildings, that the Cantonese are not convinced the totalitarian Communism, as preached from Peking, is the complete answer to their troubles.

The ordinary man in the street will go along with Communism if it provides him with more food and a better life, but he will do so on his own terms.

By now Nossal had spent eight months in China. No non-Communist reporter from the West had ever been permitted to stay as long. In early spring, the Chinese had allowed Nossal's wife and their four children to join him in his Peking hotel. But before the family had settled down, Nossal was told that his visa would not be renewed and that he would have to leave Peking in the first week of June. According to the Chinese, his reports "had not been, in all respects, accurate." Consistently, however, they refused to cite any specific inaccuracy. Rather than nominate a successor, *The Globe and Mail* closed its Peking bureau, and Nossal began to report from Hong Kong.

Some time before he left, Nossal wrote about the difficulties facing a correspondent in the Chinese capital.

The grave error often made in the West is to brand anyone who paints an honest picture of China as a Communist — or at least a very pink Socialist. There is the same tendency in China toward putting tags on people. If you do not agree with everything that goes on here, many Chinese immediately call you an enemy of the state.

This is the problem facing the Westerner who comes merely to look and whose duty it is to tell others what he sees. He may come to report facts, but finds that even facts alter depending on whether you are inside or outside the Bamboo Curtain. Here in China the facts are that the nation is growing richer and more powerful with every moment of each day and that the majority work and live for the state. The people do so willingly for the most part because no past Chinese government has had the physical success of the present regime. The Communist Party has proved to the people that only by grim determination and hard toil can they lift their land from the misery of the past into the brighter future.

It is a fact of life, too, that the average Westerner must find the new Chinese way of life unbearable. To quell all individualism within yourself, to let a single political party mold your mind in such a way that you want to follow its every whim, is a concept utterly beyond the comprehension of most men who live in a Western democracy. . . . But the West must accept the facts. To argue about principles is a waste of time. Let us state them by all means, but let us not pretend that we can convert China for the wishing.

From Hong Kong, Nossal reported on the signs that China's relations with the Soviet Union were slowly but steadily worsening; he also described Peking's new drive to band all the Afro-Asian nations in a common anti-Western bloc. There was also increasing evidence — some of it from official Chinese sources — that in 1959 and 1960, China had suffered the worst natural calamities since the Communists won control of the mainland. There were more floods and droughts in 1961, and food was strictly rationed in all the major cities. As a dramatic result of the food crisis, Chinese refugees began pouring across the border to Hong Kong in May of 1962.

For three weeks Chinese border guards did nothing to stop the mass exodus; at times they even pointed out the best crossing points along the 22-mile land-and-river frontier. Already overcrowded with 3,250,000 residents, and with water supplies rationed to four hours every day, the British Crown Colony mobilized police and troops to stem the tide. About 50,000 refugees were arrested and sent back across the border; thousands more eluded the patrols and found sanctuary with friends and relatives. As their main reasons for crossing into the colony, most of the refugees mentioned intense hunger, dimmed prospects for a good summer harvest and fewer opportunities to cultivate their private plots.

At the end of May, the exodus abruptly ended. Obviously acting on instructions from Peking, Chinese border guards stopped the flood; once again, they threatened would-be escapers with drastic penalties. A few days earlier, Nossal had found himself helping a group of refugees.

HONG KONG — First there were the eyes, brown eyes wide with fear. The Chinese refugee peered out from the high grass by the river at the lush green paddy fields behind Sheungshui Township in the Hong Kong New Territories.

His two companions crouched even lower, using the sharply sloping bank as cover against prying police binoculars. All three wore only thin shorts and singlets, dripping wet after their river crossing.

They were terrified that the two-man border patrols picking up refugees singly or two at a time would pick on them. When I spotted the frightened eyes that belonged to the leader of the trio, he motioned frantically that I should not stop to talk in

31

A construction project in Tiensin. Youths share a laugh with a boy beating a drum with crudely fashioned drum sticks.

case this attracted attention. His anxiety was understandable.

The three were no more than a mile from freedom. They had caught a train from Canton, left it two stations before the frontier, had managed to find a gaping hole in Hong Kong's new border fence and had spent two nights eluding guards in the rugged hills beyond Sheungshui.

Now the milling township with its food and clothing stalls and its barber shops was not far off.

But I did stop briefly, handed the three some bread and cigarettes and then waited for my Chinese friend who had stopped to talk to a group of local residents.

All around us Hong Kong residents were arriving with little paper parcels containing fawn or grey trousers, white shirts and Hong Kong-made shoes. But the trio had not had time to contact their relatives in Hong Kong and were saddled with their blue Communist uniforms, which lay beside them in the grass.

There was only one obvious solution to their troubles. My friend told them in Cantonese to lie low and while I talked, through some locals, with different groups of refugees about conditions in their villages, he went off to buy some clothes in Sheungshui.

In order to avoid police blockades he made a detour and it was well over an hour before he was back with a bulging paper parcel.

Although we were well inside the closed border area which is supposed to be taboo to the general public, hundreds of locals were stamping through rice fields and climbing hillsides looking for refugees in hiding.

For 10 minutes we also searched for our men. The leader, whose name was Ho, had ordered a hasty retreat when a British soldier and a Chinese policeman came too close for comfort. They had swum back across the river but quickly made the trip once again to our bank when they saw shirts flying in the wind like white flags of peace.

Ho was the first to reach shore. Clutching his bundle of ragged clothing, he climbed the bank, waved his two friends to follow him and whipped off his mud-stained singlet.

Never had three persons changed so fast. They stripped, dried themselves with old clothing and then pulled on shirts and trousers, all in 60 seconds flat.

After that Ho relaxed just a little. His face became normal for the first time. He was a handsome young chap of 21 still studying, he told us, at a technical school in Canton.

But there would be plenty of time to talk later. The main problem was to get into Sheungshui's crowded streets.

Ho and his two friends, looking highly dubious, were finally persuaded to throw away not only their blue denims but all their Chinese clothes. For anyone from China, where clothes are worth their weight in gold because of shortages, this seemed absolute sacrilege, but at last they agreed.

Before leaving their damp, crushed trousers behind, each went carefully through his pockets — for rice tickets, they said.

But Ho must have lost his during the river crossing and now scratched around in the grass. "Tell him that he won't need coupons in Hong Kong," I said to my friend. Ho's pathetic reply came back a moment later.

"He says he must have his rice ticket just in case he gets caught and is returned to China. Money's no good these days. Without rice tickets you just don't eat."

Instead of a rice ticket we thrust a camera into his hand to help his disguise and the five of us headed for Sheungshui.

As the refugees were dressing I realized to my horror that in his hurry my flustered interpreter friend had bought three identical outfits — three white shirts with a thin green check and three pairs of mid-grey cotton trousers.

We were forced to spread out. Ho, plus camera, and I led the way. Hsu, eldest of the trio, a thin electrical worker aged 25, tagged on behind a group of strangers, and 100 yards further back my friend brought up the rear with the last refugee, whose name was Tang. Tang was jauntily carrying a paper bag as if he himself had just helped someone escape by supplying a disguise.

Everyone else was tramping back into Sheungshui along the main road leading to the frontier. We did the same. Travelling in the opposite direction were several police and army jeeps. They did not give us a second glance. There were more important matters to be settled. In Sheungshui crowds of locals had tried to stop truck convoys ferrying refugees to the Chinese border and now each group of trucks was given an armed escort.

Near one of Peking's great gates a carpenter trudges to work carrying his equipment.

But the crowds grew so resentful of the police and troops that eventually refugees were transported to the border station of Lowu and across the rail bridge to China in special trains.

Ho trudged along silently, not looking at the lorries packed with refugees less lucky than he had been. From the roadside some persons threw bread and fruit into the lorries and were rewarded with wan smiles from the tired escapers.

Then the tar road winding through the frontier hills swallowed up the unhappy, hungry travellers and we marched ahead into Sheungshui. We managed to regroup, and when they all had haircuts we moved into the final phase of their escape.

The electrician was put on a train to Kowloon and Tang, a 20-year-old student, caught a community cab with a dozen other people — half of whom looked far more like refugees than he did. Both, we heard later, made it. Ho, my Chinese friend and I travelled by car.

Ho said he first tried to escape in 1961 but was caught and his hair was shaved off in punishment. This time the Communist border guards made no attempt to stop anyone from crossing into Hong Kong.

"I believe they were glad to see us go because food will be much shorter later this year," he said. "In cities we are not too badly off. I received 38 catties of grain (about 30 pounds) each month.

"It is far worse in the villages. Lots of people from Canton have been told to go to work in the countryside and that is why all the talk in the tea houses in Canton is about how to escape."

Just past the fishing village of Taipo, about 10 miles from Hong Kong harbor, there was the first big police check and for a moment Ho lost his smile.

But cars and taxis were queueing in long lines and a policeman waved us on. Ho gave a sickly grin and promptly vomited out of the car window.

He excused himself, explaining that he had not eaten in two days and what with the bread we had given him and the motion of the car, which he was not used to, and finally the dreaded police check, he felt violently ill.

But soon he was much better and we breezed past a second police check without the slightest bother.

Ho complained that in Canton you cannot buy a single thing in shops. Everything is either rationed or unobtainable.

At dusk we reached the car ferry. "How beautiful it is here," Ho said. "Just as my brother has written. I am going to live with him."

As the ponderous boat swayed gently during the crossing, I found that Ho was now a different man. His hair was neatly smoothed down, his face handsome and young and his back very straight.

And the eyes that were wide with terror at noon were shining with new life.

Charles Taylor crosses the border to China at Shumchun.

CHARLES TAYLOR

In late 1962, Frederick Nossal was succeeded in Hong Kong by Charles Taylor. Born in Toronto, Taylor was a 27-year-old bachelor who had started his newspaper career on the Toronto *Telegram*. Later he had worked for Reuters on Fleet Street and then as a free-lance journalist based in London, ranging throughout Britain and Western Europe on assignments for *The Globe and Mail* and the Canadian Broadcasting Corporation.

Throughout 1963, Taylor reported on the widening rift between Peking and Moscow. With a steady stream of government statements and bitter editorials in the Communist Party press, the Chinese pushed the dispute toward an open break. Earlier polemics had been conducted mainly in terms of Communist theory and directed against unidentified "modern revisionists"; now the Chinese were naming both Nikita Khrushchev and the Soviet Union. For the first time, Peking charged that the Russians had hampered China's development by abruptly withdrawing 1,300 technicians in 1960, scrapping hundreds of aid agreements and stopping shipments of essential materials; Moscow was also accused of breaking its agreement to help China develop nuclear weapons.

While assailing Khrushchev's policy of peaceful co-existence with the West, the Chinese also launched tirades against the United States, and predicted a total collapse of Washington and its allies in South Vietnam. By early 1964, they were making diplomatic moves to outflank both the United States and the Soviet Union. Peking exchanged ambassadors with France, and signed an agreement with Japan to open semi-official trading offices. Calling for a broad, united front against "U.S. imperialism", the Chinese also sought to mobilize the Afro-Asian nations in support of revolutionary movements throughout the world.

While reporting on these developments, Taylor had been negotiating with Chinese Communist representatives in Hong Kong to reopen *The Globe and Mail*'s Peking bureau. Permission was granted after the Canadian government agreed to allow the New China News Agency to establish its own office in Ottawa. Again there would be three Western correspondents in Peking, with Taylor joining the British and French news-agency residents. In May, 1964, he crossed the bridge at Shumchun and began the long train trip to the Chinese capital.

PEKING — It was dawn, just north of the Yellow River. Through the mist, the peasants were marching to the fields.

For mile after mile, as the train trundled toward Peking, I watched them tramp to work — men and women, some with hoes on their shoulders, others leading cattle and oxen.

It seemed an endless panorama, and it occurred to me that all over China the same thing was happening, and that five hundred million peasants were trooping to the rice paddies and the wheat fields, not to mention the millions more on their way to factories and offices.

It is easy to juggle statistics in the mind, and to have an intellectual grasp of China's size and scope. But only on that train trip from Canton to Peking was I deeply struck for the first time by the vastness that is China.

You can also take a plane, and the Viscounts now in service do the trip in less than five hours. But that way, you miss too much.

By train, it takes two days and two nights — 50 hours in all. You travel for 1,500 miles, and you cross through five provinces — Kwangtung, Hunan, Hupeh, Honan and Hopeh. At the end, you can appreciate the vast size of the task that faces China's rulers in their drive to put their agriculture on an up-to-date footing and then turn China into a modern industrial giant.

Somewhere along the way, it may occur to you — as it did to me — that given the sheer size of the country, and China's turbulent history, it is somewhat amazing that a strong central government is slowly pulling China into the front ranks of twentieth-century powers, in spite of mistakes, setbacks and methods that often seem repugnant. . . .

Several scenes stamped themselves in my mind and notebook on that long journey.

There was the mile-long bridge across the Yangtze River. It is a towering structure and a telling symbol of the partial taming of that mighty river, which for centuries has irrigated Chinese fields and, all too often, swamped them in devastating floods. Until it was completed, in 1957, train passengers were forced to disembark at either bank.

For some of the trip, we passed through wooded scrub, with hills rising many hundred feet on either side. But most of the land seemed cultivated with acute economy; even the railway embankments were used for wheat and other crops. With seven hundred million mouths to feed, every square foot is precious, and in the shadow of factories I saw carefully tended vegetable plots.

Sometimes we swept through industrial centres, and I had brief glimpses of new housing estates — grim and spartan in appearance, but with lots of trees and basketball courts. There were many factories with smoking chimneys, but sometimes there were also shells of half-built factories, seemingly abandoned after the setbacks of the Great Leap Forward.

Then there were the giant railway engines, snorting and shunting by the dozens at every major stop, or steaming past with loads of timber, coal and metal along the slender link that provides a tenuous bond between north and south in a country traditionally divided into east-west sectors.

I saw not a single tractor on the whole journey. But I must have seen thousands of peasants tending their crops with hand tools and infinite care. And, at times, there were gangs of blue-coated workers digging vast irrigation ditches by hand with similar patience.

Realistically, the Chinese rulers have said that it will take 20 to 25 years to put their agriculture on a modern footing. As seen from the Canton-Peking train, the enormity of the task is evident.

Throughout the hot summer in Peking, Taylor saw signs that Chinese agriculture had made a comeback from the disastrous years of 1959-61. Along the streets, huge piles of fruit and vegetables were an indication of China's success in growing more food for city dwellers. But rice and wheat flour were still rationed; although meat was sold on the free market, it was notably expensive. It was also evident that the Chinese had still not solved the problems of supply and distribution. In mid-summer there was so much fruit and vegetables piling up on the streets that much seemed likely to rot. In one district of the capital, more than 1,000 students and government officials volunteered as vendors, and tended temporary stalls.

Like Nossal and other Western observers, Taylor was struck by the Chinese ability to mobilize the citizens of the capital for massive demonstrations.

PEKING — It was nearly dusk, and heavy drizzle was falling on the streets of Peking. Yet, regardless of the dark and the damp, Chinese by the thousands were converging on the Boulevard of Eternal Peace.

They marched in long columns to the beat of drums, the clash of cymbals and the shrill of whistles. Many carried huge red flags, while others held bouquets of paper flowers and balloons. There were columns of young girls, each wearing lipstick and heavy rouge, and carrying a dancing costume in a small bag.

To keep off the rain, many held umbrellas made of oiled paper. Others wore bright blue plastic raincoats. They knew they were in for a long wait.

This was the start of a typical Peking welcome for a distinguished foreign visitor — in this case, General Ibrahim Abboud, the Sudanese head of state. It was also the first time I had seen the mass manipulation of Chinese crowds — with a skill, and on a scale, that would seem fantastic in any other country.

As we started our drive to the airport, the general's aircraft was still an hour out of Peking, but the Boulevard of Eternal Peace was already filling on either side. This is the main ceremonial thoroughfare of the capital. Eight lanes wide, it runs a straight course for more than 20 miles and passes through the vast expanse of Tien An Men Square.

Preparations for the welcome had been evident the day before, as workers dug holes for lavatories behind the sidewalks. These were now screened off with blue and grey canvas tents.

As we drove, we weaved our way through young men with tape measures who were staking out the two middle lanes as a narrow passage for the official procession. Other young men were taking up positions as markers and, between and behind them, groups of people were starting to form along the outer lanes.

Already some of the groups were singing, and there was a steady din made by drums, cymbals and an occasional band. Overhead the darkening sky was enlivened by hundreds of flags and banners strung across the boulevard. The general mood of the crowd seemed to be disciplined, but not a little festive. Many seemed to be enjoying their outing, in spite of the rain and the prospect of a long wait.

We arrived early at the airport — a new, beige-colored building, massive, spacious and oddly empty and lifeless in comparison with the usual clutter and clamor of a Western airport. I saw no sign of casual travellers or sightseers but only Chinese officials, diplomats and journalists arriving to greet General Abboud. . . .

Then we proceeded to the edge of the tarmac, where the welcoming committee had formed three sides of a large square. There was an honor guard of soldiers, sailors and airmen, a military band and hundreds of young girls in the vivid costumes of China's national minorities, many holding flags and paper streamers. The foreign ambassadors also had their place in line, standing patiently in the drizzle under black umbrellas.

Suddenly the Chinese leaders were among us, passing a few feet from where I stood with my colleagues — two other Westerners and a cluster of Russians and Eastern Europeans. I was seeing for the first time the tall, grey-haired Liu Shao-chi — the Chinese head of state and second in the hierarchy only to Mao Tse-tung — as well as Premier Chou En-lai, Foreign Minister Chen Yi and other top members of the government and Party. (As Party Chairman, Mao usually comes to the airport only to greet high-ranking Chinese officials returning from abroad.) With the exception of the generals, all wore the typical high-collared tunic, usually grey or blue, severe in cut, but rather smart and neat.

(I was struck by the apparent lack of security, both at the airport and during the drive back to town. There was no one who looked like a guard or a plainclothes policeman. Of course, everyone at the airport was known to the officials, and as we approached I saw a policeman apparently noting the numbers of all cars without diplomatic plates. But on the long drive back, there was a policeman only every 100 yards, directing the stream of cars. The open road was bounded by trees and ditches for several miles, and groups of workers and farmers walked right to the edge of the pavement to watch the procession. I could only conclude that the Chinese leaders had no hesitation about moving freely among their people.)

Then a Comet of the Sudanese airline roared down the runway and taxied in to complete the square. It was now raining fairly hard, but all formalities were observed. Cannons boomed a salute, the band played the national anthems, General Abboud inspected the honor guard and small boys ran up to press flowers on his entourage. All the time, the young girls shouted, sang and waved their streamers.

While General Abboud went down the line of diplomats, I watched the Chinese leaders, standing in a group. Liu Shao-chi stood straight, stiff and unsmiling, looking very much like his reputation as a stern, unbending ideologue. Chou En-lai was much more vivacious. His expression changed constantly under his bushy black eyebrows, his eyes darted everywhere and, as the band played, I saw his foot beating out the time.

When the official party moved off in its black limousines (mostly Russian, but there was also one modern, fish-tailed U.S. car), we rushed to join the procession. Back on the great boulevard, our car was the last to be allowed into the heart of the demonstration.

I have seen rallies and demonstrations of all sorts in many cities of Europe and Asia, but never anything like this. It was a Santa Claus parade, an Aldermaston march, a mass rally in Tokyo or Jakarta — rolled in one, magnified many times, infused with a particular Chinese character, laced with political purpose and presented with triumphant precision. It was vastly impressive, and even moving in a disturbing way. It was also somewhat frightening, this superlative marshalling of so many thousands.

It was dark now, the street lights were on and the rain still fell. Although we were the last car — and the official party was about a mile ahead — the people still cheered and shouted. Although they had been standing in the rain for at least three hours, they still waved their streamers and beat their gongs.

Some old Peking hands estimated that the crowds were lining the road, three deep on either side, for five miles, and that their number was something between 200,000 and 300,000. I was also told that one slogan they often shouted was: "Long Live Mao Tse-tung."

There were many adults among them, but the majority seemed to be young. By now, some of the adults wore expressions that were distinctly glazed; but many, especially the young, still seemed to be enjoying themselves, and there was no lack of vitality.

Few were standing still. Some waved banners and balloons. Others were dancing, some wore huge clown heads and others pranced in traditional lion costumes. There were giant drums, beaten by four men at a time, and there were endless clashing gongs and cymbals.

But the best was still to come. Ahead of us lay Tien An Men Square, with huge red balloons wafting high overhead. On all sides, the massive Great Hall of the People and other buildings were outlined by thousands of electric lights, and even in the trees were clusters of colored bulbs.

Suddenly we were sweeping around the square, but a square very different from its huge and empty, every-day self. Now it was filled with troops of girls, dancing on the glistening pavement to the clang and clatter of gong and cymbal. As the lights picked out the swirling yellows, pinks and greens, Tien An Men became one vast kaleidoscope.

As we left the square, the demonstrators began to disperse. Far from merely drifting away, they moved off, as they had gathered, with military precision. An hour later, I could still hear the shouts, the singing, the whistles and the tramp of marching feet as the last of the people returned to their homes.

Before long, Taylor was watching such mass demonstrations from the inside, and marvelling at the sophisticated logistics. In Tien An Men Square, he joined a procession of young boys and girls gathering to greet a delegation from Tanganyika and Zanzibar.

. . . They seemed in high spirits. It was a bright, sunny day, and they probably welcomed the holiday from school, as well as a chance to make a lot of noise and wear fancy dress.

Similar processions were converging on the square from all sides, filling it with clamor and color and a mounting sense of excitement. Each contingent marched directly to some prearranged location.

While they waited, cadres went among them, distributing balloons and paper streamers. On cue, whole groups suddenly broke into frenzied activity, practicing their shouts and cheers and waving their banners.

Here and there, a few young people sat down on the pavement for a rest, some sheltering themselves from the sun by pulling red flags around their heads. Some played cards, but most stood patiently in line, as loudspeakers blared martial music.

All the logistics had been carefully worked out. On several corners, there were ambulances and first-aid teams.

Most remarkable of all were the precautions taken to ensure that no unauthorized persons (or genuinely spontaneous demonstrators) should join the crowds. Stretching across the centre of Tien An Men Square, about 100 yards behind the demonstration, a long line of cadres, clutching small paper flags, squatted on the pavement, forming a human barrier against intruders. Further on, a second line of cadres blocked the entrances to the square.

It was clear that no one could get anywhere near the demonstration without permission.

With a visiting television cameraman, I walked back from the demonstrators to take some pictures of the lines of cadres. Immediately there was trouble. A young man rushed toward us, shouting, shaking his head, putting his hand over the camera lens and shoving us aside.

His meaning was evident. We could take all the pictures that we wanted of the demonstrators, but we were not allowed to show on film how carefully contrived the demonstration was.

On October 1, 1964, the Chinese celebrated the fifteenth anniversary of Communist rule with the usual massive parades, proud boasts of economic achievements and strong declarations of support for revolutionary movements throughout the world. Despite the rhetoric, however, Taylor reported that Mao Tse-tung and his

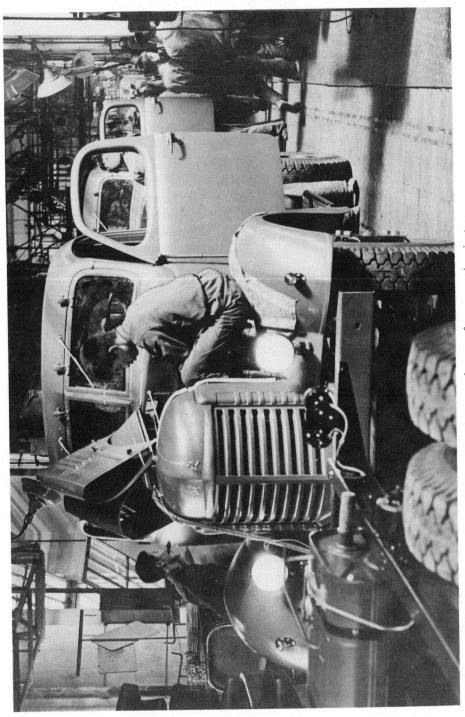

Trucks come off the assembly line at Changchun, Manchuria, at the rate of one every six minutes.

colleagues were facing the future with considerable apprehension. Every year there were about fifteen million new mouths to feed, and the better harvests were barely keeping pace. Economic planning was more pragmatic than during the heady period of the Great Leap Forward, but industry was still recovering from those months of over-hasty expansion, and many branches were operating below capacity.

Above all, the Chinese leaders were troubled by the enormous task of maintaining revolutionary fervor among the masses. Intellectuals, artists and young people in general were marked out for special attention and intensive political education. Otherwise, it was feared, they might well succumb to Soviet-style "revisionism" and abandon the official doctrine of hard work, plain living and dogmatic devotion to Communist goals. Reading between the lines of speeches and editorials, Taylor detected the start of a new rectification campaign, which was similar to some of the mass drives of the 1950s and that was aimed at tightening Party control at every level of society. The Party watchdogs were worried by the presence of "degenerates" and "careerists" in key Party and government posts, and Taylor predicted that the campaign could bring major changes even among the top leaders.

In fact, Taylor was reporting the start of a drive that would burst into the open, two years later, as the Great Proletarian Cultural Revolution and engulf the whole nation in political turmoil and violence. For the moment, the initial attacks in the official press were directed mainly against writers and artists for their alleged bourgeois tendencies. But Taylor discovered that the new campaign was aimed much wider and was reaching even into the countryside. This was a crucial development: artists and intellectuals had long been suspect to the Communist rulers, but the Chinese revolution had been based on the peasants and its survival depended on their loyalty and hard work. From one of his few unofficial sources in Peking, Taylor learned details of Si Ching, the new campaign on the communes.

PEKING — While the harvests continue to improve, Chinese leaders are taking strong steps to tighten their control over the 74,000 rural communes. After early mistakes and setbacks, these giant farming units are apparently making steady progress in raising yields and pooling manpower to build irrigation works and other needed projects. But on many communes, progress is threatened by poor management and what Chairman Mao Tse-tung has called "spontaneous tendencies toward capitalism on the part of small producers."

Now, according to several reliable sources, a massive new campaign has been launched to combat tyranny and corruption on the part of commune managers and individual peasants. There is still no official confirmation of this campaign and it has yet to be mentioned in the Peking press. But while officials plead ignorance, it is widely discussed in several circles in the capital, and there seems no doubt of its existence.

The name of the campaign is "Si Ching", or "Four Cleanouts". By the thousands — and possibly by the millions — Communist Party officials, office workers and even students are said to be travelling to the communes from the cities. According to one source, more than two million persons are involved — from Peking University, whole classes have already left for the countryside.

This drive is different from the general campaign that sends out office workers and students for regular short periods of physical labor on the communes. Under Si Ching, the city dwellers will stay in the countryside for six months or even longer. Instead of doing physical labor, they are living with the peasants and making thorough investigations of their working habits and political ideas.

Most are being billeted singly with peasant families but they are tightly organized in groups under the direction of Communist Party officials.

Reliable sources state that the Chinese leaders launched the campaign after receiving reports that many commune officials and individual peasants had lapsed into despotic and even degenerate habits.

Some have established black-market links with the cities and are lining their pockets from so-called sideline enterprises that are not listed in the commune records. The same sources report that some commune leaders have gone further, and are virtually running their districts like warlords of old, with some of the attendant vices.

It is not clear whether Si Ching involves all the Chinese provinces. Those mentioned include Heilungkiang in former Manchuria and Shantung on the Yellow Sea — both poor and backward. It is thought likely that Szechwan and Yunnan in the south are also involved.

First mooted several months ago, Si Ching seems to have got underway in the last few weeks. According to early reports, it is meeting with opposition on some communes, with peasants and officials conspiring to fool the interlopers from the cities. There have been some unconfirmed reports of violence.

The name "Four Cleanouts" is a typical Chinese title for a typical mass campaign. Apparently, each of the four points is a paragraph of crimes and vices in the general field of corruption and tyranny.

Such campaigns are a constant feature of life in China, where the Communist authorities deliberately create an atmosphere of tension and struggle in order to expose and eradicate anti-Communist tendencies. . . . As seen from Peking, tremendous discipline, loyalty, hard work and self-sacrifice are needed in the countryside to overcome the inertia of centuries, to put Chinese agriculture on a modern footing and to guarantee every Chinese a decent standard of living.

In this official view, any backsliding or self-seeking on the part of significant numbers could imperil the whole project. This is especially true if the backsliders are the commune managers themselves — hence Si Ching.

While the Chinese leaders were tightening their political control at home, they continued to trumpet their defiance of both the United States and the Soviet Union. Then, on October 16, 1964, they exploded an atomic bomb. For the first time, an emerging Afro-Asian nation had broken the nuclear monopoly of the advanced nations. It might be years before the Chinese could develop an effective delivery system for their nuclear weapons, but the successful test strengthened their pretensions to be a major power.

On the same day, Chinese prestige received another boost with the ouster of Nikita Khrushchev by his Kremlin colleagues. Taken together, the two events could only increase Peking's standing at the expense of Moscow, both in the developing world and in the international Communist movement. Yet they were announced in Peking with little fanfare. *The People's Daily* delayed publication for several hours to carry the Soviet announcement of the Kremlin

Chinese teenagers taking part in a mass rally in Peking.

shake-up. But it appeared under a modest, two-column headline ("Khrushchev Steps Down From the Stage"), and there was no editorial or other official comment. At midnight, there was a brief flurry of excitement outside the newspaper's office, when special broadsheets announcing the Chinese test were distributed, and trucks toured the streets hawking the one-page announcement. This was a low-key government statement, which pledged that China would never be the first to use nuclear weapons.

In Taylor's hotel, waiters and room boys showed less restraint, waving the broadsheet proudly and shouting "Boom, boom!" There was equal elation over the ouster of the man described throughout China as a traitor to international Communism. Crowds in Peking and other cities flocked to newspaper stalls in a festive mood and in some cases soldiers and police had to impose order.

For the time being, the Chinese suspended their polemics against the Russians while they assessed the new leadership in Moscow. But in editorials and speeches, they gave strong hints that any closing of the breach could only come on Peking's terms. At the same time, the Chinese greeted the election of President Lyndon Johnson with contempt and abuse. Newspapers relegated the story to a few brief paragraphs on inside pages, and one dispatch said that Johnson was against the working people, had violently oppressed U.S. blacks and was pushing aggressive policies abroad.

Taking a break from all such heavy polemics, Taylor travelled west to the ancient Chinese capitals of Sian and Loyang, and to the mountain stronghold of Yenan where Mao Tse-tung had made his revolutionary base at the end of the Long March in 1937.

LOYANG — Between Sian and Loyang, the train pulls slowly through mountain gorges of wild and rugged splendor.

This is cruel country. Rushing down to the Yellow River, the mountain streams can wash away the sparse fertile soil and drown the plains in devastating floods.

On the mountain sides, peasants were scratching the soil with their hoes. The hills were banked with intricate, narrow terraces. Some had already given grain and were now in seed. On others, men, women and children were carefully picking the last bolls of cotton from the spindly plants.

They were working the land right up to the railroad track — often in strips only three feet wide — with the careful cultivation that has been the mark of Chinese peasants through the centuries.

They were also taking steps to check the timeless ravages of nature. Dotted by the dozens across the hillside, some were planting trees to stop erosion of the sparse and sandy soil. On the plain below, hundreds of peasants were painfully hauling slabs of rock to the river bank, for a dam that will control the torrent.

Along the Yellow River, old and new live side by side. On the plain, smoking factory chimneys and blocks of apartments were signs of progress.

But on the hillsides, dozens of villages, and perhaps whole communes, were living in caves. For mile after mile, the peasants had burrowed out their homes, giving the hills the look of gigantic Swiss cheeses.

These were sophisticated caves. Some had several rooms, and were possibly commune offices or assembly halls. Others had earthen-walled rooms with thatched roofs built on front.

Many entrances were symmetrically arched; most had wooden doors and some had glass windows. At dusk some of the windows lit up, and it became evident that many of the caves had electricity.

For centuries, the Yellow River has been a tremendous menace to hundreds of millions of Chinese peasants. Often it has swept away whole villages, bringing death and famine.

Always there has been the problem of erosion — the loss of fertile cropland and the accumulation of silt and sediment in the river bed.

With some fanfare, the Chinese government announced ambitious plans to tame the torrent. Blasting started in 1957 on a series of major dams and reservoirs — to control the floods, to provide water for irrigation and to generate electric power. All told, the works would irrigate seven per cent of all the arable land in China, and produce eleven billion kilowatts a year.

By far the biggest project was the San Men Gorge Dam, 1,200 feet high, which was to have a vast reservoir and to generate much of the projected power.

Much of the money, the machinery and the engineering skills were to be provided by the Soviet Union. But these projects evidently suffered when the Sino-Soviet dispute worsened; aid was suspended and Soviet experts withdrawn from China in 1960.

To some extent, the Chinese may have filled the gap through their own efforts. In the Taiyuan Heavy Machinery Factory, the chief engineer said his workers had designed and built a 350-ton crane for the San Men project, to replace a promised Soviet crane that had never arrived. It had taken two years to build, and had been in operation for three years, he added.

But it is far from clear how much of the San Men project has been completed. Observers think that much of the work, especially the power side, has been in virtual abeyance since the Soviet pull-out and the setbacks of China's Great Leap Forward.

At any rate, it is impossible to find out by direct observation. Like other foreign journalists, I was refused permission to visit the San Men Gorge.

Travelling across the Chinese hinterland can often entail hazards — political and otherwise. Taylor encountered some in Mao Tse-tung's old redoubt of Yenan.

SIAN — It was all because of some Japanese fellow travellers (and the fighting in the Congo) that I missed my plane to Peking and spent two days on a bus, struggling against blizzards and landslides in rugged north Shensi.

We were in Yenan, the remote mountain base where, for more than a decade, Mao Tse-tung and the other Communist leaders had directed their battles against the Japanese invaders and the troops of Chiang Kai-shek. There were myself, a lady interpreter from Sian, 11 members of a Japanese delegation with the euphemistic title of "Listeners to Radio Peking" and their four Chinese guides.

Winter had set in after our arrival, darkening the skies, grounding our plane and covering the mountain sides with heavy snow. There was only one way out — a long bus ride through the mountains of Tunchuan, where we would catch the train to Sian. If we set out early we could do the trip in one day, and I could make my Peking connection.

We were up at six. By seven, we were waddling toward the bus in splendid fur hats and the bulky, blue, cotton-padded greatcoats that are favored by northern Chinese.

Then came the news. Chairman Mao had spoken out against so-called U.S. aggression in the Congo, and millions were to march that day in Peking and other cities. For my fellow travellers, this was a clarion call — the bus must wait while they wrote a message of support to the rally.

We had lost 90 minutes, and by now the dirt road through the mountains was a morass of muck and slush. For mile after mile, the bus pulled painfully along the narrow trail, skirting the side of towering peaks and circling the deep and deadly gorges.

At times a sudden snowstorm would cut visibility to a few inches, and we would round a hairpin turn to find ourselves bumper-to-bumper with an oncoming truck. Often we had to disembark, to clear a small landslide or to climb a bad hill on foot, lightening the load so the bus could reach the top.

For us, it was a freezing, muscle-cramping ordeal. After seven hours, we had covered 90 miles. It was dusk and there was no question of reaching our train, so we stopped at a wayside inn in Huang Ling, a village where the Yellow Emperor, legendary ancestor of the Chinese people, is said to be buried.

At last there was food. There were also bottles of Eastern Phoenix, a colorless liquid of alarming potency and one of the eight great wines of China.

Some of the Japanese sang mournful *haikas* to drink and women, I contributed a stirring chorus of "Frere Jacques" and even the Chinese unbent to the extent of a few operatic arias. After a final rousing rendition of the "Internationale", we staggered through the snow to our beds.

After breakfasting on sea slugs and other delicacies, we set out again and it took all morning before we finally left the last gorge behind, descended to the plain and reached the railhead of Tungchuan, a grim industrial city of 240,000 people.

We were greeted by the mayor, a charming little man with a wise and wizened face and a ready smile. He laid on a sumptuous banquet lunch and warmed us with another of the eight great wines, equally potent, waving on the waiters at the first sight of an empty glass and encouraging endless toasts and speeches.

It was a stirring spectacle. Around us, Japanese heads were falling heavily to the table and, at last, there were only the mayor and myself on our feet. His Worship's cloth cap was askew and his eyes were watering as we solemnly clinked our glasses in a final toast to the unbreakable friendship of the Chinese, Japanese and Canadian peoples.

However, the unbreakable friendship, etcetera, has its limitations. After the mayor showed me to my room and suggested that I take the customary "short rest", I slipped out of the hotel for a walk around the town. From the start, I was followed, although I could not be certain whether this was an official job or the amateur effort of a zealous cadre.

But after 90 minutes of wandering through the muddy streets, I was glad of my tail. At that point, I was hopelessly lost. Time was running out when he politely tapped me on the shoulder and gently led me home.

In the first week of 1965, more than 3,000 delegates to the third National People's Congress ended their deliberations in Peking and headed back to their towns and villages to propagate official policies at a grass-roots level. Speaking to the Congress with a mixture of caution and confidence, Prime Minister Chou En-lai announced modest and pragmatic goals, indicating that the economy was still in no shape to permit a new leap forward. Instead, he called for more hard work and frugality and indicated that the third Five Year Plan, already delayed for two years, might begin in 1966, and that an upsurge in production might then be possible.

As always the Congress had met in total secrecy, and the key speeches and resolutions were made public only after it was over. Frustrated in his attempts even to approach the meeting hall, Taylor reported that while no real opposition is permitted in China's parliament, the carefully selected Congress did represent a cross-section of the nation — including peasants, workers, soldiers, intellectuals and even chiropodists in public bath houses. "Glimpsed in their hotels, many were clearly local officials of some sophistication. Others, however, were more rude and rustic, and seemed overawed by the comparative splendor of Peking and the chance to meet Chairman Mao Tse-tung and other leaders."

The Chinese leaders made clear to the Congress that there

would be no let-up in Peking's militant opposition to so-called U.S. imperialism and Soviet revisionism. In February, Soviet Prime Minister Alexei Kosygin received a frosty welcome when he arrived in Peking on his way to North Vietnam. Watching the airport scene, Taylor reported that Kosygin and Chou had given each other a very stiff and brief embrace; their smiles were just as short and frigid. In contrast to the military bands and the thousands of Chinese always assembled to greet visiting African and Asian leaders, only a handful of officials were at the airport. Instead of the usual sea of banners, only two solitary flags — one Chinese, one Soviet — fluttered forlornly over the tarmac.

With Kosygin in Hanoi, the Chinese massed millions of marchers in Peking to protest against U.S. strikes in North Vietnam. These marches had long been a regular feature of life in the Chinese capital, but in early March there was a different kind of protest: the first anti-Soviet demonstration in Peking since the Communist victory in 1949. It followed a nasty incident in Moscow, where Soviet soldiers and police used violence to disperse Chinese and other foreign students when they massed outside the U.S. Embassy in support of North Vietnam. While the demonstration in Peking was relatively tiny — it involved only a few hundred young Chinese who marched on the Soviet Embassy, carrying placards and shouting anti-U.S. and anti-Soviet slogans — it was totally without precedent and had obviously been ordered at the highest level. With wry irony, a Soviet source told Taylor that only once before had the Soviet Embassy been the focal point of Sino-Soviet hostility — in 1927 when it was raided by troops loyal to the Chinese Nationalists.

The Chinese leaders were now just as disillusioned with the new Soviet regime as they had ever been with Nikita Khrushchev. At the same time, there was no let-up in their campaign to weed out their own Khrushchevs: backsliders with bourgeois tendencies who were bent on betraying the Chinese Revolution. From the official newspapers, it was evident that a new heresy was gaining ground, and that significant numbers of intellectuals, artists and even bureaucrats were increasingly unhappy with the political pressures that were part of their every-day life. As Taylor reported: "They resent the political meetings that take up so many hours each week. They deplore the ideological strait-jacket that stifles pure research and free expression. They regret their loss of status, their low wages and their 'voluntary' physical labor in factories and farms."

According to the Chinese press, the malcontents summed up their new heresy in the slogan: "To be passable politically, to be very good professionally, and to be comfortable in daily life." (Like most Chinese slogans, it sounded less cumbersome in the original.) The Chinese leaders condemned this doctrine because it ran counter to their demands that young scientists and intellectuals should be both "Red and expert", with a strong emphasis on "Redness", or loyalty to the Party line. And it violated the dogma that no Chinese should be too concerned with material comforts or personal status.

While the campaign continued in the press, Taylor reported an extraordinary incident that indicated the depth of frustration in at least one malcontent.

PEKING — A remarkable hoax has angered and bewildered Chinese officials.

Violent anti-Communist propaganda has reached all parts of China, cleverly concealed in an oil painting that won official approval and was reproduced in *China Youth,* a magazine for young people that has mass distribution.

When the hoax was finally discovered, officials called in all copies from every school, library and private home. They have launched an inquiry into the incident and are forbidding public discussion, especially with foreigners.

In spite of the crackdown, news of the hoax has reached a few embassies and foreign students.

The painting is titled "You Go Ahead, I Follow". It was shown at an exhibition in Peking and was reproduced, in full color, as the back cover of the last issue in 1964 of *China Youth.*

In the painting, young peasants are surging through a cotton field, hauling bursting bales on the end of bamboo poles. At first glance, it looks like a typical painting in the approved style of socialist realism, with the smiling youngsters as loyal followers of the Communist cause.

But in the tangled stalks of the cotton plants, two slogans are spelled out in Chinese characters: "Long Live Chiang Kai-shek" and "Kill Communism".

Actors in a morality play taking part in a three-day demonstration in Peking in support of North Vietnam's position in the Gulf of Tonkin.

In the distant background, more peasants can be seen as tiny figures marching along under three red banners. This seems a clear allusion to the favorite Chinese slogan: "Hold Aloft the Three Red Banners of the Party's General Line, the Great Leap Forward and the People's Communes".

Just as clearly, the second red banner has fallen to the ground, just as the Great Leap Forward floundered amid serious setbacks from which the Chinese economy is still recovering.

There is no doubt about the fallen banner. Given the sensitivity of the Chinese to symbols and slogans, the allusion could hardly be coincidental or unconscious.

Several experts in the Chinese language have carefully examined the slogans amid the cotton plants. They report that the characters are far from perfect reproductions, but seem much too close to the originals to be coincidental.

There are also reports — so far unsubstantiated — that more anti-Communist slogans are concealed in the painting. Just as human figures can be discerned in clouds, so amid the cotton plants can be seen a recumbent figure that bears a striking resemblance to Lenin — his body being trampled in the dust by the cheerful peasants.

There must still be some doubt whether the anti-Communist propaganda is intentional, or a series of remarkable coincidences, misinterpreted by suspicious and imaginative minds.

But there is no doubt that Chinese officials are treating the hoax as real. It was reportedly discovered — too late — by a senior official who viewed the painting at the exhibition.

Immediately, all copies of *China Youth* were recalled. Officially, issue No. 24 (1964) of the magazine has ceased to exist, never did exist and never will be mentioned, except in whispers or behind closed doors.

Many are under suspicion, and the editors of *China Youth* are being subjected to strenuous investigation. The artist, Li Tsehou, is protesting his ignorance and innocence. Real or imagined, the hoax must claim its scapegoats, and the reprisals will certainly be stern.

All this may make little sense to foreign readers. To understand the audacity of such a hoax — if hoax it is — it is necessary to live in the completely closed society that is China. Given the stringent supervision of mass communications, it is equally startling that the hoax went so far before it was detected.

But Chinese history is full of precedents for such a stunt. Through the centuries, poets and painters have expressed their opposition to tyrannical dynasties in a similar way — by concealing slogans and double meanings in their work.

It should also be said that the hoax — if real — does not indicate a strong undercurrent of opposition to the Communist regime or widespread support for Chiang Kai-shek. Neither exists to any significant degree.

If real, the hoax shows that someone felt so oppressed by the stifling demands of the Communist society that he abandoned all caution to express his opposition in a reckless but traditional fashion.

News agencies picked up Taylor's story and carried it around the world. It was a sensation on Taiwan, where Nationalist newspapers printed retouched reproductions of the painting, which crudely exaggerated the anti-Communist propaganda. With that, Taylor was summoned to the Foreign Ministry and given "a very serious warning". Officials told him that his story was totally untrue, had been written with political aims and called for subversive activities. A few weeks later, the Chinese found a way of telling their own people that there had never been any scandal. It was a very Chinese way, subtle and oblique. One day the *Peking Daily* simply reproduced the painting, without any stated reason, somewhat blurred and possibly retouched. In a lengthy caption, an anonymous critic took great pains in praising the artistic manner in which the stalks of the cotton plants had been portrayed, and said that the painting had won "rather good comments". As for the painter, another choice sentence stated that he had "recently returned from the countryside". In other words, the hoax and the scandal were non-events.

(Later, a European diplomat in Hong Kong told Taylor that when he first heard the news, he gave his copy of *China Youth* to his Chinese assistant, telling him that there might be several unusual things concealed in the painting, but without giving details. Half an hour later, the assistant returned, highly excited. On a piece of tracing paper laid over the painting, he had outlined all the slogans and symbols mentioned in Taylor's report.)

Although under an official cloud, Taylor was allowed to travel to Kunming, the capital of Yunnan Province in the remote southwest of China, immediately above Burma, Laos and Vietnam. He was one of the very few foreigners permitted to visit the area in recent years; it seemed further proof of China's steady recovery from the setbacks of the Great Leap Forward and the three years of natural disasters.

KUNMING — Outside the city, the roads curve through blue hills, beneath ancient temples and beside the lake, with its flotillas of square-sailed fishing boats. Six thousand feet above sea level, Kunming basks under brilliant blue skies and justifies its title: "City of Eternal Spring".

Marco Polo came here, and was surprised to find the natives eating their meat raw. On their march to the Bay of Bengal, the Mongol cavalry of Kublai Khan drove their way between the mountains, across the high plateau of Yunnan.

Yunnan means "South of the Clouds". Remote and rugged, it forms China's southwest wedge between Tibet, India, Burma and Indo-China.

During the Second World War, the streets of Kunming were filled with Flying Tigers and other U.S. airmen who had come through the clouds, over the Hump. On the Burma Road, it was a terminus for U.S. military supplies and a focal point of Kuomintang intrigue and corruption.

Old China hands say there was always a romantic, cosmopolitan air to the city, perched beneath the blue hills and beside the sparkling lake. Before the Americans, the French had used Kunming as a temperate retreat from the muggy climate of Indo-China, forcing their spectacular railway through the gorges from Hanoi and building their white-walled villas.

If there was romance, there were also poverty, slavery, dirt, disease and profiteering on an awesome scale — on this point, most old-timers are agreed.

Today, the remarkable aspect of Kunming is its similarity to other Chinese cities. Those who knew it in the old days say that they can hardly recognize the place.

On the outskirts, a host of new factories are a sign of economic progress. Kunming itself was expanded — from about 250,000 people at the war's end to 650,000 now. There are new hotels, apartment buildings, exhibition halls, department stores and wide, tree-lined boulevards.

I was allowed to wander freely in the poorer sections. Here there are ramshackle homes and shops, but the streets are clean and there is no evidence of extreme poverty.

Food seems as plentiful as in other Chinese cities. Early one morning I visited three markets, crowded with shoppers filling their bags with pork, chicken, vegetables, potatoes and eggs.

Rice is still rationed, but supplies have improved since the serious food shortages of 1959-61. My interpreter, Mr. Hsu, said that factory workers receive 38 to 44 pounds of rice a month. Government workers, like himself, get 33 pounds. This works out to about five bowls of rice each day. Mr. Hsu said he never ate that much, and often used only two-thirds of his ration.

On the streets, the people looked well-fed and healthy. But their clothing was notably worse than what you see in the north or even in Canton, another southern city. The people were not only patched — in some cases they were ragged.

Cotton cloth is still tightly rationed, and the new synthetic fibres are not very popular. It takes about 14 feet of blue cloth to make the standard Chinese suit, with its high-collared jacket. This is probably close to the average yearly ration, although it is difficult to get an exact figure.

On the back streets, small shops remain, although not so many as before. Most have only one or two rooms, with an open front, and the dress-makers, cabinet-makers, photographers and bicycle repairmen are hard at work. These are either co-operative or joint state-private enterprises. In the latter case, the former owner receives a wage and a fixed interest on his investment.

But the colorful street fairs seem to have disappeared, and the modern department store is now a point of pride. It has three shopping floors and is well stocked with consumer and household goods. Prices are similar to those in department stores in Peking, Shanghai and Canton, although the variety is not so great.

Old hands say that in Kuomintang days, Kunming smelled of opium everywhere, and the drug was as easy to buy as rice. All that has changed, although the Russians have charged that the Chinese still grow opium in Yunnan and ship it out through

Burma and Laos.

This was strongly denied by Chao Kuo-hei, deputy director of the Yunnan Institute of National Minorities. It was a smear, he said. There had been no opium grown in Yunnan since 1949, and although the tribesmen regularly cross from one side of the border to another, government officials and army units are on hand to guard against smuggling.

Back in Peking, Taylor found the Chinese leaders using their May Day rallies to launch new diatribes against the United States and the Soviet Union. More and more, Peking was turning the Vietnam War into a test of Moscow's Communist credentials, by accusing the Russians of collaborating with the United States to suppress the revolution in the south. It seemed a deliberate attempt to undermine Soviet prestige in both the Communist and Afro-Asian worlds, as well as to hide China's own failure to help both North Vietnam and the National Liberation Front with anything more than strong words and some military supplies. Pledging more support to the Communists in Vietnam, Peking said it was prepared for retaliation — even U.S. air strikes against China itself. Repeating the claim that mankind could survive a nuclear holocaust, the Chinese exploded their second atomic bomb.

Meanwhile the Chinese leaders were strengthening Party control over the People's Liberation Army. To counter the growth of a professional elite — more concerned with military efficiency than political purity — Peking stripped army officers of their ranks and insignia. Instead of wearing peaked caps, epaulettes, special belts and service badges, the former officers would dress like ordinary soldiers, sailors and airmen, with a simple red star on their hats and a red badge on their collars.

On the day of the changeover, Taylor saw several "soldiers" arriving by limousine for a conference at his hotel. They were middle-aged, portly and clearly accustomed to giving orders. Now they were dressed like any humble conscript in shapeless khaki uniforms and pudding-shaped hats. Later, Taylor observed them as they left the meeting: "Since it was a hot day, they had taken off their caps and jackets and left them on a coat rack outside the meeting room. With no insignia to guide them, the Chinese were frantically trying on each other's caps and jackets. Here, one would put on a cap that sank down to his nose; there, another

Ping-Pong is a favorite pastime in China, both in cities and in the countryside.

would have the cuffs on a jacket barely reaching past his elbows. It was pure slapstick; they switched and sweated with frantic embarrassment, a scene from an old silent movie. At that moment, I would have dearly loved to have taken a poll on their opinion of the new changes."

On October 1, 1965, China celebrated its sixteenth birthday as a Communist nation with the usual parades and pageantry. This time, however, the occasion was overshadowed by a remarkable press conference given on the eve of National Day by China's ebullient Foreign Minister, Chen Yi. Smoking cigarettes, removing his dark glasses for the benefit of the television cameras, laughing at his own jokes and growling in his rough Szechwanese accent — sometimes amiably, sometimes ferociously — the tough old warrior put on a virtuoso act for the benefit of resident correspondents and a few dozen reporters flown in for the occasion. Press conferences were a distinct rarity in Peking and so was Chen Yi's unscripted, free-wheeling performance. There would be headlines around the world the next day for the Foreign Minister's challenge to the United States and its allies — a challenge that they should invade the Chinese mainland.

"The Chinese people are ready to make the supreme sacrifice," Chen said, his voice crackling with anger. "I hope that tomorrow the American imperialists will fight into China." Almost shouting, he added: "We welcome them to come — to let the Indians come with them — to let the British Imperialists come with them — to let the Japanese militarists come with them — and to let those (Soviet) revisionists co-ordinate the attack. But even then we'll win victory. For the U.S. and their puppets to send a few million troops to China will not be enough."

Moments later Chen laughed and implied that he did not really expect to be invaded. China was patient and China was responsible — those were the points he went on to emphasize. But the main impression he left with his listeners — and their vast reading public — was that China was in a mood of angry defiance, and was willing to match its might against the United States, the Soviet Union and all their allies.

For all the bluster, Chinese foreign policy in the autumn of 1965 seemed in disarray. It was also on the defensive. Where they had once threatened to send volunteers to Vietnam, the Chinese were now stating that the Vietnamese Communists would have to win their own victories. Although there had been more border skirmishes with Indian troops in Sikkim, Peking was avoiding any major offensive. China had notably failed to organize a strong bloc of Afro-Asian nations to support its revolutionary policies, and the abortive Communist coup in Indonesia was another major embarrassment.

Then, too, China's real priorities were still on the home front. On a trip to Manchuria, Taylor observed both the problems and the progress.

PEKING — With bold claims about a new upsurge in production, Chinese leaders are again hopefully hatching plans to overtake the expanding economies of the Western world.

But in northeast China, the heartland of the nation's heavy industry, progress still seems slow and there is scant indication of any dramatic breakthrough.

This is evident from an eight-day tour of the four major industrial centres of former Manchuria — Anshan, Shenyang, Changchun and Harbin.

In each, there is great bustle on the streets and signs of growing prosperity. There is no shortage of basic foods, and retail stores are well stocked with cheap consumer goods. Row after row of newish red-brick apartments are a further sign of the state's concern for workers' welfare.

But many of the leading factories are suffering from a strange malaise. Most seem to have made only a partial recovery from the double disasters of the Great Leap Forward and the abrupt ending of Soviet aid. And these, it should be emphasized, are the plants that are selected to be shown to foreign visitors.

Yet all of them, including such show places as the giant iron-and-steel works at Anshan and China's leading truck factory in Changchun, are clearly operating well short of capacity. In most workshops, one shift each day is more common than two, and three shifts are a rarity.

It is also difficult to become enthusiastic about the heavy machinery and cable-and-wire factories, both in Shenyang, and Harbin's ball-bearing and electric-generator plants. In each, I noticed idle machines and idle workers. Allocation of space seemed inefficient, as did the random storage of spare parts and raw materials. Many of the workshops are dark and dingy, with crooked floors and scant safety precautions.

Although the Russians and Japanese developed an industrial base in Manchuria before the Chinese Communist victory — building railways, mines and factories — there is still something of a makeshift atmosphere to many of the plants. In Harbin, the ball-bearing factory is lodged in two old Japanese flour mills, divided by more than a mile of other factories, which creates a transport bottleneck. While officials proudly demonstrate workers' "technical innovations", these devices mainly reveal a shortage of modern machinery.

Production figures are rarely given. In general, it seems that output has barely regained pre-1960 levels, after several years of consolidation and recovery. . . .

Yet present economic policies are pragmatic and make sense. If many of the larger factories in Manchuria seem so stagnant, it is because agriculture — and industries serving agriculture — must still have priority, until the time when China can gain a sure and sizable surplus from the land. There is no sign of this policy being reversed during the much-delayed Third Five Year Plan, which starts next year, nor any indication that the follies of the Leap will be repeated.

In all fairness, Chinese industry is not exactly standing still. With the repayment of the last debts to the Soviet Union this year, there are signs of increased expansion in some key sectors, including steel, oil, chemicals and machine tools.

Allowance must still be made for the chaos created by the Russians — in many factories, the 1960 pullout was a staggering blow. Credit must be given for the extent to which most factories have recovered, mainly through native wit and a desperate ingenuity.

And while actual production in many northeastern factories may still be low, the area has become a vast training ground for young technicians. Each of the major cities has a dozen or more institutes of higher learning, while nearly every factory has its own part-work, part-study school to teach simpler skills. Proudly boasting of their self-reliance, officials are determined to train a technical force that will be second to none.

Finally, it is not fair to judge Chinese progress entirely by a visit to the northeast, even though it has the largest and most developed industrial base. Some of the most striking advances have been made in the cities of the interior, where there was often virtually no major industry before the Communist victory.

In Manchuria, the Chinese were building on a Japanese base; in cities like Sian and Taiyuan, they were often starting from scratch. In Loyang, in central China, and Kunming, in the far southwest, I have visited ball-bearing factories that were more efficient and up-to-date than the one in Harbin.

David Oancia with a Chinese acquaintance at a reservoir near Peking.

CHAPTER THREE: 1965–1968

DAVID OANCIA

In October, 1965, Charles Taylor was succeeded by David Oancia. Born in Stonehenge, Saskatchewan, the 36-year-old correspondent had started his career on newspapers in Moose Jaw and Regina before joining the Canadian Press and serving in the news agency's bureaus in Edmonton, Calgary, Montreal, Ottawa and London, England. For the previous three years, he had worked in *The Globe and Mail*'s Montreal office, specializing in financial and business news. Oancia would be joined by his wife and infant son. While his two predecessors had lived in the Hsin Chiao Hotel, it was now time for the *Globe*'s bureau to acquire less transitory quarters: an apartment with office space was leased in San Li Tun, a new embassy area in Peking's northeastern suburbs.

Although he managed an early trip across the North China plain, Oancia was soon back in Peking and busy reporting new moves in the campaign to purge both the Communist Party and the Chinese government of their backsliding cadres. During the next two years, he would have little chance to travel again, but his dispatches from the capital would be carried on the front pages of newspapers around the world. For he was heralding — in the spring of 1966 — the massive upheaval that would soon burst forth as the Great Proletarian Cultural Revolution.

By May, Oancia was reporting that the drive against suspect intellectuals had reached almost feverish intensity and predicting that the campaign would be extended to include political and military figures. Then, in early June, the first prominent victims were named: Peng Chen, the mayor of Peking, Lu Ting-yi, director of the Central Committee's propaganda department, and Lu

Ping, the president of Peking University. According to Oancia, their disgrace hit Peking like a thunderclap.

PEKING — The news broke late in the afternoon and it was broadcast repeatedly through the night. It was given top prominence on the front page of the Peking evening newspaper and long queues formed outside news vendors.

Hastily organized demonstrators started to gather in front of Peking Party headquarters to chant their support for Chairman Mao Tse-tung, the Party's Central Committee and socialism, and to pledge determination to destroy "all monsters and freaks".

The sound of gongs, drums and cymbals punctuated hoarse-voiced men and women who read slogans into microphones on the steps of the five-storey white-brick building across from the International Club in the old foreign legation quarter.

Firecrackers crackled like gunfire as a crowd of several thousand cheered and raised clenched fists. Such a demonstration in favor of the Party is unprecedented in the 17-year history of the Communist state. It continued until well after midnight.

This was the first demonstration of the Cultural Revolution. It continued for three days and nights as columns of marchers gathered outside the Party headquarters amid a din of gongs, cymbals and brass bands playing rousing martial music. Other columns descended on Peking University on the outskirts of the capital. In both places, the demonstrators waved placards and shouted slogans that supported the purge of what was now called the "anti-Party, anti-Socialist counter-revolutionary clique".

Soon after the demonstrations began, Chinese foreign ministry officials warned Oancia and other correspondents about making unauthorized visits to the university or trying to gain unauthorized interviews. Apart from representatives of Communist nations, the foreign press corps now included Oancia, correspondents from the British, French and West German news agencies, and nine Japanese reporters. Throughout the next two years, their attempts to make some sense of the tumultuous events would involve them in frequent confrontations with their Chinese guardians. (Oancia's vivid reports of the turmoil would also earn him a National Newspaper Award.)

Aside from the evidence of their eyes, the foreign correspondents relied initially on the official press for hints about the direction of the Cultural Revolution and its probable next victims. In June, it was announced that entrance examinations would be abolished in the universities, and that fall enrolment for the coming academic year would be postponed for six months. As Oancia reported, the goal was to absorb more students from the families of peasants, workers and soldiers — and to undermine the ancient Chinese tradition of developing intellectual aristocrats who gradually took over positions of power.

It soon became evident that the Chinese army had emerged as a key factor in the political struggle and that its leader, Defence Minister Lin Piao, had become the official interpreter of the words and thoughts of Chairman Mao Tse-tung. In July, Mao took a much-publicized swim in the Yantze River: in flamboyant prose, the Chinese press developed the theme that the 72-year-old Chairman was in robust health, and that his people must follow Mao and advance in the teeth of great storms and waves. In early August, Mao and Lin appeared together on the Gate of Heavenly Peace and accepted the accolades of one million Chinese gathered in the square below. Both wore simple military uniforms — a further indication that Mao was relying heavily on the army. Watching the other leaders on the rostrum, Oancia found it significant that Liu Shao-chi, the Chinese head of state, had slipped from second to eighth place in the line-up.

By then, too, an important new faction had entered the fray. The Red Guards were teenagers who were mobilized — first in the thousands, later in the millions — to aid Mao and his supporters in their struggle against a Party and government bureaucracy in which their opponents were firmly entrenched. In August, Oancia had his first glimpse of Red Guards in action.

PEKING — The operator of the small store was miffed. A brawny, unsmiling man and his girl comrade had put up a ladder to his midtown store front and started to smash his sign.

"It's the will of the masses," said the Communist Party activist, who stopped chipping away at the sign. "They want to carry the Great Proletarian Cultural Revolution through to the end."

"But I'm a part of the masses, and nobody has even bothered to ask me," the store man protested.

The activist fixed the man with a severe stare. "Comrade, are you in favor of the revolution or not?"

The store man's head bowed and he walked inside as though in a daze. The activist chipped away until the last Chinese character had fallen as plaster dust on the pavement below. Then he and his friend moved on to another store.

Neon tubes were dropped and shattered on the street. Heavy Chinese characters were knocked from their supports to smash on concrete walks.

Overseeing this wave of destruction were members of the Red Guard, China's new paramilitary force of red-arm-banded girls and boys in the 10-to-16-year-old bracket.

When they barked orders at the waves of humanity that turned out to watch the weekend spectacle, the crowds moved without question. The police work they did and the effort they put into their orgiastic attempt to break with China's venerable past are part of a program evolved by Chairman Mao Tse-tung and his closest colleagues in an effort to ensure that the revolution they created will not pass to successors liable to fall into the pitfall of revisionism.

Their weekend assignment was to carry "the great proletarian cultural revolution" a stage further by shaking up trade establishments, changing street and store names and issuing sweeping warnings about teddy-boy haircuts, permanents, blue jeans, rich living and tight high-slit skirts. . . .

Photographers have been warned to avoid provocative poses or displays glorifying styles accepted as part of normal life in the British colony of Hong Kong. Cosmetics are being removed from stores and hairdressers and barbers have been ordered to give no-nonsense short revolutionary-type hair cuts.

People who were businessmen in pre-Communist society and who became part of the joint state-private enterprise schemes, receiving small interest payments on their investments, are being urged to turn over their holdings to the state. They are being told also to cut down on their high living, to eliminate wines and rich foods from their diets and to live modestly without luxuries. The young activists promise to "help" them if they don't.

There were complaints, too, about the use made of neon signs. Some posters note they are used mainly for advertising such things as toothpaste. This will have to cease. From now on they are to bring to public notice Chairman Mao's thoughts and image. . . .

Taking a pedicab is now considered bourgeois: anyone wanting to do so must let the driver ride and pedal himself. Taxis are considered decadent and are being dispatched to the country. Restaurants on which China's world reputation as the centre for excellent food depended have been ordered to prepare food inexpensive enough for workers, peasants and soldiers.

Public bath houses have also come under fire. Pedicures, manicures and massages are said to be for bourgeois people only and hence taboo. . . .

There were also demands that the traffic-light system used generally throughout the world — red for halt, green for go — be transformed. Red, the revolutionary color, they argued, should mean that the motorist may proceed; on green he would halt.

Soon the Red Guards were pouring into Peking from all parts of the country. They ransacked private homes for jewellery, cosmetics and suspect literature. Occupying Protestant and Roman Catholic churches, they smashed crucifixes and statues of the Virgin Mary. Throughout the capital, foreigners watched as the militant teenagers marched their victims through the streets and sometimes beat them viciously in full public view.

PEKING — The couple looked sheepish trudging among the cyclists on the packed earth of the *hutung*, with bundles of personal belongings in their hands and the searing stares of their neighbors on them.

The cyclists were their teenaged captors, the paramilitary Red Guard, who had gone through their homes and questioned their neighbors and friends for evidence they felt showed there were crimes or sins against the mores of their society.

Like the Jews in Nazi Germany who were branded with huge Stars of David, captives here also had their badge of shame. It took the form of a notice board on which their alleged crimes or sins were written for all to see.

At worst, if their crimes are judged counter-revolutionary, that walk in the *hutung* could lead rapidly to the grave. At best, to a mighty conversion resulting from a remolding through labor, in which the human psychological and physical resources of this huge land are focused — a redemption of souls brought about by inducing individuals to shed revisionist or bourgeois habits and patterns of thought.

That couple marching through the crowds was not an isolated phenomenon. Hundreds, perhaps thousands, were following a similar course through this city of seven million. And the drive is picking up intensity in other major centres in China.

By September, Party leaders were moving to impose discipline on the Red Guards. Truckloads of troops were moved into Peking after reports of bloody clashes causing death and injury in several cities outside the capital. Even the official press was openly discussing Red Guard battles with peasants and workers, while calling on the young storm troopers to stay out of factories, mines and farms, and not to disrupt economic activity. Meanwhile, Oancia was reporting more apparent changes in the highest Party ranks. Premier Chou En-lai seemed to be slipping in authority, while Chairman Mao's wife, the former Shanghai movie star Chiang Ching, was clearly rising in the hierarchy. In October, wall posters in the capital attacked senior officials for "taking the capitalist or revisionist road" — including head of state Liu Shao-chi and Teng Hsiao-ping, the Communist Party general secretary. For the first time, official journals admitted that significant segments of the population (and, by implication, the leadership) were opposed to the austere revolutionary policies of Mao and Lin Piao, the man who was now described as the Chairman's "close comrade-in-arms". In November, Oancia watched a massive rally in Tien An Men Square at which a tearful Mao indicated his continuing support for the Red Guards.

PEKING — The battle-scarred architect of China's Communist Revolution, a man usually considered unsentimental, appeared to be in the grip of a deep emotion yesterday as he stood on the gilded, vermilion Gate of Heavenly Peace and watched a stream of 600,000 of his nation's seven hundred million people pass before him.

Several times, as the television camera held him in its gaze, 71-year-old Chairman Mao Tse-tung brushed his cheeks with his forefingers as though he were wiping away tears. Once he pulled out a white handkerchief but the scene on television swiftly changed to a procession of trucks rolling through Tien An Men Square along Cheng An Boulevard.

Most of the time China's leader stood in the centre of the balcony, waving and clapping often to the crowds, but seldom allowing his serious visage to relax into a smile. Around him were his closest associates — Defence Minister Lin Piao, Premier Chou En-lai and standing committee members Tao Chu and Chen Po-ta.

A mist hung over the city, with its mixture of traditional curved-roofed buildings and modern brick structures, as the demonstration got under way about 10 a.m. It was the seventh rally since mid-August, but it was the first in which the demonstrators rode rather than walked.

Three thousand trucks, many of them bearing the markings of the armed forces and carrying a total of 100,000 persons a trip, passed the reviewing stand three times. When the last truck rolled by, half the 300,000 persons standing in the square moved up to the balcony to be reviewed by the Chinese leader.

As they did so, Mao was walking to the right and left of the rostrum and when he returned to the centre he stood before the microphone and shouted: "Long live the people", one of his rare public declarations.

It was the climax of a day in which the cheers of thousands, amplified throughout the city by specially placed loudspeakers, filled Peking with calls of "Long Live Chairman Mao".

It was a day devoted almost entirely to Red Guards, students, teachers, troops and commanders who participated in the rally. A massive convoy filled the streets and made impossible the normal movement of traffic for the six hours that it lasted. When it was over, tens of thousands congregated in the main square, many of them wearing traditional colored costumes from the country's mysterious western regions.

None of the leaders made any speeches, but a radio announcer described the demonstration as a review of the masses by Chairman Mao after their "victory for the proletarian revolutionary line".

While Oancia and the other foreign correspondents were permitted to attend some of the mass rallies — and while they could read between the lines in the official press — they were also making

Passersby examining wall posters going up on a building in central Peking.

A church near Shanghai's famous Bund was turned into a factory. Doorways are blocked by packing cases.

Demonstrators aboard a truck on their way to a rally.

cautious but increasing use of unofficial sources. Although difficult to confirm, dramatic developments in the Cultural Revolution were constantly reported by the Red Guards in their own crudely printed newspapers and in wall posters, which they plastered up around the capital. Frequently Oancia struggled through excited crowds to read the latest Red Guard pronouncements. They were now claiming that both Liu Shao-chi and Teng Hsiao-ping had been forced to make self-criticisms, but that these had been spurned as being insufficiently sincere. While neither the head of state nor the Party's general secretary had been officially denounced, calls for them to bow their heads and "acknowledge their guilt to the whole nation" were in evidence throughout the capital.

By the end of 1966, Peking had endured the Red Guards for five months. It had been a massive influx, which had brought millions of teenagers from various parts of the nation. As Oancia reported, it had also caused considerable vexation among many in the capital.

PEKING — It was late in the year, and the bitter wind whistling out of the Gobi Desert snapped at the 2,500,000 Red Guards still roaming the streets of picturesque Peking to "exchange revolutionary experiences".

Some who came from such tropical centres and provinces as Canton and Yunnan were dressed in paper-thin cotton suits and wore rubber sandals attached to sockless feet by thongs. The luckier ones had warm, padded overcoats, sometimes so big that they reached down to their ankles. Others sought warmth wherever they could find it.

In the radio repair shop on Wang Fu Ching, Peking's Fifth Avenue, we had to struggle through a crowd of Red Guards to get to a counter to pick up a shortwave radio that had been repaired. Shop assistants spoke without passion or anger when they exhorted the red-arm-banded youngsters to clear the way.

"We don't sell anything here," one said in a tone that indicated little hope of impact. "Why don't you go out and read your damned posters?"

A few sheepish teenagers shuffled out of the warm shop but their places were taken by others and the crush was as great as ever.

In the streets, hardy Mongolians in massive fur hats and brilliantly hued gowns to their boot-tops, turbaned Uighurs from Sinkiang wearing skirt-like robes over their trousers and Tibetans who never seem to put their right arms in their coat sleeves provided exotic contrasts to the Peking residents in their padded blue frigid-weather suits.

Visitors glanced desultorily at the *tatzebao* — wall posters criticizing the leaders — spawned during the Great Proletarian Cultural Revolution. They reserved their keenest interest for the dazzling (to them) display of consumer goods in stores and for the wonders of the legacy of Chinese civilization in Peking.

This done, they seemed at a loss. For they were roaming the streets at a time when the Cultural Revolution appeared to have hit dead centre after the last of the Red Guard mass rallies in November. They would not be seeing Chairman Mao Tse-tung, Defence Minister Lin Piao — described as Mao's closest comrade-in-arms — and other leaders.

In eight rallies held since August 18 — including the October parade marking the seventeenth anniversary of the People's Republic — Chairman Mao and his colleagues are reported to have reviewed 11 million students, teachers and Red Guards.

At the start of 1967, the Cultural Revolution entered a new phase with signs of growing opposition to the Maoists and their Red Guard allies. In early January, Oancia stood outside Peking's railway station and watched a new invasion of the capital. This time it was not teenagers, but columns of factory workers: burly men and women from all parts of the nation. Within a few days, it became evident that they had been mobilized — and financed — by opponents of the Maoists.

PEKING — Tens of thousands of persons — many of them unwelcome workers from other major centres in the land — strolled through the streets of the capital yesterday.

Painted on the workers' handbags were the names of the cities they came from — Changchun, Chengchow, Shanghai, Tientsin, Harbin, Darien, Sian, Tsinan and Shenyang. Many of them have come to the capital with funds given to them either by factory managements or local officials opposed to Chairman Mao's revolutionary line.

They seem to have plenty of money to spend and the central leadership supporting Mao is going out of its way to make it difficult for them to do so. A quick tour of the People's Market in midtown Peking provided some idea of the goods they were interested in.

Wristwatches — both Chinese and Swiss-made — radios and bicycles, usually plentiful in the well-stocked shopping centre, had disappeared. Departments selling furs, woollen goods and some types of ready-made clothes were closed. On Wang Fu Ching, one of the city's main shopping streets, radio shops and tailors' establishments were closed.

In addition, authorities have taken steps to seal off points of interest for sightseers. The Summer Palace of the last Ching emperor has been closed. So have many of the parks and historic sites in the city itself. These measures seem to have had some effect. The size of the crowds in the streets seems to be diminishing.

Central authorities who control the major propaganda outlets such as the press are not criticizing the workers. They are laying blame on "the handful of persons in authority who are taking the capitalist road or are clinging to the reactionary line".

"They stir up parties of workers to leave their production posts, bring about partial suspension of production and disruption of communications to undermine the national economy," said an article yesterday in the *Kwangming Daily*. "This is a new form of counter-attack by the bourgeois reactionary line."

These bourgeois authorities are being accused of bribing workers to oppose Mao's line. The Chemical Industry Ministry was accused of giving away more than 40,000 yuan (about $18,000) in the past eight days and with giving $2,300 away in six hours. The Peking Institute of Chemical Engineering has been charged with spreading 48,000 yuan (about $21,000) among its students and teachers.

"Some of the revolutionary organizations have closed down the financial departments of the Ministry of Chemical Industry, the Ministry of Forestry and the Peking Institute of Chemical Engineering," the newspaper reported.

As the political struggle intensified, new wall posters in the capital criticized Premier Chou En-lai for defending many of his senior colleagues in the government. Other posters listed a growing number of veteran Chinese leaders who had been arrested by Red Guard factions, including former defence minister Peng Te-huai, army chief of staff Lo Jui-ching and Vice Premier Po I-po, one of the architects of China's economic development. It was claimed that Lo Jui-ching had committed suicide and that others, including Teng Hsiao-ping, had made unsuccessful attempts to kill themselves. As clashes were reported in Shanghai and other centres, Defence Minister Lin Piao was quoted as stating that the nation was engulfed in civil war, and that Chairman Mao himself had called on the army to abandon its stance of non-intervention and come to the aid of his supporters.

Then, for several days, the internal struggle was overshadowed by fresh demonstrations against the Soviet Union. These followed reports that 69 Chinese students in Moscow had been savagely beaten by Soviet troops and police. Hundreds of thousands of Chinese marched on the Soviet Embassy in Peking, plastered anti-Soviet slogans on the walls and chanted slogans demanding that Soviet leaders Leonid Brezhnev and Alexei Kosygin be either hanged or boiled in oil. At Peking airport, Oancia witnessed other dramatic scenes as the Russians began to withdraw the wives and children of their embassy personnel. Before reaching their aircraft, the Russians had to fight their way through Chinese demonstrators and crawl under portraits of Mao, Lenin and Stalin.

All these upheavals disrupted Spring Festival, China's great traditional holiday. But Oancia discovered that ordinary citizens were reluctant to abandon their old habits.

PEKING — Traditions die hard in eternal China, despite the upheaval known as the Great Proletarian Cultural Revolution, launched to eliminate old customs and habits such as yesterday's Spring Festival holiday — the nation's equivalent of Christmas festivities — which officially was suspended for the duration of the drive.

For centuries this has been a day Chinese looked forward to, a day of family reunions, good food, toys and new clothes for children — perhaps even a game or two of cards and Mah Jongg.

Each year since the Communist victory in 1949, the authorities have encouraged the people to discard some practices considered feudal, superstitious, wasteful, unrevolutionary or bourgeois.

A year ago people queued for hours to get delicacies for the festival-eve banquet, gifts for the family and special prints for their homes. Sons and daughters in distant cities made special efforts to join the family and the state then provided free transport and travel time to enable families to celebrate reunions.

During and after the banquet the children set off fireworks variously called "double-kicking feet", "peonies strung on thread", or just plain "fire devils", to drive away unfriendly spirits. We heard firecrackers again this year, but the bangs that punctuated the usual stillness of the Peking night were sporadic. Few of the families scattered across this vast and populous land were reunited.

Needless to say, in a nation led by people determined to rekindle revolutionary ardor and to remove the deadweight of unproductive traditions, some practices followed for thousands of years disappeared early in the history of the Communist state. Children have not kow-towed to their elders for years. Paper money and joss (incense) sticks are no longer burned in the worship of dead ancestors whose names traditionally are inscribed on a tablet given a place of honor in every Chinese home.

Family reunions were impossible to arrange this year, because of the disruption that has developed in transportation services and in factories, mines, farms and offices as a result of the mass movement brought about by the power struggle. Trains still are jammed with revolutionaries gallivanting around the country to "exchange revolutionary experiences". Even if the authorities had wanted to permit family reunions, it is doubtful if the transport system could have handled the extra travellers.

Then, too, the authorities are showing increasing uneasiness over walk-outs, which they charge are being fomented by Chairman Mao Tse-tung's enemies who use money and increased welfare benefits to sabotage his austere revolutionary line.

Recent directives clearly indicate a sense of urgency on the part of Mao and his supporters to maintain production on farms and in factories while their shake-up of the country continues.

One edict from the Shanghai Workers' Revolutionary Rebel General Headquarters — the standard label for Mao's supporters — charged class enemies with having fomented new schemes. "At present they make use of the peasants' custom of celebrating the Spring Festival to throw out to them a hint to carry out feudal and superstitious activities, to buy festival goods in quantity and to visit relatives and friends, abandoning the struggle and their current production tasks."

The Shanghai notice called on "revolutionary rebels and peasants" to rebel against the Spring Festival, to abolish feudal superstition and to carry out resolutely the State Council decision on banning festival holidays.

In large measure the decision was obeyed, perhaps with some grumbling. But the urge to buy remains. Markets selling toys, wristwatches and radios were more crowded than usual, as were those selling sweets, pastries and other delicacies.

Women on the streets of the capital yesterday obviously had been to hairdressers and many of them — and their children — were dressed in colorful clothes.

In the countryside many of the children were flying kites, playing with specially made toys or carrying colorful windmills made from bamboo and brilliantly hued paper. I used about a dollar's worth of gasoline before I found the peasant who had made and was selling them. His price was the equivalent of about two Canadian cents.

Although attempts were made to remold Chinese society holus-bolus, Oancia also discovered that the Cultural Revolution had hardly altered certain Chinese traits, including their demonstrative love of little children.

PEKING — It's the little things — like the time our son cussed in Chinese at a Chinese child — that forcefully draw attention to other facets of the character of the Chinese nation's millions at a time when interest is usually riveted on street demonstrations and the dramatic, big character posters of the cultural purge.

Our two-and-a-half-year-old son was sketching on the sidewalk with a piece of chalk, receiving only sidelong glances from Chinese parents strolling with their children, when one child, engrossed in a new toy, stepped on his primitive sketch. Our son let loose with a sharp untranslatable expletive.

Red Guards and Mao supporters storm the gates of the Soviet Embassy in Peking to hang up straw effigies of Soviet leaders.

Peking residents stop to read posters pasted to the wall of the Imperial City in central Peking.

Students waving their red-jacketed Quotations from Mao Tse-tung.

The mother's reaction was not one of haughty disapproval. It was, instead, astonished delight.

"He speaks Chinese!" she exclaimed, breaking into a smile that unmistakeably displayed her appreciation that a foreign child was learning her language.

Other mothers who heard her exclamation crowded around and began a delightfully animated conversation with our boy. Husbands, embarrassed by the public display of emotion, tugged insistently at their wives' sleeves in an effort to restore decorum by inducing them to resume their walks.

Even when the Red Guard movement was at its peak, people still had time to display their delight over children, their hospitality and their desire to please. It was not uncommon, when strolling with holiday throngs, for a child to dart out and press something into our son's hand and disappear again. Some of these gifts — expensive toy cars and a brilliantly colored drum, for example — must have represented real sacrifice for the donors.

It has become ritual for us to have a family lunch in a rooftop restaurant of the Hsin Chiao Hotel. Again it is the child who gets attention. The headwaiter, whom we have come to know well, rushes off and returns with a warm moist towel to wipe his face and clean his usually grimy hands.

The waitresses, some of whom baby-sat for us when we lived at the hotel, hurry over and remark excitedly on his growth. They pamper and help feed him, and when he has finished eating they keep him entertained so that we can lunch in relative peace.

After one such recent lunch these same people descended in a body to the lobby to "struggle" against the hotel manager who was accused of taking the capitalist road. They helped load the manager into the back of a truck, put a peaked cap on his head and a signboard listing his crimes on his chest, forced him to bow and then drove with him through the streets of the capital to show him off to the populace.

By early spring, the Cultural Revolution seemed ready to devour new victims. Although some Red Guard groups in the capital urged that Chou En-lai should not be criticized, there were growing attacks on at least six of his vice-premiers and government ministers. Columns of marchers in the capital also denounced Liu Shao-chi, at the same time as the official press launched a systematic campaign to discredit the man once considered Mao's likeliest successor. Soon mass rallies were castigating the head of state as "China's Khrushchev", and newspapers charged that Liu had backed purged members of the Communist Party's Peking Committee in plots to stage a *coup d'etat*. In late April, hundreds of thousands of residents took to the streets to hail the creation of a new Peking Revolutionary Committee, a move they described as the death knell for Liu and his followers. Despite the inflammatory slogans, Liu, Teng Hsiao-ping and other disgraced leaders were reliably reported to be still alive, and under house arrest behind the vermilion walls of the Imperial City. As Oancia reported: "The troops carrying bayonet-mounted rifles or submachine guns who now patrol these walls are there as much to keep angry 'revolutionaries' out of the compound as to keep distinguished and once-powerful leaders inside it."

In fact, the "revolutionaries" were showing little inclination to obey official calls for greater discipline. In the heart of the capital, Oancia watched a typical demonstration by Red Guards and their supporters.

PEKING — The scene in the rain-washed square in front of Peking's five-storey department store could have been the setting for an act in a surrealistic drama.

Half a dozen trucks, cars and buses, each mounted with powerful loudspeakers, expelled declarations that reverberated across the square and along the main shopping street.

Other loudspeakers, pushed through open windows in the store and mounted on roofs of buildings making up the covered market complex across the street, sporadically joined in the exchange. And late in the day youths shinnied up light poles to put up more speakers, which they connected to heavy-duty amplifiers carried in jeeps or trucks.

Around these vehicles stood blue-clad men and women, many wearing dark-hooded raincoats, under scarlet banners on which the names of their revolutionary groups were emblazoned. Sometimes they argued so passionately that it seemed they were near blows, but they invariably stopped short of such action.

Along the street stood throngs watching soberly for the most part but always ready to cheer or laugh at some unexpected act by one of the groups under the banners. There was a big round of applause when about a dozen youths clambered onto the slate-grey roof of a single-storey Chinese house beside the store and planted their banner on it.

The policemen, dressed in khaki tunics and blue trousers, watched good-naturedly when they were not confronted with the ticklish task of squeezing a bus or car through the crowds and made no effort to interfere. This was another of the struggles that have characterized the "great proletarian cultural revolution" and, as in the past, the police let the contending groups argue and struggle it out among themselves.

The struggle yesterday could hardly have been welcomed either by the central leadership or by the new Peking Revolutionary Committee, which has assumed both the state and the Communist Party powers once held by deposed former mayor Peng Chen and other members of the leadership of the Peking Party branch.

Hsieh Fu-chih, the Security Minister and commander of China's police forces who heads the new committee, called on Maoists last week to avoid allowing divergent views to develop into "civil wars", thus "confusing the general orientation of the struggle and even giving the enemy a chance to sabotage our great alliance and great unity".

His plea obviously made little impact on the hundreds of workers in the department store. Their multi-sided conflict for power in the establishment burst into the open after a fistfight between members of two different groups over who should get first use of the loudspeaker system to denounce Liu Shao-chi, now freely described as China's Khrushchev, and others associated with him.

The result of this struggle was that the store remained shuttered and barred all day. Just how the new conflict will be resolved is not yet clear, but if the past is any guide chances are good that the Chinese army will move in to end the bickering and promote an alliance under a strong centralized leadership, a step that has been taken previously in a number of establishments.

By May, Oancia was reporting increasing tension in the streets of the capital, with clashes between rival groups of Red Guards and workers, each claiming to be more Maoist than the others. Troops with bayonets patrolled the streets at night, as the army was given sweeping powers to put down the wave of plunder and violence. Then, in July, Oancia himself became a victim.

PEKING — A Chinese mob smashed the car belonging to *The Globe and Mail* in Peking and attacked its three occupants outside the gate leading to the foreign ministry compound yesterday.

Two of the occupants — Norwegian broadcaster and journalist Harald Munthe-Kaas and Swedish cultural attaché Jon Sigurdson — were cut superficially by pieces of glass. All of us were punched and spat on in a 90-minute ordeal with Red Guards that was followed by a five-hour session at the aliens' section of the city's security bureau.

The incident began when we were driving down the Boulevard of Eternal Peace watching truckloads of troops and civilians in a massive demonstration. A jeep carrying troops roared up and seized the Norwegian radio man's tape recorder.

When the masses closed in on us, the troops obligingly cleared the way through them for us and we drove on for 100 yards before we were stopped by a second and more threatening crowd. Once again the troops came to our rescue and persuaded the mob that the foreign ministry should handle the matter.

Then, escorted by two military jeeps and a motorcycle, we drove to the ministry on the street once occupied almost exclusively by foreign legations and commercial establishments.

The jeeps stopped in the middle of the entrance to a possible haven in the ministry compound, leaving us exposed and unable to move in the crowd outside.

For almost 45 minutes they pummelled the car and shouted anti-Soviet and anti-imperialist slogans at us. Then a new group arrived and with clubs and bars they began to pound the car. They smashed the windshield, the rear window, a side window, bashed in the roof and dented the luggage compartment and engine covers.

Then they began to spit at us. The troops who led us to the

ministry tried occasionally to intervene and then gave up until someone suggested we should be taken to police headquarters for punishment. Then, surrounded by jeering Red Guards, we moved along at a snail's pace to the destination about 300 yards away.

One Red Guard who climbed into the car through the open rear window told me to drive right up to the steps or we would face a beating. We took his advice, climbed out and were escorted into a haven of cool tranquillity inside. We spent roughly half an hour waiting before an officer came in and led us out through the back door to a waiting car in an adjoining courtyard. We were driven by a roundabout route to the aliens' section.

There we were questioned separately. I was accused of allowing an illegal tape recording to be made, thereby co-operating in breaking Chinese law. The masses had a perfect right to take measures against anyone who broke the law.

I was given a serious warning about committing a similar mistake in the future. As I was leaving, the interrogating officer said: "The masses have pushed your car here. It's waiting outside in the street."

I drove the battered Midget home without further incident.

Revolutionary rebels, as supporters of Chairman Mao Tse-tung's revolutionary line are known in Peking, have begun vetting press dispatches sent by foreign correspondents and have refused to authorize transmission of at least two cables during the weekend.

Both my French colleague and I were informed Saturday morning that cables we had written on street demonstrations and other matters Friday night were not transmitted. Some Japanese colleagues have reported similar experiences.

This appears to mark a new phase in the operations of foreign correspondents in Peking and the beginning of *de facto* censorship — a measure Chinese authorities have spurned in the past.

The refusal to transmit Oancia's earlier dispatch was the first time that the Chinese authorities had invoked censorship against *The Globe and Mail*'s Peking bureau. It did not occur again, although officials continued to warn correspondents against reporting information gained from wall posters and Red Guard newspapers. On the day after his car was mobbed, Oancia was summoned to the foreign ministry and told that the Red Guards who wrecked the car were "fully justified and have our full support". Oancia was accused of violating revolutionary orders and refusing to sign a document admitting his mistake. (During his interrogation, he had maintained that he was merely performing his normal duties as a reporter.)

It was becoming perilous to be a Western correspondent in Peking. A few days earlier, Reuter correspondent Anthony Grey was placed under house arrest. The move came after British authorities in Hong Kong sentenced the New China News Agency correspondent to two years' imprisonment for activities during pro-Maoist riots in the Crown Colony. It would be two years, two months and 13 days before Grey was released.

That summer, Oancia took a furlough. When he returned to Peking in September, he found that much had changed in the capital. Most visibly, the office of the British *charge d'affaires* was a smoke-stained shell — it had been ransacked and gutted by a Chinese mob in further retaliation for the suppression of Maoist rioters in Hong Kong.

The Cultural Revolution was entering a new phase with a call for the hundreds of contending "revolutionary" groups to end their strife and join in three-way alliances with civilian officials and the armed forces. The army was also instructed to send special units to factories and communes, to restore order and revive production. Chairman Mao himself had placed his immense prestige behind the drive. At the same time, there were concerted efforts to reopen the nation's schools and colleges. For 16 months, the students had enjoyed an extended vacation so they could participate in the Cultural Revolution; now the leadership was clearly concerned that much valuable time had been lost in training scientists, technicians and others needed in the drive to make China a modern industrial power. With the onslaught of winter, Oancia reported on the vast problems the political upheaval had notably failed to solve.

PEKING — The first blast of winter that swept across the Chinese capital from the direction of the Gobi Desert signalled a change in the cadence of the lives of the northern Chinese; a new stage in the rhythmic pattern governed by the seasons that almost two decades of Communist rule have modified only slightly.

The winds were not whipping before them the fine yellow Gobi dust. These storms will come later and they are the closest thing on the North China plain to a genuine blizzard on the Canadian prairies. The fine dust turns the thin winter sunlight into an eerie amber glow and street lights turned on during bad storms shine white and hard as diamonds.

The recent wind abruptly signalled the decisive change in the warm colorful autumn, which most people who live in Peking view as the best season of the year.

Almost overnight it swept the yellow and red leaves from the trees and blew them along the streets, leaving bare branches silhouetted starkly against blue sky. It ended the long, lazy walks and picnics in the city's picturesque parks and in the rugged hills in the western suburbs.

For city dwellers, it signalled a change in diet, the quest for winter clothes and for fuel for the tiny coal stoves used to heat individual rooms of those who live in the low slate-grey-walled houses with curved gables.

Melons, including those from the western region of Sinkiang (scarcer this year because of transport problems that developed during the Cultural Revolution), have disappeared. Apples and pears, freshly harvested, and the brilliantly orange persimmon (considered at their best after being nipped by frost) are in their places in the fruit stalls. Soon beside them will be the Mandarin oranges and lichees from southern China.

This is also the season for vegetables harvested in the communes of Peking. Carts pulled by donkeys, horses, oxen and occasionally the peasants themselves creak along the paved roads leading into the capital, laden with long white cabbages, carrots, sweet potatoes, beans and grain. Usually they go to a central market, but in the last year or two they have been taken, with increasing frequency, to various residential areas where they are unloaded on to the sidewalk to make it easier for people living some distance from the markets. Cereals, which are strictly rationed to ensure that everyone gets a share, are sold only in approved stores.

And this is the time when people switch to winter dress. Coal is an important source of energy for China's industry and northerners, who treasure warmth at almost any cost, are facing an intense barrage of exhortation to economize on heating.

City dwellers compensate with warm clothing. Men and women frugally save cotton ration coupons to make sure they will have the warm quilted capes that reach almost to the ground for their infants, padded pants and jackets for themselves and quite often long thick padded coats to wear over them. I once wore one of these topcoats on a day-long jeep ride from Tsinan, the provincial capital of Shantung, to the coast a couple of winters ago, and found it as warm as an eiderdown-filled parka I had used in the Canadian Arctic.

The peasants, who represent eight out of every 10 of China's seven hundred million people, find warmth is almost a luxury item. Their toil, which is governed by the seasons, still produces an income only a fraction of what many city workers receive. Padded clothing and a sufficiency of coal are beyond the reach of many.

There has been progress in the countryside in the past 10 years, but an immense amount of work still remains to be done to raise standards and close the gap between the cities and the eternal villages where the peasants live.

Given an absence of international tension and pressure, the tasks faced by the Chinese are staggering. In the present atmosphere, when average literate Chinese read daily about the ring of hostility encircling their nation in official newspapers, the problems assume awesome proportions. They must, as Chairman Mao has declared, prepare for war, for natural calamity and for the people. In practical terms this means build up an efficient military establishment, store grain for years of crop disasters and at the same time strive to raise living standards.

It is against this background that the Cultural Revolution, with its emphasis on destroying old customs, habits and ideas, and its attempt to remold Chinese men and women into selfless, dedicated and determined individuals, must be viewed. One by one those in the upper echelons of the Communist leadership who opposed the current upheaval launched by Mao are being swept from office.

The upheaval has caused considerable dislocation in schools, factories and on farms. But leaders like the indefatigable Premier Chou En-lai insist that this is temporary and will be overcome rapidly.

Whatever the outcome of this drive, one thing is certain: the peasants, working to the rhythm of the seasons, will face decades of staggering labor. For their labor generates capital to finance factories and mines, atom bombs and other weapons and the pressing programs of conserving water and soil and extending the use of fertilizers and machines on the land where they work.

Despite the official campaign to restore order and revive production, it was clear that the Maoists had not abandoned their drive to purge their high-placed opponents. Although he had still not been specifically named in the official press, Teng Hsiao-ping was under mounting attack. Before the Cultural Revolution, the short, rough-hewn Teng had seemed in full control of the Communist Party apparatus; now he was clearly "the other top person" (with Liu Shao-chi) who was accused of taking the road of capitalism and revisionism. In particular, Teng and Liu were criticized for policies aimed at increasing farm production during the hard years of 1959-61, including the return of private plots to commune families and the extension of free markets. It was evident that the Chinese leadership intended to restore the full commune system as originally proclaimed by Mao; as Oancia reported, the Chairman may well have launched the Cultural Revolution mainly to preserve such cherished programs.

While every Peking directive was laced with quotations from Mao, Oancia and the other correspondents were not certain whether the elderly Chairman was in full control. Judging by the prominence the press gave to her activities, Mao's wife, Chiang Ching, had assumed vast powers. An even greater propaganda build-up was portraying Defence Minister Lin Piao as the unquestioned successor to Mao.

Whatever its exact composition, the Chinese leadership had still not succeeded in controlling the violence and the crime that had been engendered across the nation by nearly two years of political upheaval, as Oancia reported on the eve of the 1968 Spring Festival.

Peking stadium crowd protests America's role in Vietnam.

Female swimmers parade in Peking, where fitness programs call for mass participation.

PEKING — The Chinese leadership, in a dramatic display of the power of "proletarian dictatorship", is seeking to assure the population generally that the state has the authority and the force needed to halt a wave of bloody fighting, black-market operations, robbery, ransacking of homes and other crimes including the reappearance of prostitution.

Public conviction rallies broadcast on television on the eve of the three-day Spring Festival have been held in Peking and Shanghai.

The rallies resulted in the immediate execution of four persons. For the first time since the Cultural Revolution was launched almost two years ago, it has been made unmistakeably clear that political crimes can lead to heavy penalties.

In extensive publicity campaigns associated with these conviction rallies, officials disclosed that violent fights involving dissidents and regular troops have occurred in Peking itself and in a suburban commune and coal mine.

Peking has been bristling with soldiers carrying bayonet-mounted rifles and automatic weapons for almost two weeks. This display of force involving patrols on virtually every main thoroughfare in the capital has no precedent in recent years.

It was against this sombre background that this city's people began the celebrations that once were the occasion for the annual family get-togethers, feasting and drinking. Now the reunions and associated events this year are officially discouraged.

Students at higher institutes have been told there will be no winter holiday and that permission for home visits will be granted only in cases where there is a family emergency. The strictures on travel during the festival for workers are equally severe.

Despite appeals to avoid rush buying of key commodities and festival candies and other goods, long queues formed outside food markets and other stores. In many of these line-ups stood children, all of whom purchased a share to build up the family larders.

One violent clash erupted last Thursday at the huge Peking central railway station, which was jammed with people who somehow had managed to get travel permits or tickets for the holiday.

A group of workers and staff from the Peking knitting mill had gone to the station to "propagate Mao Tse-tung's thought and maintain revolutionary order". They complained that as they were doing this, they were attacked by 29 men from the Subway Engineering Bureau who "professed to be checking on passengers' tickets and were searching and blackmailing people and beating up passengers wilfully".

When troops began to interrogate them, the people from the Subway Engineering Bureau sent out a call for their own forces. Fireworks were tossed into the station concourse from the second floor as about 100 persons armed with axes, picks and shovels broke into the station.

There was a struggle over army weapons but none seem to have been stolen or used.

In the ensuing melee, 49 of the 50 knitting-mill workers were beaten, 19 of them being seriously wounded. More serious was the fact that 32 soldiers were also beaten and one was sent to hospital with severe wounds.

The *Peking Daily*, in reporting the incident, described it as teaching by negative example.

"Shouldn't those who have fallen victim to factionalism draw a deep lesson from the case and awaken promptly?" it asked in an editorial. "Today, when the Great Proletarian Cultural Revolution has won a decisive victory, a handful of renegades and spies mingle in our ranks. The handful of diehard capitalist roaders in the [Communist] Party and the ghosts and monsters in society are not reconciled to their defeat."

The second and equally serious incident occurred at the Mentoukou commune, site of one of the country's important coal mines. The Peking garrison and the Peking Committee have issued a joint order calling for the wiping out of enemies creating trouble. Instigators in this area manipulated a group called the Red Flag commune to start fights in which many persons were said to have been wounded or killed.

This group has been accused of precipitating a blood bath at the local hospital, setting up private courts and taking captives from buses and trains.

Little space has been given in the Peking press to the operations of what can be called the ordinary underworld. Shanghai newspapers, however, reported two sweeps by a group called the Army of Ten Thousand against profiteers and criminals.

The newspapers said that those carrying out the sorties fought not only profiteers who bought and sold a whole range of goods including iron and steel, building materials, farm and industrial machinery, food products, coal and cigarettes. They also found gold, land deeds, underground factories, guns, ammunition, daggers and other weapons in the fluid society of people who live on river boats.

They discovered as well people trafficking in human beings and private prostitutes, an illicit trade systematically eradicated in the years following the Communist victory in 1949.

By now, Oancia belonged to a dwindling band of foreign correspondents. Many of his colleagues had been forced to leave China because of incidents connected to the Cultural Revolution (and Anthony Grey was still under house arrest). Those who remained — from East and West — were united by bonds of shared adversity that transcended their political differences. Also in early 1968, Oancia reported on the ritual farewell given to a Czech colleague.

PEKING — The luncheon at the Feng Tze Yuan was excellent, as are all meals in this famous Peking restaurant. It featured many specialties, representative of China's regional differences of approach to the preparation of food.

It began with large plates of *hors d'oeuvres,* which included duck eggs buried and cured in lime for at least a month until they had turned gelatinous and green. They were followed by northern soft-fried prawns and chicken that must be dipped in small plates of black pepper before being eaten, bits of pork fried with hot chili peppers and mellow smoked chicken cooked in the Shantung style. The fish was not overlooked. It was baked whole in pungent spices and hot colorful chilis in the style of the central southern provinces.

Three different drinks accompanied the meal: powerful *mao tai,* a beverage so potent it burns as readily as gasoline, hot yellow rice wine made in the Shanghai region and Peking beer.

But the tantalizing foods and the free-flowing spirits were not enough to make the luncheon a happy one, for it was an occasion at which the Peking press corps had gathered to say farewell to another colleague. Miroslav (Mirik) Strouhal, the Cze-

Anthony Grey, Reuters correspondent, was arrested in Peking, in retaliation for the jailing of Chinese correspondents in Hong Kong.

choslovak news-agency correspondent, was leaving after four years in the Chinese capital; the authorities had refused to extend his press credentials following accusations that he had slandered the Cultural Revolution.

His departure meant, in effect, that the Czech news agency office in Peking was being closed. In November, Strouhal's intended successor had made the 10-day journey from Prague to Peking on the Trans-Siberian Express without authorization from the Chinese authorities. When he asked for credentials at the foreign ministry he found they were unavailable, and after a brief stay in Peking boarded the train again for the long journey home.

Strouhal was only one of a number of correspondents who, during the last year, either failed to get their visas renewed or were expelled outright. Among them were four Russians, one Yugoslav and perhaps half a dozen Japanese. The Norwegian correspondent left voluntarily following an incident last July and did not return before his re-entry visa had expired, and Reuters correspondent Anthony Grey was still under house arrest at the year end.

These departures have not only reduced the number of reporters covering critically important developments in a nation that has one quarter of the world's population; they have also introduced a rough balance between the numbers of Communist and non-Communist journalists working in Peking.

The chairman of our farewell luncheon for Strouhal was East German correspondent Walter Eckleben, a thoughtful Sinologist more concerned with long-term trends than the day-to-day fireworks of the Cultural Revolution. He spoke in both Russian and English when he proposed the general toast for the guest of honor.

Tass correspondent B. A. Borodin, also a China scholar, followed with a toast in Russian and halting English. The toast on behalf of the non-Communist correspondents was made by the West German news agency's Hans Bargmann, dean of a tiny corps present that included two reporters from Japan, one from France and one from Canada.

The luncheon was only part of the traditional way of saying farewell to departing colleagues. The final act was played out on a platform at the monumental Peking railway station just before Strouhal boarded the Russian section of the Trans-Siberian Express. There were decorous handshakes from the Western correspondents and lusty bear hugs and kisses from the European Communists.

The mournful wail of the locomotive whistle in the darkness signalled the train's imminent departure. Strouhal struggled free from well-wishers. He stood on the platform of his sleeping car, a lonely figure with moist eyes, holding flowers in his left hand and waving with his right a farewell to the people he had worked with and the city he knew so well.

Colin McCullough poses against a sparsely treed hilly backdrop.

CHAPTER FOUR: 1968–1969

COLIN McCULLOUGH

In the spring of 1968, Colin McCullough succeeded Oancia in Peking. McCullough, 38, had been assistant editor of *The Globe and Mail* and editor of *The Globe Magazine*. On May Day, he joined other members of the dwindling band of correspondents to watch the festivities in Tien An Men Square and to catch a glimpse of Mao Tse-tung as he made a brief appearance before 500,000 cheering Chinese. Amid the continuing struggle of the Cultural Revolution, McCullough was struck by the growing cult of Mao and the overwhelming authority bestowed upon his every utterance.

PEKING — In China, the recorded thoughts of Chairman Mao Tse-tung are omnipresent. As I write this, I can look up and read a quotation by Chairman Mao on the calendar tacked to my office wall. A quotation on cardboard is pinned to the upholstery in the taxi that takes me downtown. When I light a cigarette, the wood match comes from a box with a quotation printed on it. My cook, Chen, drinks tea from a white cup inscribed with a quotation.

Peking airport, the anti-imperialist hospital and other public buildings have quotations by Chairman Mao hanging on the walls. They are pasted up in restaurants and along the corridors of the Hsin Chiao Hotel.

When the Peking Friendship Company's transport service packs goods to be sent out of China, you are given an export-application form that begins with a quotation. When you enter China, you fill out a foreign-currency declaration. Glued to it is a quotation printed in red: "If the U.S. monopoly capitalist groups persist in pushing their policies of aggression and war, the day is bound to come when they will be hanged by the people of the whole world. The same fate awaits the accomplices of the United States."

This statement — and more than 400 others from interviews, speeches and essays by Chairman Mao — can be found in the little red book entitled *Quotations From Chairman Mao Tse-tung*. And in the massive ideological campaign that is being conducted with the avowed purpose of uprooting revisionist and bourgeois beliefs by turning the whole of China into "a great school of Mao Tse-tung's thought", the little red volume is the textbook. It is, indeed, the symbol of the Cultural Revolution.

In the foreword to the 33-chapter book, Vice-Chairman Lin Piao has succinctly set out its purpose: "We have compiled [it] in order to help the broad masses learn Mao Tse-tung's thought more effectively."

What this means in the lives of the Chinese people can perhaps be illustrated by a few vignettes.

Ride the train from Canton to Peking and through the window you capture some snapshot glimpses. A bullock waiting beside a wooden plow that is hooked into the ground like a grey finger, while nearby is a circle of peasants squatting in the field reading the red book. A woman with two pails of water strung from a shoulder pole, walking up a hillside path to a small grey house that has a red poster quotation stuck to the front door. A railway worker standing motionless beside the tracks, holding up a red book as the train sweeps past a village station too small for a stop.

Or see these things in Peking. A group of soldiers sitting on the ground near the Forbidden City, reading aloud from their red books. Three drivers standing inside a small taxi office, facing a color portrait of Chairman Mao and repeating a quotation in unison. A class of eight-year-olds walking in twos along the street, each with a red plastic shoulder bag containing the little red book. An open truck jammed with standing soldiers holding the quotations aloft as they speed along the Boulevard of Heavenly Peace. Four little girls standing by the curb and waving their red books at passing motorists.

Most memorable of all: to be in the stands at Tien An Men on May Day and look down into the great square rippling like a forest of red leaves as half a million Chinese greet the appearance of Chairman Mao on the rostrum.

Behind these scenes is the decision made in the early days of the Cultural Revolution that the quotations from Chairman Mao were to be the means by which a nation of seven hundred million people was to have its thinking "revolutionized". This meant, first of all, that the books had to be printed — not by the hundreds of thousands, but by the hundreds of millions. And quickly.

The order went out suddenly to mobilize China's printing plants to this one task. The results were staggering. In 1967 alone 350 million copies of *Quotations From Chairman Mao Tse-tung* were printed. And that was only part of the story. The quotations are, after all, only extracts from longer works: these also had to be printed in great quantity. They were. . . .

Getting the books to the people is only one part of the campaign. As Vice-Chairman Lin Piao has written, it is not only necessary to study and restudy many of Chairman Mao's basic concepts. Important statements should be memorized and should be applied creatively to solve specific problems. . . . What the result will be has already been predicted by Vice-Chairman Lin: "Once Mao Tse-tung's thought is grasped by the broad masses, it becomes an inexhaustible source of strength and a spiritual atom bomb of infinite power."

Shortly after settling in Peking, McCullough went out to Hong Kong to meet his wife and their eight-year-old daughter, Katharine. On the trip back, he discovered that the constant propaganda — and the normal Chinese suspicion of foreigners — is somewhat mitigated if you travel with a blue-eyed little girl.

PEKING — We were somewhere over Kwantung Province, flying from Canton to Shanghai, when I noticed the Chinese soldier in front of us was peering at Katharine through the narrow space between the seats. At least, I thought he was staring at her. And why not? An eight-year-old Western girl with blue eyes is a rare sight in China.

Then I realized he wasn't looking at her at all. What had caught his attention was the comic book she was reading: "Archie's Pals 'n' Gals".

Katharine and her mother and I were not the only foreigners in the plane. Seated at the back, surrounded by large white canvas bags marked "On Her Majesty's Service", were two tall grey-haired and moustached British couriers, also on their way to Peking via Shanghai. Earlier, we had nodded to each other across the waiting room during a performance by the Canton airport propaganda team. Katharine had rather liked the show.

All the passengers had been seated on benches placed in a semi-circle facing a large color portrait of Mao Tse-tung on the wall. About 30 men and women stood in three rows, below Mao, and sang revolutionary songs.

Then a group of dancers, young boys and girls who were also airport workers, took the place of the choir. They wore white shirts and grey cotton trousers. The music was militant and lively, the dancing vigorous. They also acted out the story of Men Ho, the soldier hero who died when he threw himself on a rocket to save his comrades. I explained the story to Katharine, but she said she much preferred the dance in which the boys and girls twirled long red streamers.

Once aboard the plane, the unbearable wait began. The two grey-trousered stewardesses handed out broadleaf fans, but they barely stirred Canton's humid heat and the soldiers began to take off their tunics. Katharine and her mother didn't seem to mind the heat, but this was their first trip to China and they were busy just looking.

"There's Chairman Mao," Katharine said in a loud voice, pointing at the small framed picture over the passageway. Then she began to read aloud the red, framed quotations from Mao's works (printed in Chinese and English) that were hanging on both sides of the cabin. At this point a stewardess, who wore her long black hair in two thick braids, came along with a tray of candies and chewing gum. She chatted away with Katharine and insisted with gestures that she take several pieces.

Now, I should point out that such hospitality has nothing to do with the policy of the civil aviation administration of China. Nor, for that matter, was Katharine receiving extraordinary treatment by Chinese standards. The simple fact is that the Chinese love children, all children.

At Shanghai, where we used up part of the hour stopover by having supper in the airport restaurant, the waiter hovered over Katharine and the food came promptly. Alas, she found the food strange and the chopsticks unco-operative. And she shot envious glances at the next table where the two dignified British couriers stoutly demanded, and got, fish and chips, bread and butter and tea, please.

From Shanghai to Peking the trip went quickly. Katharine had hardly finished her paper cup of ice cream and dived into her comic book when the stewardess passed out song books.

Then, with one holding a microphone and the other shaking a tambourine, they led the army and navy officers in revolutionary songs.

It didn't occur to me that my translator might not have got the telegram I sent from Shumchun earlier in the day telling him to arrange for the Volkswagen to be at the airport. But, indeed, he hadn't and it wasn't.

So there we were in the Peking airport at about 10 p.m., miles and miles from the apartment, with no car or taxi (the airport doesn't have buses, limousines or taxis just standing by) and with only 12 Archie comic books to while away the time.

It was then that the British offered us a lift in the minibus that had come to pick them up. When they had let us off, I realized I didn't have a key to the apartment. For a few minutes we sat on the luggage in the quiet Peking night. Katharine was half asleep. My wife, being kind, said nothing.

At that point a Dutch couple who live in the same apartment block came strolling along. Why not stay in the empty apartment next to theirs (it belonged to a departed Dutch diplomat who had not yet been replaced)? It had three beds, and they would supply the linen. We practically fell on their necks.

And so, for our first night together in Peking, we slept on borrowed sheets in borrowed beds in a borrowed apartment. And we were glad to.

Incidentally, the telegram from Shumchun still hasn't arrived.

By late summer, it was evident that the Chinese leaders were taking further steps to bring the Cultural Revolution under control, and especially to restore order in the cities and to have factories resume normal production. Their chosen vehicles were the "revolutionary committees": the three-way alliances of the army, cadres who had survived the Cultural Revolution and Red Guards and other "revolutionary rebels". These committees now governed every Chinese province; they also controlled most municipalities, communes, factories and other institutions. In September, McCullough became the first foreign correspondent to be allowed to visit one of the committees.

PEKING — There were nine of us sitting at one end of a table that was long enough to take 30 more people easily. On the white linen tablecloth were plates of cigarettes and cups and saucers.

We had just begun to talk when from the hall outside came shouts and the beating of drums so loud that we laughed and gave up.

"What's going on out there?" I asked my translator. "Oh, it's some of the revolutionaries bringing good news from one part of the plant to the other," he said.

While we waited for the marchers to pass, the People's Liberation Army soldier at my right offered cigarettes and poured another cup of Chinese tea for me. Beside him sat a political cadre wearing a blue cotton jacket and trousers.

Across the table from us were three women with their hair cropped short and two men. One looked to be about 30. His hair was neatly combed and he wore a short-sleeved shirt open at the neck. The other, about 50, had a brush cut and wore the same dark blue work clothes as the cadre.

The older man, I later learned, had been a deputy director of the Peking general knitwear factory — which was where we were meeting. He was now vice-chairman of the factory's revolutionary committee. The soldier, the cadre, the young man and one of the women were also committee members. The other two women were on the staff of the committee.

Three weeks earlier I had asked the foreign ministry's information department for permission to visit a factory and to talk to members of its revolutionary committee. It was not surprising that the knitwear plant was chosen: it is one of the most famous in China.

This mill was in the vanguard of the Cultural Revolution: its workers seized power from the old management six months

Two thousand young people walk through the snow to the Soviet Embassy in Peking to join a demonstration protesting Russian actions along the Ussuri River.

after the revolution began and — despite some difficulties — eventually set up a revolutionary committee. Stories about the factory appear frequently in Chinese magazines and newspapers, and it often is included on the itinerary of foreign dignitaries visiting Peking.

As far as I know, I was the first foreign correspondent to visit the mill since the revolution, and the first to talk to members of a revolutionary committee anywhere in China.

Revolutionary committees — three-way alliances of cadres, soldiers and workers — are the new instruments of power created by the Cultural Revolution. They have replaced the old administrative and political structures not only in factories, schools, hospitals and communes, but also at municipal and provincial levels.

I had arrived at the plant in the northeast outskirts of Peking at 8 a.m. Slogans were on the pillars of the gate leading to the mill: standing by the road were two rows of about 20 persons being led by another worker in reading aloud from the famous little red book, *Quotations From Chairman Mao Tse-tung*. About 10 men and women wearing the army's green uniform and cap with red star passed by in single file.

The revolutionary committee members were waiting at the main building entrance, and as we shook hands I asked if I would be able to take photographs. The soldier nodded approval.

I followed them into the room with the long table, where tea was poured and cigarettes lighted. On one wall were framed portraits of Marx, Engels, Lenin and Stalin. The attractive and self-confident woman sitting across from me (she was on the committee staff and appeared to have dealt with visitors before) led the talk.

After welcoming me, she said she would first describe the general situation at the mill, and then I would be taken on a tour. Afterward I could ask questions and they hoped I would suggest ways in which they could improve their work.

The following is a summary of what she said:

The factory was opened in 1953, employing 400 persons. It has 3,300 workers, including those at two sub-mills. The main product is cotton underwear. Shirts, trousers and other kinds of cotton clothing are also produced for export and domestic use.

At the start of the Cultural Revolution, in August, 1966, revolutionaries in the factory criticized authorities and workers who were following the capitalist line of Liu Shao-chi, now always referred to as China's Khrushchev. A fierce struggle took place, with many revolutionaries being suppressed.

On January 20, 1967, however, they took over the mill, and a provisional committee was chosen in a factory-wide election. The revolutionaries had split into two large organizations, the Red Rebels with 800 members and The East Is Red with 1,200 members, and they disagreed about the committee.

One side thought the committee was decadent; the other side thought it was basically sound, although it had made some mistakes. Soon the two organizations, which had fought side by side to oust supporters of the capitalist road, began to criticize each other.

By June, antagonism had reached a point where many workers were not speaking to one another and although there had not been any fighting, production had been affected. In late June, the army answered Mao's call to support the left and entered various mines and factories, including the knitwear mill.

The soldiers organized study classes of Mao's thought and, through working with both groups, gradually reduced tensions. After several meetings of the faction leaders and the soldiers, an alliance (the preparatory group for a revolutionary committee) was formed on September 19.

More study classes were held among the workers and their families. On November 11 the revolutionary committee was established. Unification had spurred production and the factory completed its 1967 quota 20 days ahead of schedule. This year the six-month target was reached 11 days early. In addition, more than 30 innovations were made to improve production.

The woman ended her talk by saying: "There are still many things to be desired here, and compared to the advanced work of other units, what we have done is not satisfactory. We are determined to make revolution all our lives and turn our factory into a great school of Mao Tse-tung's thought."

We were about to start the tour when a committee member pointed with pride to a letter that had been framed and hung on the wall. It was, he said, the message of salute the revolutionary committee had sent to Chairman Mao when it was established. The letter had been returned to the committee with the words written across the top: "I have read it. Very good. Thank you, comrades."

In the autumn of 1968, with revolutionary committees in place across the nation, Peking launched a major campaign to revive China's educational system. For two years, the universities had seen some of the worst clashes of the Cultural Revolution; as Red Guards rampaged around the country, most primary and secondary schools had closed their doors. Now special propaganda teams were being sent to restore order in the universities, and tens of millions of younger students were returning to their schools. In September, Shanghai reported that all its schools had reopened for the new term, while in Peking, McCullough noted that the school yards were filled with children every morning.

At the same time, Peking announced Mao Tse-tung's own long-awaited program for the reform of higher education. In essence, high-school graduates would no longer automatically go on to universities. Instead they would do manual labor for a period of years — then their fellow workers would judge whether they should be allowed to have a higher education. This new program was designed to break the academic framework of the past: in 1949 the Communists had inherited an education system that had been Western-oriented for more than 50 years. University programs followed Western patterns, many foreign textbooks were used and many leading teachers and scholars had received their education in British and American universities. Inevitably, many graduates were motivated by Western concepts of professionalism and individualism rather than Communist ideology.

Once again, Mao was trying to ensure that future generations would be both "Red and expert"; once again, he was moving to prevent the growth of a new intellectual elite that would question Communist goals. As he wrote in his directive: "Students should be selected from among workers and peasants with practical experience, and they should return to production after a few years' study." According to McCullough, some clever and talented young people would undoubtedly be denied a higher education because they were judged to be politically unsuitable: "This sacrifice is probably deemed necessary and desirable to keep the course of the revolution Red."

As winter closed in on the capital, McCullough discovered that the festive season was a strange and lonely experience for the small foreign community.

PEKING — It just doesn't seem like Christmas.

My wife and I miss the Santa Claus parade, the harried last-minute rush to Toyland, the elbowing crowds of last-minute shoppers, the constant blaring of carols, Christmas lights along the streets — all the trappings of the cash-register atmosphere we once deplored and wished were gone.

We do have a Christmas tree in our apartment, bought from a small stock of trees laid in for foreigners at a flower shop on the Boulevard of Eternal Peace. And we do have two poinsettias.

Christmas here is a very private, almost lonely thing, celebrated quietly and in small groups by foreigners like ourselves and perhaps a few scattered Chinese Christians.

From old Legation Street, now called Dung Jiao Min Hsiang, you can see the twin grey gothic spires of Saint Michael's Church rising behind high courtyard walls.

It seems a rather pretty church and I often wonder what it is being used for. Some people think it may be a school, but it always appears deserted when I pass by.

Its doors were closed last night, as the doors of all Peking churches have been closed on Christmas Eve for the past two years of the Cultural Revolution.

For Peking's diplomatic community, though, there were Christmas services last night, and today a French priest from Cambodia will sing mass at 11 a.m.

It would have been earlier, but the British Office had already arranged a morning service — which will be conducted by acting *chargé d'affaires* Percy Cradock — and a lot of people want to attend both.

I think I will, although I usually leave church-going to my wife and nine-year-old daughter, Katharine.

For the past couple of weeks, Katharine and her mother have been making decorations for the tree. They found some gold and silver wrapping paper in a side street in downtown Peking, and a Danish friend lent them some designs for paper stars. The gold stars look best.

One minor tragedy occurred. The box marked "Christmas lights", which we discovered two months ago in a closet, was finally opened on Monday night. The string of lights was cut in four pieces. Our *amah* explained with little English but many gestures that last Christmas my predecessor's five-year-old son had discovered how to use scissors.

Our translator made a telephone call and two Chinese electricians duly appeared with a box of tools and a long ladder. They worked until noon, with our *amah* and cook hanging over their shoulders. They left for lunch, warning us not to move anything because they would be back. Yesterday they reappeared and we now have lights for the tree.

For Katharine, Christmas is a magic thing, even in Peking. A few days ago she stopped saying she didn't believe in Santa Claus and began trying to decide where she will hang up her stocking. She knows a good thing when she sees it.

She already has received one Christmas present. The French Embassy school held a party for students and parents last week. The children from 11 different countries had a good time, eating chocolate cake and drinking orange juice and getting presents from Father Christmas himself.

That, she said confidently, was the French Embassy's radio man. She was wrong, but I said nothing. Why should I spoil a child's illusions about Christmas, especially when her gift was a Scrabble set?

Today we plan to open presents early and then attend the two church services. Afterward, we will drive to the Summer Palace for a walk. We are taking along skates, just in case the lake ice is thick enough for skating. In the evening, the three of us will dine on the turkey that our cook, Chen, cooked.

Western diplomats spend Christmas Eve quietly. The Scandinavian ambassadors gave dinners for their staffs in their embassies and, later, a choir from the British Office made the rounds singing carols.

New Year's Eve, however, promises to be lively. There will be dinner parties in the diplomatic community, with the Scandinavians more or less dividing among them unattached Westerners like us. Afterward, we will repair to the French Embassy for one of three major New Year's Eve balls. The two other big parties are being given by the African embassies, collectively, and by the Soviet Embassy.

The Russian party, basically for diplomats from socialist countries, begins an hour before midnight. Toasts are drunk every hour on the hour as midnight arrives in Omsk and other Russian cities until 5 a.m. when 1969 begins in Moscow. Then the party ends.

I supposed we could do the same, toasting Charlottetown, Halifax and so on. But midnight in Toronto is one o'clock in the afternoon in Peking. Somehow I don't think we would make it.

Amid the harshness of winter, everyone — Chinese and foreigners alike — enjoyed the novelty of a Peking snowstorm.

PEKING — Snow is a rare sight in Peking, but not because the weather is mild.

In winter the wind whips down from Siberia, charges across the Gobi Desert and hits Peking with stunning force, rattling windows and prying at ill-fitting doors.

Bicyclists, muffled in padded cotton clothes, fur helmets and white face masks, seem held back by an invisible giant's hand as they pump against the gale.

Even Peking's housing authorities take it into account. Rents are higher for flats that face the south and need less fuel for heat because they are sheltered from the biting north wind. (They also enjoy exposure to the sun.)

But the wind is dry and brings little snow to Peking. Last winter, for instance, Peking had only one snowfall, as far as most foreigners remember. And many of them didn't even see it because it began at night, lasted only about an hour and was blown away by the wind before dawn.

' This December, though, thick snowflakes began to fall one night and were still swirling down on the next morning.

Peking was transformed. The snow softened the stern walls that line almost every street, and lent new grace to the curved tile roofs of the Chinese houses. Temples were capped with white, providing a startling contrast to their intricate and brightly colored wood carvings.

Everyone enjoyed the snow. Even cyclists seemed amused

117

when their bicycles slowly slid out from under them at slippery corners and they bumped to the ground. Of course they were so well padded that it was difficult to be hurt.

Many Chinese armed themselves with cameras and set off for the city's parks, particularly Coal Hill and Pei Hai, both of which are located near the Forbidden City and offer spectacular views of Peking. Near the park entrances, the old women with pushcarts who sell glasses of hot tea poured from oversized vacuum bottles were doing a brisk business.

At some busy intersections, pedicarts arrived loaded with ashes, which workmen spread on the road. No salt was used, which may explain why one sees in Peking gleaming Packards, Hudsons and Buicks 20 years old and older that a vintage-car collector would snap up at double the original price.

There were no snow plows in evidence, but street cleaning was not a problem. By noon the snow had stopped and an hour later most of the roads had been cleared. This was done by street committees or neighborhood organizations which quickly marshalled thousands of women to shovel snow from roads near their homes.

Still, there was enough left for children to enjoy. They were out in force, laughing and shouting as they pulled and pushed each other on the packed snow. Even toddlers wearing the split trousers that make diapers unnecessary were clambering about in the snow — though many were also wearing a sort of padded apron for rearguard protection.

A number of simple home-made wood sleds appeared, just large enough for one child to sit on cross-legged. Many of the children took turns riding and pushing, but others had two short metal picks that they used like ski poles to speed their sleds along the frozen snow.

Only one winter item was conspicuous by its absence — a snowman.

For nearly three years, the Chinese had seemed almost totally absorbed by the trauma of their internal political struggle. But in March, 1969, an armed clash on Chenpao Island — along the disputed border between the Soviet Union and Chinese Manchuria — led Peking to launch massive anti-Russian demonstrations across the nation. In the capital, McCullough observed one of the largest rallies.

PEKING — The two tall Chinese boys were good actors. They shuffled along the Boulevard of Eternal Peace, their heads and shoulders bowed to express abject defeat — and also to hide the occasional grins they shot at each other.

One boy was wearing an ill-fitting suit-jacket and a high cardboard top hat painted with red and blue stripes. He was U.S. Imperialism. The other boy wore a brown tunic and breeches. He was Soviet Soldier. Behind them, stepping proudly, came four boys holding wooden rifles and wearing the uniform of the Chinese People's Liberation Army.

And behind them came a long column of 2,000 teenaged boys and girls holding aloft red flags, pictures of Chairman Mao Tse-tung and signs denouncing the "new czars" of Russia. In unison they raised their red books of Mao's quotations as they shouted "Down with Soviet Revisionism".

On they marched to Tien An Men and their cries soon became muffled in the cloud of sound hanging over the Square of Heavenly Peace where another 40,000 Chinese were also parading and shouting slogans.

At least a million persons marched through the streets yesterday in one of the largest demonstrations Peking has had. Yesterday's was the third and probably last day of organized public protest over the armed clash between frontier guards at the Sino-Soviet border in Heilungkiang Province, northeast China.

At times it seemed that almost all of Peking's estimated seven million people were taking part. Old men with long, grey beards, their padded trousers tied at the ankles, walked with factory workers, housewives, children, office clerks and commune peasants. Even the staffs of some foreigners — translators, cooks, drivers, *amahs* — asked for the afternoon off to join the demonstration.

Some carried signboard drawings of Alexei Kosygin, Soviet premier, and Leonid Brezhnev, Soviet party secretary, with their noses painted green and ropes around the necks. Others waved little colored paper pennants bearing slogans: "We vow to defend the sacred territory of our motherland at all costs."

Throughout the day convoys of 10 to 15 trucks jammed with standing men and women rumbled back and forth across the city. Many were bound for the Soviet Embassy where demonstrators have paraded for three days, effectively sealing off the street leading to the main entrance. Trucks with loudspeakers blared slogans at the embassy, but they and the marchers disappeared early in the evening.

The demonstrators have not been allowed to approach the embassy or to put posters on its walls as was done during some phases of the Cultural Revolution.

Many soldiers and policemen marched with the demonstrators to emphasize discipline and orderliness. In the downtown area, paraders parted lines to allow foreigners doing their shopping to cross the street.

According to the New China News Agency, demonstrations involving millions of people are also being held in cities across the country.

No figure has been released on the number of Chinese casualties in the border battle but official reports have used the word "many", whatever the figure may be. An observer in Peking gets the impression that the armed clash has intensified the unity of the Chinese people and provided them with final proof that their country is indeed endangered by their once friendly neighbor, the Soviet Union.

Later in March there was more fighting on Chenpao, with Peking charging that the Soviet Union had sent a large force of tanks on to the island and had also shelled the Chinese mainland. By April, however, the anti-Soviet clamor had died down, as thousands of beating drums and millions of marching feet in the capital signalled a major domestic event — the long-awaited Ninth Congress of the Chinese Communist Party. It had been 11 years since the Eighth Congress, and the fact that the Party's Central Committee was expanded by almost 100 new members was a further indication of the changes wrought by the Cultural Revolution. Yet the top leaders remained in place: Mao Tse-tung, Lin Piao and Chou En-lai, followed by Chiang Ching and others who had risen to prominence during the recent turmoil. No startling policy changes were announced: speeches and editorials stressed the importance of achieving unity and avoiding a resurgence of bitter factional-

Peasant children join in the harvest at a commune outside Peking.

A large Mao button adorns an industrial complex.

ism. By summer there were further signs of consolidation. The People's Liberation Army, which had been a major stabilizing force in the Cultural Revolution, began to loosen some of its control over civilian affairs; in a parallel move, there was a drive to rebuild the shattered Communist Party by recruiting new members from the ranks of the "revolutionary rebels" and by re-accepting veteran cadres who had been criticized and since publicly admitted their errors.

McCullough's time in Peking was nearly at an end. Before he left, he filed some vignettes of every-day life in the Chinese capital.

PEKING — We bought our daughter a pair of Chinese shoes. They were well made with thick rubber soles and tough suede uppers. The heels and soles, we discovered, had been made of old car tires: the tread was still visible.

Fifteen Russian technicians, travelling from Hanoi to Moscow via Peking, sat in the Canton airport waiting room muffled in heavy overcoats and fur hats. They stared impassively at the choir of smiling Chinese airport workers who stood before them singing songs praising Stalin — in Russian.

A sure sign that a major demonstration will be called for the next day is to see workmen late at night putting up canvas-walled portable latrines along the Boulevard of Eternal Peace.

It costs about five cents to enter the Summer Palace grounds. More often than not, the ticket taker says "Long life to Chairman Mao" as he hands you your change.

Some nights, if we are lucky, we go to sleep hearing faintly the twisting and sweet melody of a Chinese song being played on a flute by someone, somewhere. In the morning, at six, we awake to the sound of "The East Is Red" being played on nearby loudspeakers.

The Chinese press hasn't mentioned the subject for about a year, but work is proceeding rapidly on a subway being built on the site of the thick wall that once encircled the city. A night shift works under lights in the open-cut line. One long section has already been filled in and it appears that at least part of the subway line will be open in time for China's National Day, October 1.

The old man pumped the pedicart slowly along the road. There was one passenger, a boy about 12. His shoulders shook uncontrollably, and he did not wipe away the tears that ran down his cheeks. He sat cross-legged, with one arm stretched across the pine board coffin beside him.

Sometimes, late at night, we hear a roar like a football crowd and see lights against the sky from the nearby Workers' Stadium. It is disconcerting to know that about 50,000 people are meeting just a few blocks away, and yet not have the faintest idea of what they are doing, or why.

The fronts of railway engines are bedecked with little red flags and a framed color portrait of Mao Tse-tung.

Without doubt, the most popular stores along Peking's main shopping street, Wang Fu Ching, are those that sell Chairman Mao badges. There is always a line of people waiting to buy badges of a new design. Most are bright red plastic, but I have seen others made of porcelain and bamboo. They cost from one to five cents each and some are as large as saucers. Every Chinese wears one badge.

Men's long underwear can be bought in shades of bright blue, green and yellow.

Norman Webster skating with his son at the International Club in Peking.

CHAPTER FIVE: 1969—1971

NORMAN WEBSTER

In the autumn of 1969, the *Globe and Mail* bureau entered its second decade as McCullough was succeeded in Peking by Norman Webster. A Rhodes Scholar, Webster, 28, had been a member of the editorial board, editor of *The Globe Magazine* and assistant editor of the newspaper. He was accompanied by his wife and their two sons, aged one and nearly three. (By the time of their return, a third son had been added to the family.) Although the political scene still seemed quiet, it was evident that Webster would be even more restricted in his movements — at least initially — than McCullough and Oancia had been. Chinese authorities were ignoring requests by diplomats and correspondents to visit cities such as Shanghai, Nanking and Hangchow — all of which had been accessible in the past. Even in the Peking area, such favorite weekend spots as the Great Wall, the Ming Tombs and the Western Hills had recently been declared off-limits to foreigners.

These moves seemed linked to Chinese fears of a major attack from the Soviet Union. After the Chenpao Island battles in the spring there had been further clashes in the northeast and along the Sinkiang border in the far northwest. Negotiations on the disputed boundaries had started in Peking in October, and continued fitfully throughout the winter. But there was no apparent progress in the talks, and the Chinese press continued to assail the Soviet "revisionists". Peking seemed to be preparing the Chinese people for more extensive hostilities, as well as taking practical measures such as increased army and militia training, the stockpiling of food and strategic metals, and some decentralization of industry. Most visibly, they were also building air-raid shelters and labyrinths of underground tunnels in Peking and other major cities. At first there was no official mention of the shelters, but Webster reported that huge piles of loose earth around the capital were signs of extensive digging. Then, in early 1970, he witnessed his first air-raid alert.

PEKING — When the sirens sounded, children at the nearby primary school formed up in ranks with their teachers. Then, directed by soldiers, they set off up the street at double time. After several hundred yards they came to the farm fields that form the northern boundary of the diplomatic area known as San Li Tun.

Still jogging in step, they ran from the street out into the bare brown earth. Then, like little field mice, they disappeared into an underground bunker.

That was on Friday when the children, and many others, participated in an air-raid exercise in northeast Peking. Along the main boulevard that runs between San Li Tun and the other main diplomatic area, Wai Chiao Ta Lou, rows of Chinese apartment buildings stood empty, doors and windows open, their inhabitants removed by truck.

Monitors with arm-bands stood by each building. Cyclists and donkey carts stood still on the streets, under the direction of soldiers. The area, usually filled with men, women and chattering children, was eerily quiet.

Evidently the exercise was not held throughout the city. Nor, apparently, was it the first such practice alert here. At least one is said to have been held earlier in January. Peking is a city of seven million people, a vast area and, for a foreigner, one of remarkable impenetrability.

It is perhaps significant that Friday's exercise was held in and around the diplomatic areas. It would indicate that an element in China's preparation-against-war campaign is to be seen to be doing it.

There can be no doubt that, for whatever motives, the campaign is continuing. Air-raid shelters are still being dug all over the city, and the pace has, if anything, increased. Blocks of flats have rough wooden fences around adjacent vacant spaces, behind which digging machines operate. A similar barricade surrounds an area at the side of the Great Hall of the People down-

At the Liu Lin production brigade near Yenan, a barefoot doctor gives acupuncture treatment to a peasant suffering from a cold. The poster is of Dr. Norman Bethune, the Canadian surgeon who died while treating Mao's soldiers thirty-two years ago.

town. Men wield shovels in the courtyards of the walled Chinese dwelling compounds.

Most of the work is more or less out in the open, however. Sidewalks along Wang Fu Ching, the main central shopping area, are blocked in many places by dirt being brought out from shops that are "closed for repairs". On Chien Men Wei, a shop-filled avenue leading south from Tien An Men Square in the city's centre, even the old Peking Duck Restaurant is putting in a shelter, and the avenue's eastern sidewalk is filled block after block by piles of earth often 10 feet high.

Men and women carry out full wicker baskets on shoulder ropes and add to the piles. Mortar is mixed on the sidewalk and bricks passed hand to hand along lines leading inside. Supplies are brought by truck and pedicart. Work continues at night.

As work on the shelters continued through the spring, the Chinese became more active on the diplomatic front. This, too, seemed a response to Soviet threats. During the Cultural Revolution, Peking recalled most of its ambassadors and sank into diplomatic isolation. Now the envoys were back at their posts, and the Chinese were pursuing some tentative openings to the West. Negotiations with Canada and Italy over diplomatic recognition were proceeding at a leisurely pace; more significantly, the Chinese had resumed ambassadorial talks with the Americans in Warsaw (although these were suspended in May when President Richard Nixon ordered the U.S. invasion of Cambodia). Peking's claims to great power status were underlined in April when the Chinese launched their first satellite: this was seen as an important step forward in the development of Chinese rocket and missile technology.

Throughout the summer, there were further signs that the Communist Party was being steadily rebuilt and reactivated. At least at lower levels, party groups were taking over from revolutionary committees. But Chinese newspapers and other official sources gave few details of the changes, and diplomats and correspondents were reduced to speculating on the basis of the scantiest evidence, such as the sudden disappearance of Red Guard dolls from Peking toy counters. On a less trivial level, Webster found confirmation of a return to normal conditions in the way the Chinese were once again enthusiastically engaging in sport.

The Red Detachment of Women perform a morality play, with a poster of Mao on the backdrop curtain.

PEKING — The man who may be the best high-jumper in the world stares at the bar through the rain. Ni Chih-chin has already won his event at the track meet on the forty-ninth birthday of the Chinese Communist Party. Now the bar has been raised to 7 feet 5 inches, higher than anyone has jumped in recent years, and the rain has started. Ni is of stout heart. "In order to win honor for Chairman Mao and the motherland I must make it, no matter how bad the weather is!" And so saying, runs up and clears it first try.

In an indoor stadium, 20,000 fans are silent as two of the best table-tennis players in the world battle for a key point. You can hear the squeak of their white sneakers right up in the last row as they struggle — one man smashing, smashing and smashing again, the other making dogged, impossible returns from more than six feet back of the table. It is fierce and dazzling, laughably unlike anything you ever played in the basement.

At the Summer Palace of the Chings, swimmers stroke and splash under the eye of whatever spirits still reside in the Buddhist pagoda on Longevity Hill. Military swimmers, male and female, march along in a platoon of blue tank suits and make an orderly entry into Kunming Lake.

It is Sunday, and on an open athletic ground in downtown Peking all the basketball courts and soccer fields are in use. No grass grows, and a tumble on the rough dirt means a scrape or a bruise, but the games are still played vigorously. Thousands line the main soccer field to follow the action.

On a country road on the outskirts of the city, a man in shorts and singlet puffs along rhythmically, dodging donkey and horse carts, peasants, children and marching soldiers. Here even the long-distance runner finds little loneliness.

Sport has returned to China — and the Chinese are returning to sport — as life continues to settle down and the wave of the Cultural Revolution to subside.

It is not, perhaps, generally realized that organized athletic competition virtually ceased here in the years 1967-69. An awareness of just how profoundly the Cultural Revolution gripped most areas of Chinese life comes when one remembers that by 1966 China had become a country with more than a hundred million sporting participants.

Schools emphasized games. Factories and offices provided sports breaks during shifts. In the villages of the countryside, China's peasants were introduced to athletics for the first time.

"Sport has become an inseparable part of the life of the Chinese people," *The People's Daily* declared in 1965 — the year Ping-Pong ball production reached a whopping seventy million. Table tennis, basketball, volleyball, soccer and swimming were most popular, followed by mountaineering, badminton, track-and-field and gymnastics. (Some hockey was played, mainly in the northeast.)

The development of champions was not neglected. In all, in the 16 years after the Communist takeover in 1949, Chinese athletes were said to have broken world records 115 times in track-and-field, swimming, weightlifting, archery and other events.

China's greatest triumphs, though, came in table tennis. The game was brought here from Japan around 1904 by a merchant from Shanghai, but the Chinese did not enter world competition until 1957. In 1959 they captured their first world title — the men's singles.

China retained this title in the succeeding biennial world competitions in 1961, 1963 and 1965. Chuang Tse-tung won it in each of these three years, while his teammates added other trophies. In 1965 the Chinese nearly swept the board — winning the men's and women's team championships, the men's singles and the men's and women's doubles.

China's athletic triumphs were credited to the beneficial effects of having applied Mao Tse-tung's thought to arrive at the correct motivation. The theoretical journal *Red Flag* made it plain sport was more than fun and games: "To play table tennis is a revolutionary endeavor and serves the interest of the people. It is not for fun or for the opportunity to show off."

Hsu Yin-sheng, who with Chuang won the men's doubles in 1965, added a practical tip: "If we take the ball as Chiang Kai-shek's head and smash it with our bats, how powerful will be our strokes!"

Young children perform for their friends before a billboard of Mao Tse-tung and Lin Piao.

Snow-clearing operation after one of Peking's infrequent snowfalls.

Pat Webster, wife of Globe correspondent Norman Webster, strolls across Tien An Men Square with her children.

Observers were tempted to credit the Chinese superiority also to technique — notably to the pen-holder grip favored in Asia and used by most of the top Chinese. In the classical grip the bat is held roughly like a tennis racquet and different surfaces used for forehand and backhand shots. Pen-holders take the handle between thumb and forefinger, with the remaining three fingers acting as support behind the bat. Only one side is used for striking.

The grip sounds unworkable until you see slight pigtailed girls using it to hit savage forehand drives. This stroke is considered the most powerful in table tennis, and the best pen-holders use it a majority of the time, standing close to the table and forcing their opponents on to the defensive.

It was, in a way, an athletic feat that signalled the beginning of the end for the first golden age of Chinese Communist sport. In July, 1966, Chairman Mao, then 72, took a highly publicized swim in the Yangtze River, reportedly covering nine miles in just 65 minutes. Having made plain to his people that he was fit and vigorous, the Chairman proceeded to put his full weight behind the Cultural Revolution, then building for some months.

China still participated in the Games of the Newly Emerging Forces in Phnom Penh, Cambodia, in November of that year, but after that almost everything stopped. No Chinese teams went abroad. No foreign teams visited China. Public sporting performances were almost as rare as Brezhnev bumper stickers.

Even pick-up games of basketball and soccer became rare. The clacking of Ping-Pong balls on public tables was no longer heard. Athletic fields and stadiums were used for demonstrations as China's energies were absorbed by political struggle.

The country's top athletes disappeared from view. Some, notably Ping-Pongers Chuang and Hsu, were criticized for having indulged in a capitalist way of life.

There was still militia training, of course, and with it certain sport-related activities — shooting, parachute jumping, grenade throwing. (You can buy wooden-handled models of Chinese hand grenades at Peking sports counters: about 55 cents each for the top line.) Mountaineering and swimming continued, and school children never ceased their year-round outdoor calisthenics, route marches and jogging. But organized athletic competition ceased.

It now seems clear that at least some of China's top athletes were allowed to train behind the scenes, many at the Peking Institute of Physical Culture. Last summer, favored foreign guests began to be treated to exhibitions at the institute.

Then last October the public got a peek at a gala sports evening in Peking's beautiful 20,000-seat Capital Stadium. There were exhibitions of table tennis, gymnastics, basketball and volleyball. Star of the evening was erstwhile world champion Chuang Tse-tung, making his first public appearance in three years.

Then the curtain fell again, although occasional articles in the press indicated sport was once more being encouraged at factory and village level. It was not until June that the full go-ahead was given. In the space of a few days three things happened. A Chinese table-tennis team was sent to Nepal to play during King Mahendra's birthday celebrations. Regular sports performances for the public began. And *The People's Daily*, in a front-page article, gave the kiss of the leadership once more to sports and physical culture.

As for the masses, signs of a sports resurgence are apparent. Youngsters play soccer on school fields, teenagers practice lay-ups beneath outdoor basketball hoops and fathers and sons play badminton beside apartment buildings.

Again, as before, fun comes well down on the list of the benefits of sport. Of prime importance is building up the people's health so they may better fulfill their tasks of production, socialist construction and national defence. Militia training and sports are closely linked.

Sports also "foster the sense of revolutionary discipline and organization". In other words, they are another means of strengthening social organization and structuring the leisure time of persons who might use it for private, suspicious activities.

Late in 1970, Webster was permitted to travel to Shanghai and Nanking — two cities rarely visited by foreigners since the Cultural Revolution. This was further confirmation of the return to more normal conditions. But in both cities, Webster found that political activity was still fervid.

SHANGHAI — For the traveller from Peking, Shanghai is a political massage.

Banners bearing slogans overhang the streets and cover the fronts of buildings both horizontally and vertically.

The store windows are full of battle scenes starring grim-faced stalwarts of the army, navy and air force. Others depict heroic characters from China's revolutionary theatre.

Ranged along the famous riverside Bund and spreading throughout the city are the mass criticism posters that foreigners are forbidden to photograph or even to read.

Every half hour the great clock on the old Customs House chimes "The East Is Red". Red Guards worked without rest for two days and nights during the Cultural Revolution to manage that.

At night orange neon characters blaze out high atop the buildings along the Bund and across the Whangpoo River. "Long Live Chairman Mao", they read, over and over. "Long Live the Communist Party of China".

Factory workshops are festooned with slogans, covered with big-character posters, filled with political blackboard newspapers.

And always, everywhere, portraits of Mao Tse-tung.

Residents in China during the Cultural Revolution say this was the pattern for Chinese cities at that time. But Peking no longer looks like this.

Shanghai, where the Communist Party of China was founded in 1921, is traditionally more political and volatile than the sleepy northern capital. . . .

NANKING — On a huge billboard in the centre of Nanking, Chairman Mao Tse-tung looms in full color before a representation of China's proudest feat of engineering, the great bridge here across the Yangtze River.

On the street in front of the billboard, men and women strain and sweat in harness as they pull carts of bricks, coal, wood and vegetables.

The contrast is striking. It gives something of the feeling of this ancient centre, poised between its imperial past and the Communist vision of its future.

Ancient it is. The site of Nanking has been inhabited for about 6,000 years, and the city was the capital of many of China's dynasties — most notably, for a time, the Ming.

More recently for Nanking, Sun Yat-sen proclaimed the first Republic of China in 1911 and the city later served as a capital for Chiang Kai-shek's Kuomintang regime.

Since the Communist takeover in 1949 the city, long an artistic and educational centre, has been rapidly industrialized. More than 400,000 in the population of 1.7 million are said to be industrial workers. Chemical fertilizer, textiles, iron and steel, machinery, trucks, cement, optical instruments, radios and foodstuffs are important products.

Nanking's importance as an industrial and communications centre can only be enhanced by its prize asset, the bridge. It makes Nanking the key link between the country's north and south.

Before the bridge was completed, in December, 1968, trains had to be loaded onto ferries and crossing the Yangtze barrier was a slow, laborious affair. Today 90 trains a day rumble swiftly over the river and projections are for greatly increased traffic.

Nanking has shops of every description beside sidewalks lined with parked bicycles. The People's Department Store has a reasonable selection of goods (including, believe it or not, baseballs), although inferior to the selections found in Peking and Shanghai. Clothes, too, are a bit more faded and patchy than those in the other two cities.

The pace generally is slower. Workers fixing a roof take their time. Tea vendors on sidewalks do a brisk business as people break from their labors.

There is little motor traffic. Instead there are donkey and horse carts, pedalled vehicles and, as often as not, conveyances pulled by men and women in traces.

It makes for interesting sights. Pedicab drivers pump past in a line, their passenger seats heaped with hunks of red, raw meat on the way to market. A big block of reinforced concrete rolls along on a cart pulled by a team of men and women.

Those omnipresent fixtures of the new China, public loudspeakers, carry revolutionary music, news and political material to every corner of the city from 6 a.m. on.

There are mass-criticism posters, slogans on walls, political displays in store windows and revolutionary drama in the theatres and cinemas. In the evening, low-watt bulbs illuminate rooms with groups facing portraits of Mao Tse-tung and reading their red books.

By early 1971, the Chinese leaders were facing the world with renewed confidence. Diplomatic relations had been established with Canada, breaking the recognition logjam and setting a pattern for other nations to follow. In March, Premier Chou En-lai visited Hanoi, and a joint communiqué denounced "the recklessness and madness of the Nixon Government" in Indo-China. This was followed by more strident attacks on Washington in the Chinese press. Behind the scenes, however, the Chinese had been preparing a major diplomatic initiative to improve relations with the United States. In April, a 15-member delegation of U.S. table-tennis players and officials suddenly appeared in China. It was the start of "Ping-Pong diplomacy" and the biggest story to come out of China in years.

The invitation had been issued in Nagoya, Japan, at the world table-tennis championships. Players from Canada, Britain, Colombia and Nigeria were also invited, but it was the Americans who stole the show when they reached Peking, followed by a host of U.S. reporters. It was the first time that a U.S. delegation had been received in China since the Communist victory in 1949, and the Americans were deluged with speeches of friendship. As Webster reported: "The smile on the face of the dragon was dazzling." At the climax of their visit, a relaxed and jovial Chou En-lai greeted the Americans in the Great Hall of the People. Surrounded by U.S. newsmen and television cameras, he said the visit had opened a new page in Sino-U.S. relations. In future, he added, the two peoples "will be able to have constant contacts". At the end of an extraordinary week, Webster summed up the highlights and speculated on the significance.

PEKING — If there's a diplomatic hall of fame somewhere, one exhibit it should place alongside the pin-striped suits and attaché cases is a certain T-shirt.

White, with long sleeves, it sports the U.S. stars and stripes on the front — except that in place of the stars there appears the peace symbol. Underneath is the slogan, "Let It Be".

The shirt was given to China's top table-tennis player, Chuang Tse-tung, by U.S. Ping-Ponger Glenn Cowan during the recent world championships in Japan.

Although it is doubtful that Chuang will walk down the streets of Peking in the shirt, he accepted the gift in friendly fashion and returned a picture-imprinted Chinese handkerchief.

The exchange was the most interesting of several friendly gestures between the U.S. and Chinese table-tennis delegations at the championships. That friendliness, and the good publicity it brought, was doubtless one of the many considerations that led to the invitation to U.S. players to visit and play in China.

The result has been an astonishing week here. Consider what your psychiatrist would have made of these fantasies a week and a half ago:

● Premier Chou En-lai meets athletes from five countries in Peking's Great Hall of the People as the event is covered by — good grief — NBC, the Associated Press, United Press International and *Life* as well as the CBC in both English and French and a number of other foreign news organizations.

● A U.S. teenager with hair falling to his shoulders asks Premier Chou what he thinks of hippies.

● Premier Chou says they should do their thing.

● On an outdoor basketball court in Peking, an American takes a jump shot. A Chinese goes up for the rebound.

● A British group tours Peking's Forbidden City, formerly the Imperial Palace of China. It has been closed to all but a favored few since the Cultural Revolution.

● Two startlingly bourgeois paintings in old-fashioned frames suddenly replace a slogan by Chairman Mao Tse-tung on a restaurant wall. The slogan read: "People of the World, Unite and Defeat the U.S. Aggressors and All Their Running Dogs".

● U.S., Canadian, Colombian, British and Nigerian table-tennis players practice in Peking's Capital Stadium as Chinese players instruct them and work on the weak points of their game.

- Chinese guides shift uncomfortably as they are grilled on sexual customs, dope and other subjects dear to the heart of North American youth. One Chinese cannot conceal his amazement when an American talks with a grin about "Happiness in a pipe".
- U.S. tourists snap photographs of the Great Wall of China as if it's the most natural thing in the world.
- "These are Americans," I announced in Tien An Men Square to a crowd of Chinese. They smile. Two months previously hundreds of thousands filed through the square denouncing "U.S. imperialsm".
- Chou En-lai says that U.S. journalists will be coming to China in batches. He says a new page has been opened in relations between the Chinese and U.S. people.

It probably has. In the past week and a half, China has shown just how supple and clever it can be in its foreign relations. And it all came off a Ping-Pong bat.

There is no doubt that it wasn't a last-minute affair. The Chinese Ping-Pongers went to the world championships in Japan with explicit instructions to smile.

Observers in Peking feel there must have been a contingency plan drawn up some time ago for a U.S. visit. When the decision was finally made and the invitation issued and accepted, the plan swung into operation, with impressively smooth results.

U.S. newsmen and organizations were probably not planned for originally. It took a couple of days to expand the plan. Decisions of this importance probably go right to the top, to Chairman Mao himself. . . .

China's dealings with foreigners have become more flexible generally in recent months. The trend is toward finding common ground instead of points of difference.

Heads of foreign missions in Peking are currently on tour in China, a rare occurrence in recent years. China and Austria have begun formal negotiations about diplomatic recognition. Since Canada opened the door last October with its recognition of Peking, seven countries have followed.

China's sights currently seem set on the United Nations, which it hopes will vote to expel Taiwan and install Peking next

Line-ups. Always line-ups. This one is at a snack bar during an outdoor pageant.

A factory worker in Sian.

fall. The new recognitions, the people-to-people friendliness, even with Americans, the opening up to newsmen — all will keep up the momentum for Chinese entry into the United Nations.

The visit of the U.S. Ping-Pongers and the full coverage of their activities should help the cause. The favorable publicity will make it that much more difficult for President Richard Nixon to fight hard to keep Taiwan in the world organization.

All in all, it was a forehand smash, one of the bolder strokes in China's foreign relations for some considerable time. And it began, in public at least, when a T-shirt was exchanged for a printed handkerchief.

Maybe the hall of fame should get the hankie too.

Webster would win a National Newspaper Award for his coverage of the remarkable visit. Soon after the Americans departed, he and other foreign residents began to benefit from the new spirit of Ping-Pong diplomacy, as the Forbidden City and the Valley of the Ming Tombs were opened to them. That spring and summer, Webster also made trips to Changsha and Canton in the south, and Sian and Yenan in the northwest: no resident correspondent had been allowed to travel so widely since Charles Taylor in 1964-65. But if the Chinese authorities were adopting a more relaxed attitude toward foreigners, they were still taking pains to impose a strict Communist discipline on their own people — especially the children.

PEKING — "Follow Chairman Mao," their voices shrill as they march past my window. "Forever make revolution. Hold high the revolutionary red flag. Brave heroes kill the enemies."

Children in China — probably the world's cutest, busiest and most indoctrinated. The molding of the new socialist man begins right after the toddler stage.

Among the first things children are taught at kindergarten are revolutionary fight songs and verses in praise of Mao Tsetung. They learn to chant political slogans and to stage routines that end with bayonet lunges to the shout of "Sha!" ("kill").

They imbibe class hatred through frequent retelling of the bitterness of the oppressed classes in old China. They hear tales of U.S. aggression in Indo-China. They are told about the sweetness of the new society, and instructed to adjure all thoughts of self and dedicate themselves to serving the people.

This continues through primary and secondary school and, if they are lucky, university. It produces young people who, when questioned, almost unfailingly reject any thought of personal ambition. They insist their only desire is to obey the wishes of the Party, to do what is best for the country.

You often have a strong urge to look into their skulls and see what they really do think. You might find it is just as they say.

Work is an important element in the molding process. An important precept of Chinese life today is that no one shall grow up unfamiliar with the bracing virtues of manual labor. For countryside youngsters, there is no end to the farming jobs they can take on, and there is plenty of work for young urban hands, too.

Much of it consists of clean-up tasks. Young people play an important role in the periodic "patriotic sanitation" campaigns in the big cities.

In Peking you can see them pulling up weeds beside the road, hauling away garbage, collecting fallen tree branches, picking up paper, sweeping in the parks. They also help dredge dirty ditches, fill in areas where insects breed, clean out public lavatories and scrape horse manure from the streets.

A principal pastime is standing at intersections — wind, rain or shine — alternately reciting the thoughts of Mao and bellowing traffic-safety slogans at the hordes of cyclists. It is, to the newcomer, one of the most startling sights in China.

An activity in which more are participating these days is long hikes in and around the city. These are supposed to emulate the Red Army's epic Long March of 1934, toughening the new generation physically and spiritually. Joe Frazier should do as much roadwork.

It isn't a grim life without fun, though. Chinese children play often and hard, enjoying themselves enormously in simple games.

In the winter, boys perch on sleds with steel runners and propel themselves, whooping over the capital's frozen lakes and canals. They fly kites, spin tops and roll iron hoops.

Young girls tend more to skipping games, one a form of hopscotch, another using an elasticized rope. Tying this be-

In Sian, a peasant pauses on his way to market to distribute some of his cabbages.

This mud-brick house in Shaoshan is where Mao was born. It is now a museum for the faithful.

A young girl uses draw reins to help her mother lug a heavy cart near Sian.

Ping-Pong diplomacy wasn't all diplomacy. A U.S. team member plays hard against his Chinese opponent.

tween two trees, they dance a complicated skipping routine one never tires of watching.

Older children and teenagers go in for sports. They swim en masse and play basketball, volleyball, soccer — and Ping-Pong.

More than in most other societies, however, the spare time and vacations of young people are organized. And the activities have a heavy political slant.

Besides physical labor and organized sports, these include revolutionary songs and dances, group self-criticism, lectures about class struggle and visits to gruesome exhibitions about the bad old days. Children are told lively stories of revolutionary heroes. These activities are overseen by carefully picked adults, sometimes attached to the school, sometimes to a local neighborhood.

Many youngsters become Little Red Soldiers, a corps for youngsters from 7 to 14. The elite of the 15-year-olds and up may join the Communist Youth League or a Red Guard group. The Red Guards these days are more like Boy Scouts than the rampaging threat to all Chinese institutions they represented during the Cultural Revolution.

These groups often carry the revolutionary message out into society. Nanking, for example, has Little Red Soldier troupes of musicians, singers and dancers as gifted and appealing as any I have ever seen. This is a clever propaganda move: Chinese will drop anything to watch children perform.

Another reason for organizing out-of-school activities is to leave little time for that old debbil the class enemy to do his thing. Reports appear periodically about the "feudal superstitions, anarchism and corruption" that these enemies spread, and about the "poisonous novels and magazines and gutter songs and stories" they pass on to the young people.

Poisonous literature apparently means literature tending to inculcate bourgeois attitudes and lacking the strictly black-and-white approach of the Chinese writing permitted nowadays.

A function of the out-of-school organizations is to bring peer-group discipline to bear on youngsters who get out of line. They are encouraged to censure those caught with poisonous novels and magazines, or those with no regard for the "revolutionary discipline" desirable in school.

If a youngster proves to be a real hard case, a delegation may drop in on his family for some Mao study and discussion of their child. This underlines another result of close control over young people — it provides a line to their parents.

Every effort is made to have the "revolutionary parents" take an active part in planning the programs for their children. On the other hand, youngsters are told to keep an eye on their parents' attitudes and not to be afraid to criticize.

It is all part of the continuing Communist assault on the old, inner-directed, authoritarian-patriarchal Chinese family unit. Probably the assault is having more success in the cities than in the countryside, where attitudes change more slowly.

But there, also, they march and work with their hands, tell revolutionary stories, dance and sing. "Chairman Mao loves the people," the children's voices ring. "Chairman Mao, he is our guide. . . ."

On a rainy day in Peking John Burns has his picture taken while getting set to take one of his own.

CHAPTER SIX: 1971—1975

JOHN BURNS

In June, 1971, Webster returned to Canada and John Burns took over in Peking. A 26-year-old bachelor, Burns had lived in Rhodesia, South Africa, Germany and Britain before graduating from Montreal's McGill University. Before he went to China, Burns had represented *The Globe and Mail* in the Parliamentary Press Gallery in Ottawa for two years. Burns was to remain in China for four years — the longest tenure of any of the *Globe* correspondents. He would report on many dramatic developments, but few would be more startling than the announcement within a few weeks of his arrival that White House aide Henry Kissinger had made a secret trip to Peking and that he would be followed by President Richard Nixon. Stunned by the news, the foreign community saw it as an unexpectedly speedy result of "Ping-Pong diplomacy".

Soon Burns was busy trying to unravel an especially perplexing Chinese puzzle. In August, Peking announced that Communist Party committees had been established in each of China's 29 provinces, autonomous regions and independent municipal districts. Five years after the start of the Cultural Revolution, it seemed that the Chinese had succeeded in rebuilding the Party framework, and that the leadership was again united. Then, in September, the Chinese announced the cancellation of their October 1 National Day parade. This was another startling development, since the parade had always been the climactic moment in the Chinese year, and since extensive preparations had been underway for several weeks. Eventually, official spokesmen maintained that the cancellation was an economy measure. To Burns and the other correspondents, however, it was clear that serious new problems

must have emerged for the Chinese leaders. Whatever their nature, a second visit by Kissinger in October indicated that the
Nixon visit would still take place. Then, while Kissinger was on
his way to Peking airport, there came the news from New York
that China had been voted into the United Nations, and that
Washington had failed in its attempt to preserve a seat for Taiwan.
Chinese officials were openly jubilant.

By late 1971, however, it became evident that something *was*
amiss at the highest level in Peking. A lengthy campaign in the
press featured attacks on "careerists and plotters who are fighting
against Marxism under the banner of Marxism". While the plotters were not named, attention centred on Vice-Chairman Lin
Piao. Three years earlier, Lin had been named Chairman Mao's
official heir. But he had not been mentioned in the press since
early September — just before the cancellation of the National
Day parade, when he would normally have stood beside Mao on
the reviewing stand. Recently, his name had disappeared from
billboards around the capital, and bookstores no longer had vol-
umes of his speeches and essays. Clearly Lin was on the skids, and
Burns speculated that he might even be dead.

Soon, however, Burns was occupied with reporting on preparations for the historic Nixon visit. The White House sent advance
parties to make technical arrangements, and other Americans set
up color-television cameras in the Square of Heavenly Peace for
their live broadcast of the president's arrival. (The 27 resident
correspondents shuddered when they learned they would be
swamped by 87 American reporters flying in for the occasion.)
The Chinese were busy sprucing up their capital: storefronts were
repainted on every major street. Visitors to finer restaurants were
told that the best chefs in Peking had been drafted for a gastro-
nomic task force that would cook the official banquets. At the
same time, however, the Chinese took pains to convince friend
and foe alike that the visit implied no compromise in their foreign
policies. To the last moment, the press was condemning Nixon's
latest Vietnam proposals as a fraud and branding his peace pledg-
es as "nothing but deceitful lies". When Nixon himself arrived in
Peking — on February 21, 1972 — his welcome was deliberately
low-key.

PEKING — President Richard Nixon arrived to a subdued welcome in the capital of China this morning at the start of a week-

long visit aimed at ending a generation of hostility between the world's most populous nation and the West's most powerful democracy.

Mr. Nixon became the first president of the United States to set foot in China while in office when his blue-and-white-painted plane, "The Spirit of '76", swept in across the frozen wheat-fields of the North China Plain to a copy-book landing in perfect springtime weather.

Members of the Chinese welcoming party provided the only moment of warmth in the reception that was decidedly cool in every other respect by breaking into restrained applause when the President and Mrs. Nixon appeared at the front door of the aircraft after their two-hour flight from Shanghai.

The time was 11:32 a.m., two minutes behind the schedule laid down before Mr. Nixon and his presidential caravan set out from Washington on their 10,000-mile journey to Peking.

Premier Chou En-lai, who had stood with his hands clasped before him during the brief applause, stepped forward to grasp the president's hand as Mr. Nixon alighted on the tarmac. Few words were spoken, but the handshake lasted several seconds, with each man smiling at the other.

With millions of television viewers around the world watching, the 73-year-old Chinese leader led the president and his wife down a line-up of his colleagues in the welcoming delegation, which included several of the most powerful men in China.

Mr. Nixon, looking fresh despite his early-morning start from Guam, appeared calm and relaxed throughout the arrival ceremonies. With the exception of his smile at the first greeting, Chou remained impassive.

Chairman Mao Tse-tung was present only by proxy, in the shape of an enormous portrait pinned to the airport terminal, which overlooks the arrival scene. But his absence was not regarded as a snub, since he has not attended an airport reception in several years.

After the handshakes with the leadership group, the premier led Mr. Nixon forward a few paces into a clear area in front of the 150-man brass band of the People's Liberation Army, which played the national anthems of the two countries while the leaders stood side by side at attention in the brilliant sunshine.

While the anthems rang out over the arrival area, the flags of

153

the two countries hung limply from twin flagpoles in front of the airport building. It was the first time that Communist China had ever flown the U.S. flag or played its anthem.

Though an interpreter was never more than a couple of paces behind, the premier could be heard saying a few words in English to the president as he led him forward toward the 400-man honor guard from the army, navy and air force, drawn up four ranks deep for the president's inspection.

The guard was immaculate, with the army and air force units in green gabardine overcoats and the navy in blue. The men stood rigidly to attention with Chinese-made semi-automatic rifles at their side, red flashes at their collars and matching red stars in their caps that glinted in the sun.

Mr. Nixon walked briskly down the line of men, hands at his side, with Premier Chou a couple of steps behind. Both men appeared to be keeping in step with the band, which played a selection of Chinese revolutionary songs, including one entitled "Song to Our Socialist Motherland".

The two men were a study in elegance, with Mr. Nixon wearing a dark-blue suit and black shoes beneath a grey herringbone overcoat. Chou wore a dark-blue overcoat over a grey Mao tunic. Both men were hatless.

Immediately behind Chou came Mrs. Nixon, in a soft red woollen overcoat. At her side was Lieutenant-Colonel Verne Coffey, a military aide to the president. He became the first man in 22 years to enter China as a guest wearing a U.S. military uniform.

Behind them followed a large group of Chinese officials, mingling easily with Secretary of State William Rogers, presidential assistant Henry Kissinger and other members of Mr. Nixon's official party.

About 15 minutes after stepping from the aircraft, Mr. Nixon climbed aboard a Red Flag limousine, pride of China's auto industry, for the motorcade into the city. Premier Chou accompanied him in the car, which flew Chinese and U.S. flags from the front fenders.

The rest of the official party followed behind, some in Red Flags and others in the less dignified Shanghai sedans. All told, the motorcade ran to nearly 40 cars.

The airport ceremony contrasted strongly with the reception

Madame Mao, Chiang Ching, wears a warm fur hat, which partly obscures Chou En-lai behind her.

Hand-to-hand combat training with staves and protective gear.

given other visiting heads of state in recent times. Normally, a state visitor is greeted by a drum-beating, cymbal-crashing crowd of several thousand, including not only soldiers but workers, peasants and teenaged dancing girls in gaily colored costumes.

For the first time ever, diplomats were excluded from the arrival ceremony, which, with the exception of about 30 foreign journalists living in Peking, was an entirely bilateral affair. Even with the restrictions, there were still about a thousand people watching the arrival, including nearly 300 U.S. officials, Secret Servicemen, broadcasters and correspondents.

For those familiar with the normal procedure for state visitors' motorcades, the drive into the city was an eerie experience. Normally, several hundred thousand people are mobilized to line a 10-mile section of the route, chanting their welcome as the visitor passes. This time, there was no mobilization, and the thousands of people who happened to be in the streets as the president passed merely stared in curious silence.

Security was tight along the eight-lane Boulevard of Heavenly Peace that sweeps across the city, with groups of soldiers carrying semi-automatic rifles with fixed bayonets posted outside every major building.

Moving on through the heart of the city, the president's route took him past the centuries-old Gate of Heavenly Peace, restored by the Communists as a rostrum for their massive National Day parades, and out to the guest house, set at the northern end of a tree-lined compound known as the Jade Abyss Pool Park.

There, behind 10-foot-high grey walls surmounted by electric fencing and the tightest security cordon in the city, he and Mrs. Nixon, together with Secretary of State William Rogers, White House aide Henry Kissinger and 11 others in the official party, were settled into plush suites occupied only three months ago by North Vietnamese Premier Pham Van Dong and a party of officials who came here from Hanoi to be reassured of China's support for them in the Vietnam War.

Within hours of his arrival, Nixon had a 60-minute meeting with Mao Tse-tung. That afternoon, and on each of the next four days, he had longer working sessions with Chou En-lai. There was also a state banquet (at which a crack band from the People's Liberation Army tackled — with notable proficiency — "Home on the Range", "America the Beautiful" and "Turkey in the Straw") and an evening of revolutionary ballet (at which Nixon, sitting next to Madame Mao, inadvertently laughed when Communist soldiers took pot-shots at a caricature of Chiang Kai-shek). The president also attended a sports display and took a much-filmed stroll on the Great Wall.

After the coolness of the airport welcome, Burns and the other foreign observers were startled by the unprecedented publicity the Chinese gave to these activities, both on their national television network and in their newspapers: "It was the first opportunity that ordinary Chinese people have had to see what Mr. Nixon really looks like. For years they were treated to grisly caricatures of him, usually focussing on his ski-jump nose. . . ." It seemed that the Chinese leaders were preparing the people for a speedy normalization of relations with the United States, as well as reaffirming their new moderate diplomacy, and possibly sending a signal to Moscow that China was no longer isolated and vulnerable.

Accompanied by Premier Chou, Nixon ended his week in China with visits to Hangchow and Shanghai, where the two leaders issued a communiqué that placed their countries on the long road back toward normal relations. There was no sign that Nixon and Chou had narrowed their differences over Vietnam, but there was a breakthrough on Taiwan, with a U.S. pledge that all U.S. forces and military installations eventually would be withdrawn from the island, and a U.S. acknowledgement of the Chinese view that "there is but one China and that Taiwan is part of China". The two leaders also agreed to open direct trade and to promote further contacts. Clearly jubilant, Nixon told correspondents that his visit had "changed the world". On the Chinese side, as Burns reported, "There seems little doubt that the visit was an unqualified success, not only in terms of the tangible agreements it produced but also in terms of the intangible factors of national pride and international image." This, at any rate, was the message the Chinese conveyed to their own people, as Burns discovered during an unusual encounter in the capital.

PEKING — A group of Red Guards gave a measure of the distance China has travelled in the past year by sitting down with

157

a group of correspondents yesterday and chatting about President Richard Nixon's visit in China.

The Red Guards, teenage zealots who gained a reputation for hostility toward foreigners during the Cultural Revolution, intercepted us during a May Day tour of the Temple of Heaven in suburban Peking.

Beaming, they insisted that we take a rest at the refreshment centre they had set up on the forecourt of the pavilion that stands guard at the entrance to the Altar of Prayer for Good Harvests, once a place of meditation for China's emperors.

After pouring tea and fruit juice and offering cigarettes all round, half a dozen of the guards pulled up chairs and opened up a lively exchange about school life, the duties of Red Guards and their career ambitions.

It was an astonishing performance, something that could never have happened a year ago, nor even as late as last fall when all contacts between foreigners and young people in China were still being closely supervised by officials.

Initially, we kept our questions to topics we were sure the guards could handle on their own without having to call in one of the teachers who were busying themselves a few tables away, out of earshot and apparently unconcerned by the spontaneous chatter between their charges and the visitors.

However, the confident manner of the teenagers — four boys and two pigtailed girls ranging in age from 12 to 27 — soon made it clear they could handle anything we could throw at them.

It was not long before the Nixon visit came up and they were obviously ready for it. Much of what they said was a word-for-word repetition of what Premier Chou En-lai said many times before the visit, but there were elements that were fresh, indicating that the topic has been aired thoroughly in the schools of China since Mr. Nixon's visit.

The 17-year-old, acting as principal spokesman for the group, declared that the decision of the Chinese leadership to invite the president had been shown to be wise. The visit had "opened the door to the development of friendly relations" between the two peoples, but the overriding problem of Taiwan still remained.

The U.S. role in Vietnam remained a matter of great concern

to the Chinese people, the youth said, but it should be viewed as distinct from the context of Sino-U.S. relations. There, the principal problem was the refusal of Washington to recognize the Peking regime as the sole legal government of all China.

What about the Shanghai communiqué with which the president and the premier concluded their talks? It was a start, but Mr. Nixon had been vague about the Taiwan question, acknowledging that Chinese on both sides of the straits maintain there is only one China, but stopping short of recognizing Peking as the legal government. That would have to be sorted out before there could be any question of a diplomatic exchange.

As the youth talked, his Red Guard arm-band catching the last rays of the setting sun, a listener could not help wondering if the Red Guards were as surprised by the pace of development in Sino-U.S. relations in the past year as he was.

The answer: yes and no. No, because the two peoples had always wanted good relations and their will was bound to be irresistible in the long run. Yes, because events had moved faster than they had expected.

It was getting late, and most of the holiday crowd had long since set off for home. A few remained behind to clear up, serenaded as they did so by the bars of the "Internationale" relayed over loudspeakers. The guards seemed willing to chat on, but a teacher eventually came over and suggested it was time to break it up.

In early summer, Burns was allowed to make a tour of Honan, the vast north-central province with a history stretching back 4,000 years to the beginning of Chinese civilization. In a county town, he saw an impressive result of the mass mobilization of the Chinese peasantry.

LIN HSIEN — Of all the memories that a visitor carries away from this dusty county town, there is none so persistent as the sight of the water tap that stands at the junction in the centre of town.

The tap must be the busiest for miles around. Small boys come to wash their feet under it, their older sisters fill heavy pitchers from it and their mothers gather beside it to do their washing.

In a region that was chronically short of water for centuries, the presence of the tap is itself remarkable. But more remarkable still is the fact that users frequently fail to turn it off, leaving the water to gather in a muddy pool at its base.

The abundance of water is something visitors come from all over China and all around the world to see, for Lin Hsien County is the site of the Red Flag Canal, the premier showcase of water conservation in modern China.

Cut through mountains and across plunging gorges by men and women working largely without the benefit of modern equipment, the canal is as much a monument to the working people of Communist China as the Great Wall is to the slave laborers of an earlier age.

Though it was later taken over by the province of Honan, the canal started out as a local project, conceived by local people as a means of bringing permanent relief from the drought that had long scourged the lives of the county's 700,000 residents.

A visit to Lin Hsien today begins with an account of the misery suffered by the people as a result of the water shortage, especially in the days before the Communists came to power. The account is spiced with lurid tales of cruelty of the landlords and rich peasants who owned most of the county's wells.

According to officials, the well owners would sell the water to peasants at exorbitant prices, or force them to pay for it with their labor. Peasants unable to do either would have to walk as much as 15 miles to one of the few common wells available, trudging homeward with the bulky pitchers slung on shoulder poles.

And that was not all. Most of the peasants worked land owned by the landlords, paying for it with as much as 70 per cent of the yield. The rate was constant, in good years and in bad, so a drought could result in a family having its entire harvest taken by a greedy landowner.

This all resulted in some curious side-effects. For example, it became customary for a young man contemplating marriage to ask the prospective bride how far her home was from the nearest well. Since it was usual for the young marrieds to move in with the girl's parents, a bad location could be disastrous for a girl's matrimonial prospects.

Nowadays, Ma Jung-shui chuckles about it all, but there was

Passengers on a Peking subway train. This was among the first pictures the authorities allowed to be taken.

a time when he didn't think it so funny. A gentle man of 63, with a weatherbeaten, bewhiskered face, he regales visitors to his peasant home with tales of the bad old days, before the Communists and the canal.

"In a way, we were lucky, because we at least had a well near the village," he says, pointing down the road that rolls through the cluster of mud-walled homes that make up the Da Tsai Yuan production brigade. "But others were not so fortunate."

Those others include relatives who lived in another village five miles to the south. "I well remember," Ma says, "going down to the well to meet them on their journeys up here for water. They used to come three times a week, trudging from dawn to dusk."

To end such hardships forever, the people of Lin Hsien drew up an ambitious plan. Since there are no major water-courses in the county, the only long-term solution was to build a canal to draw water from the Chang, a river that flows through Shansi Province, on the far side of the Tai Hang mountains that flank Lin Hsien's eastern boundary.

The work began in February, 1960. Starting at a point on the Chang where the provinces of Honan, Hopei and Shansi meet, the workers set out to build a canal system more than 60 miles long, with an additional 720 miles of irrigation channels to carry the water to the fields.

In all, it took 30,000 people nearly 10 years to complete the work. According to the official history, now chronicled in a special museum, the workers had to overcome not only the difficulties of the terrain, but also the efforts of "political saboteurs".

The saboteurs argued that the project was too costly, and beyond the capacities of the simple men and women who had set out to complete it. In the early stages of the work, their arguments nearly prevailed, and during the Cultural Revolution their feud with the canal's supporters succeeded in halting the work.

In the end, the faint hearts lost the day, but it is not difficult to see why they had their doubts. A 60-mile canal, 25 feet wide and 15 feet deep, is no easy task with mechanical drills to cut tunnels, trucks to carry quarried stone and all the rest of the paraphernalia of modern engineering; without them, the job becomes herculean.

Photographs in the museum give the visitor some idea of just how tough it was. One, typical of many others, shows a man chipping away at a sheer rock face, secured from a fatal plunge of several hundred feet by a single strand of rope.

The work produced many heroes, paraded now before the constant stream of visitors to the canal. Their stories are too often painfully long, and somewhat overdrawn, but there is enough substance in them to show that great courage and initiative were involved.

Back in Peking, Burns reported that the Chinese leaders were starting to lift the veil of mystery surrounding the disappearance of former Defence Minister Lin Piao. At a diplomatic reception, Lin's death was confirmed to foreign correspondents by Wang Hai-jung, an assistant foreign minister who was believed to be a niece of Mao Tse-tung. Answering questions, Miss Wang said that Lin — who was long called the Chairman's "closest comrade-in-arms" — had launched an attempted military coup against Mao the previous September. When his plans were discovered and foiled, Lin died in an air crash while fleeing the country. The Chinese people had still not been informed of Lin's death, and Miss Wang said she didn't know when this would happen.

Soon Burns was back on the road. He had recently returned to Canada — to marry his fiancee and bring her to Peking. Now the couple were to enjoy the odd delights of a Chinese train trip.

PEKING — When the driver pulled our Volkswagen to a halt on the broad forecourt of Peking station, the illuminated clocks to either side of Chairman Mao Tse-tung's portrait on the station facade were already showing 6:45 p.m. — 10 minutes to go before the departure of Express No. 13 for Shanghai.

Loading up with suitcases, camera bag, typewriter, shortwave radio and all the other paraphernalia of a correspondent travelling in China, we bounded into the building past clusters of curious Chinese squatting on the forecourt waiting for friends and relatives arriving aboard incoming trains.

Inside, we rode a crowded escalator to the mezzanine floor, sprinting from there to the gate leading to Platform 5, where a uniformed security officer stood ready to check our travel documents while our tickets were scrutinized independently by two severe-looking young women in pigtails.

163

Inspection over, it was down the stairs to the platform, where another man stood waiting to guide us forward to our carriage, past family groups bidding teary farewells and groups of passengers jockeying for position at refreshment booths dispensing steamed bread and other forms of sustenance for the journey.

With two minutes in hand, we found our carriage, marked "Ruanzuoche", meaning "soft-seat car", to distingish it from the hard-seat carriages in which all but the most privileged Chinese travel. Boarding, we were ushered to our compartment, as plush a sleeper as you could hope to find.

For myself, my wife and my Chinese interpreter, it had been a frantic beginning to a two-week journey that was to carry us south and east from Peking to Nanking, the ancient city on the lower reaches of the Yangtze, and then down the rail line to Wuhsi, Soochow, Shanghai and Hangchow.

It was a stimulating prospect, heightened by the knowledge that we were to travel the entire round trip of nearly 2,000 miles by train. As we already knew from previous journeys, train travel for foreigners in China is a luxury reminiscent of the bygone days of the great inter-city passenger trains in North America.

On Express No. 13, the nostalgia began as we walked down the platform and glimpsed the locomotive — a magnificent steam engine, sleek black with red wheels and a massive cowcatcher, its cabin lit by an orange glow from the boiler, its engineer standing at the door awaiting the signal to be off.

The compartment stirred childhood memories, too, with its polished hardwood, its carpeting, its velveteen seat covers, its lace curtains and such special touches as the potted plant by the window and the three pairs of leather slippers laid out neatly on the floor.

Before we had settled which of the three of us would take an upper bunk (in the end, my wife volunteered), there was a loud burst of steam up front, a lurch forward and we were on our way to Nanking, 17 hours and 650 miles to the south.

As the platform fell away, the loudspeaker in the compartment burst into life with a stirring rendition of "Sailing Seas Depends on the Helmsman, Making Revolution Depends on Mao Tse-tung Thought", the signature tune of the Chinese railways, followed by the stentorian voice of a woman announcer.

After welcoming the passengers aboard on behalf of the crew and running through the train's schedule ("from Peking, the capital, to Shanghai, birthplace of the Communist Party"), the announcer introduced the day's selections from the *Quotations From Chairman Mao,* a standard feature of any journey by air or rail in China.

"On this line," she assured us, "we are resolved to read and study seriously so as to have a good grasp of Marxism, as Chairman Mao instructs. We aim to do our work well, and we hope that revolutionary passengers will help us by voicing their opinions and suggestions to this end. Let us unite to win still greater victories!"

A barrage of quotations from the Chairman followed ("The force at the core leading our cause forward is the Communist Party"), interspersed with exhortations to the passengers to study each one during the journey, and to debate each among themselves, so that their political consciousness might be heightened by the journey's end.

Next came a catalogue of the services aboard the train. Among these were a medical clinic staffed by a first-aid team, a service counter dispensing such items as soap, toothpaste and stationery, and an attendant in every carriage who was ready and equipped to patch passengers' clothes and sew on buttons — free of charge, of course.

A good deal of attention was paid to meal service. Passengers with all-in tickets (about $22 for the 900-mile run between Peking and Shanghai) would be served in their carriages, with each receiving a bowl of rice, meat and vegetables, and a cup of tea. Those without all-in tickets could buy the same for the equivalent of 10 cents.

Those with the money could book a meal in the dining car, where the equivalent of about a dollar would buy a bowl of soup, three or four Chinese dishes, as much rice as you could eat and a couple of glasses of a red wine that tasted rather like sweet sherry and was nearly as powerful.

After outlining the meal service, the announcer had some tips for passengers. Those travelling on business should take good care of their papers. Those with children should take them to the toilet regularly and keep them from sticking their heads out the windows. Everybody should try to keep the train clean.

One other point, a little strange to foreign ears but apparently necessary in China: "Passengers travelling with quantities of gasoline, dynamite and nitroglycerine, or any other substances that are explosive, inflammable or radioactive, should hand them over to the crew members in carriage No. 7 for safekeeping."

With that in mind, and with the train thundering on under a half-moon that hung suspended over the endless grain fields on either side of the track, we settled down to a lesson in the intricate stratagems of Chinese chess, with Tang Kwang-ting, the 31-year-old interpreter, as a patient instructor.

Next door, in an identical compartment, three officers of the People's Liberation Army were well into a game of cards that they called Pu-ka, and which looked suspiciously like five-card stud — without, of course, the gambling that usually accompanies it in the West.

I have travelled across China three times by train, and on each occasion most of the other soft-seat compartments have been occupied by soldiers, apparently on business and almost certainly officers, to judge by their age and bearing since they wear no badges of rank.

The soft seats are a privilege worth having, affording a degree of privacy and comfort not available in the hard-seat carriages, where passengers are ranged row upon row on twin-tiered bunks, each equipped with two pillows, a blanket and a soft Chinese-style quilt, the whole heated in winter by means of a small coal furnace at one end of the carriage.

Before turning in for the night, I switched on my shortwave radio to pull in the BBC's late news. I was sharply reminded of where I was when I paused for a moment to listen to a broadcast in Mandarin, only to have Mr. Tang advise me rather curtly that it was not coming from Peking, as I thought, but from Taiwan. I switched quickly to the BBC.

In the morning, it was up early for a wash and shave in the cleanly kept washroom at the end of the car, then along to the dining car for a breakfast of scrambled eggs, toast and jam and coffee.

Before breakfast was over, we were joined at our table by the head of the train crew, anxious to learn if all was to our liking. Named Liu Ke-kuei, 42, he told us that we were the only foreigners among more than 1,000 passengers aboard, "so we should like to see to it that you are comfortable in your journey". He beamed when we told him we had never ridden a more comfortable train.

In Shanghai, Burns found further evidence of China's tentative opening to the West — in this case, a craze for learning English.

SHANGHAI — It's a curious reversal. A full generation after pidgin English went out of fashion along Nanking Road, it's back again at the instigation of the regime that abolished the Little England that once ranged on both sides of Shanghai's main shopping street.

Walk down this once-grand avenue in the small hours of the morning, and the youths pedalling their vegetable carts to market will cry out in unison as they pass: "Hello! How are you? Good-bye!" Wait for a second wave of carts, and their riders in turn pick up the refrain: "Hello! How are you? Good-bye!"

It is the same everywhere you go in the city these days, for Shanghai is the site of a pilot program in language instruction by radio. The language is English, and any one of the ten million people living in the Shanghai district can have a crack at it by tuning in to the thrice-daily lessons beamed over the city's radio network.

When the lessons started in the spring they caught on quickly, and reports that spoke of a craze to learn English were not exaggerating. It is perhaps just as surprising that their popularity continues unabated after the first five months, even if the results in terms of spoken English remain something less than startling.

The lessons are conveniently scheduled at breakfast, lunch and supper times, and it is hard to find any spot in the city out of earshot of a radio when the half-hour programs are on the air. Even where there is no radio available, the chances are better than even that there will be a loudspeaker in the vicinity blaring out one of the programs.

The lessons have a universal appeal. They are most popular among middle-school students, but within the space of three days a visitor also sees how the craze has caught on among boys

Chinese Premier Chou En-lai greets U.S. President Richard Nixon.

Canada's Progressive Conservative Party leader Robert Stanfield is measured for a "Mao suit" during a visit to China.

Teng Hsiao-ping, recently resurrected from obscurity after being purged during China's Cultural Revolution in 1966, faces Vice-premier Li Hsien-nien.

in his hotel, workers in factory canteens and even among the pedicab drivers in the street, some of whom have equipped themselves with transistor radios.

Enthusiasts will go to considerable lengths not to miss a lesson. One example among many is a cook in the eighth-floor restaurant of the Peace Hotel, the imposing edifice on the waterfront that was known as the Cathay in the days when it was one of the finest hotels in the Orient.

The cook, a portly fellow in his thirties, likes to see guests in the hotel eat their dinner by 7:30, when the evening lesson begins. Then, or shortly after, he can be seen making his way to a small room that leads off the hotel's main lounge, which happens to house the only radio in the vicinity.

Leaving the door to the lounge slightly ajar, and so positioning himself that the light from the lounge falls across the five-cent textbook in his lap, he follows the lesson through to the end, moving his lips in time with the broadcaster. Interrupted by a stranger, he beams and declares: "Hello! How are you?"

There were further diplomatic moves that autumn, as China established relations with Japan and West Germany. At the same time, the Chinese were gradually abandoning the strict puritanism that had been imposed upon them during the Cultural Revolution. Burns noted that women were curling their hair again and wearing brighter clothing; men were back on the streets playing poker, and soldiers and their girl friends were strolling hand-in-hand in the parks. It was also announced that examinations were to be brought back in Chinese schools and colleges. During the Cultural Revolution, exams had been condemned as "an instrument for fooling the people and for grooming successors for the ruling classes"; many students had rejoiced when they were abolished, but academic standards had fallen drastically.

In early 1973, Burns took time off from his reporting to establish a new milestone for the *Globe* bureau — and for the whole foreign community.

PEKING — I shudder to think what the Manchu emperors would have made of it — a foreigner, within the very precincts of their palace, being mobbed by Chinese athletes after finishing next to last in the Spring Festival foot race.

That was the scene yesterday as I became the only foreigner on record to participate in the annual round-the-city race, a seven-mile contest that winds its way around the vermilion walls of the Forbidden City in central Peking.

Wearing a maple-leaf T-shirt, I was cheered along the way by thousands of amused spectators, many of them shouting "Jia-na-da" ("Canada") or "Jia-you" ("Canadian friend") as I trundled past, others simply dissolving into helpless laughter at the unfamiliar sight of a foreigner exerting himself.

For all the cheers and the weeks of severe training that had gone into the effort, the best I could manage was to finish 1,165th out of 1,500 contestants, and that after nearly 300 of the starters had dropped out along the way, victims of cramp and blistered feet.

My time for the event, as clocked by my graciously unembarrassed wife, was 51 minutes 32 seconds — nearly 15 minutes behind the winner, a 31-year-old railway worker named Wang Fu-hsin, and a goodly distance behind a number of contestants in their forties and fifties, compared with my youthful 28.

For all its mediocrity, the performance earned a tumultuous reception from Chinese newsmen, officials and other contestants at the finish, who seemed to think it little short of miraculous that a foreigner — and a journalist at that — should be capable of completing the course.

From the finish line I found myself swept through the great archway beneath the golden-roofed Gate of Heavenly Peace into the sprawling, snow-covered forecourt of the Forbidden City, where film cameramen and still photographers finally got the mass of humanity stopped long enough to record the scene.

With a massive portrait of Chairman Mao as a backdrop, the photographers snapped shots of me standing arm-in-arm with two steelworkers who fell in alongside me as the race began and escorted me step-for-step the rest of the way, sacrificing their superior speed in the process.

Afterwards, officials of the Peking Revolutionary Committee approached, forgave me for entering the race without their permission and pinned commemorative badges on my wife and me, the scene once again being recorded by the cameras.

Appropriately enough, another badge went to my interpreter, Tang Kwang-ting, who unwittingly launched me on the path to the contest with a chance remark some months ago to the effect that I was looking overweight.

All my life I had been told I was too thin and here was a spare-looking young Chinese telling me I was getting fat — a reverse of such demoralizing proportions that I determined immediately upon a crash fitness program.

At first it was a matter of modest jogs around the block, but once the problem of blistered feet and sprained ligaments had been overcome I stepped up the program, making daily forays of four or five miles to neighboring areas of the city.

To avoid the chaos of Peking traffic, and to gain a measure of privacy for my efforts, I scheduled most of my runs at night — often in the small hours of the morning when the roads are deserted, save for soldiers on guard duty, shift workers cycling home and the occasional horse-drawn cart.

Apart from paring my weight down, the running served to introduce me to a new side of Peking — the city by night about which I, like most foreigners living here, knew precious little.

I learned, for example, that the Chinese capital has 24-hour cycle-repair shops — logical enough in a city where there are 1.7 million bicycles and the private car is unknown.

I also discovered the whereabouts of half a dozen all-night restaurants, rough-and-ready places where shift workers, carters and soldiers can gather over a jug of draft beer, a bowl of noodles and a plate of delicious boiled dumplings called "Chiao Tzu" — a complete meal that costs about 30 cents.

I developed a special affection for the carters, homespun fellows from the countryside who, ignoring traffic regulations, contrive to spend almost all of their journeys in and out of the city bundled up in their sheepskin coats atop their loads — fast asleep.

Often, as I loped past a convoy of carts, one of these gentlemen would spy me, shoulder himself into a position to get a better look and alert his companions to the curious-looking foreigner puffing by in his tracksuit.

After a while, even the soldiers on guard outside embassies — normally reticent fellows — began to respond to my greetings, but it was the shift workers on bicycles that I came to know best.

Often, the cyclists would glance at the stranger as they pedalled by, think it over for a moment or two, then drop back and start a conversation — where do you come from, what do you do, and why would you go running at this hour?

From time to time another runner would pass me on the road, pounding by at a speed that made me feel that I should have stayed home in bed — or at least chosen some less demoralizing way of getting fit.

It was only when I developed the power to keep pace with these speedsters — if only for a few blocks — that I decided to enter the round-the-city race, a project I had to keep to myself for fear of a veto from Chinese officials, ever careful of the health of foreigners.

Right up to the start of the race, I kept my plan to myself, swaddled in a Chinese padded overcoat until the starting gun fired — a disguise that fooled other competitors for about as long as it took them to spot my tracksuit bottoms and sneakers.

As it developed, I need not have worried, for officials made no move to stop me and other competitors made it clear that I was welcome, running alongside to read the Chinese inscription on my tracksuit — "Long Live the Friendship Between the Peoples of China and Canada" — and to shake my hand.

With the Spring Festival holiday at its height, the streets were lined with tens of thousands of spectators, but we had hardly skirted Chairman Mao's residence — about 500 yards from the start — when the two steelworkers fell in alongside to run interference.

The two — Kao Chao-hsiang, 31, and Wang Ta-keng, 27 — remained there to the finish, calling out the distance covered as we passed each landmark and urging me into a sprint at the end.

As well as the fun of it, I discovered as a friend drove me home after the race that there are certain practical benefits to being a minor celebrity in China, even if it lasts only a couple of hours.

As we drove off, a policeman stopped my friend for making an illegal left-hand turn, demanding his driving licence and waxing indignant when told that the licence was at home.

Just then, a passer-by looked in the passenger's side, saw me and told the policeman that I was the foreigner who had just run the race.

In a flash, the indignation turned into a smile, with the policeman not only waving us on our way but halting other traffic to allow us to do so. It is a pity there is but one Spring Festival a year.

Attending a state banquet in April, Burns and the other correspondents were astonished to see the diminutive Teng Hsiao-ping walk into the Great Hall of the People with top government and Party officials. Formerly the secretary-general of the Communist Party, Teng had not been seen in public since 1966 when he was denounced as one of a handful of leaders who had "taken the capitalist road". Later, Red Guards accused him of other offences, such as transporting his card-playing cronies around the country in government aircraft. At the time of his downfall, Teng ranked fourth in the Party hierarchy. Officials at the banquet made clear that the 69-year-old veteran was appearing in his capacity as vice-premier and that he had still not regained any Party rank. But the re-emergence of the man who had day-to-day control of the Party machinery for more than 12 years showed the leadership's determination to rehabilitate most of the senior officials purged during the Cultural Revolution.

It was more than three years since Norman Webster had reported that the Chinese were building air-raid shelters in their major cities. Now Burns became one of the first foreigners to be granted a look at the vast underground labyrinth in the capital.

PEKING — It is vintage stuff. A sales clerk steps from behind the counter in a crowded little clothing store, slips his fingers behind a calendar hanging on the end of a display case, presses a hidden button and presto — a section of the pink-tiled floor rolls away, revealing a subterranean staircase.

With the clerk leading the way, a party of Western visitors moves behind the counter and starts down the staircase, a steep spiral of 35 steps that emerges into a brightly lit tunnel. As the last of the visitors reaches the foot of the stairs, the clerk pauses, turns and announces: "You are now eight metres (26 feet) below the surface of Peking!"

It is a moment of carefully contrived drama, for the tunnel and the web of others that run off from it are a visitors' showpiece, presented as an example of the thousands of miles of tunnels that have been built in cities throughout China in response to the threat of war with the Soviet Union.

In recent months, the tunnels beneath the Chianmen clothing store on Peking's Ta Sha Lan street have become a staple of most visitors' tours, but it was not always so. Indeed, for nearly three years after the first digging began in December, 1969, the project was shrouded in secrecy, with even high-ranking officials disclaiming knowledge of it.

For all that, it took no great feat of sleuthing to figure out what was going on. First there were the huge mounds of loose earth lying along the streets and alleyways, and later the long rows of semi-circular concrete beams that appeared by the roadside all over town. Clearly, the order had gone out for the masses to get tunnelling, and it was not difficult to guess why.

The digging began about four months after the last of three serious border clashes with the Russians that year. Talks on the border dispute had begun in Peking in the late fall, but had quickly bogged down in a stalemate that has lasted to this day. As anti-Soviet propaganda reached a new level in the Chinese press, the nation-wide tunnelling program began.

For children, the program provided endless scope for new games amid the piles of earth and rows of concrete beams. But for adults, mobilized in their millions, it was no game. Several hours of extra toil were added to the day's work in an office or factory.

Most of the digging took place beyond the view of passersby, behind hoardings or inside buildings. But the occasional glimpse — from the roof of a high building or through the open door of a vacant store — told the story: teams of men and women working feverishly, often with only the crudest implements, and through every kind of weather.

Until recently, that was about all that was known about the project. Then, late last year, the first groups of foreigners were taken to Ta Sha Lan, treated to the mystery of the hidden staircase and introduced to a subterranean world that makes the catacombs of ancient Rome look like child's play.

Officials say the pattern is repeated throughout the city, with every factory, school, restaurant, apartment block, government office and almost every shop having its own access to the tunnels.

In fact, officials say 80 per cent of Peking's inner population of four million could be safely inside the tunnels within 10 minutes of a warning — and the percentage will go higher as the capacity of the tunnels is increased.

The claim is impressive, but the swiftest evacuation system in the world is little use without an adequate warning system; and even then, with the closest Soviet missiles located only a few hundred miles to the north, 10 minutes may be too long. In that event, how much use would the tunnels be?

Chinese officials smile when such difficulties are raised. They say provision has been made for early warning, but they do not define the means or say how much time there would be. They do concede, however, that it would be a close-run thing: "The warning is inclined to be sudden. We try our best."

There are other problems. The tunnels are designed chiefly as a means of dispersing the population to the countryside in the event of an attack. But they are narrow on the average, seven feet high and five feet wide — and reach only as far as the suburbs. Is it conceivable that more than three million Pekingers could be accommodated by such a system in a space of 10 minutes without causing catastrophic congestion, leading to panic?

Officials acknowledge that crowding is a worry, but say measures have been taken to minimize the problem. Every citizen is briefed on the trap door nearest his home or place of work and instructed on emergency procedures. If there is any confusion, markers every few yards signal the shortest route to the suburbs.

Nobody pretends the system is a foolproof defence against all-out nuclear attack, but the officials say it would be effective against all but a direct hit and would provide temporary defence against radiation — long enough for most to escape the tunnels and head for open country.

Eventually, the tunnels will be turned into a proper shelter system, if technology provides answers to such vexing problems as the purification of radiated air. Officials say scientists are working on the problem, in the hope the tunnels can be developed into a subterranean city, where people could work and live until the radiation dispersed.

Already, the tunnels boast a number of home comforts, some

A Chinese hockey goaltender practises in the summer.

Kindergarten children in a Peking suburb.

of them a little incongruous to a Westerner accustomed to an earlier generation of air-raid shelters. There is a loudspeaker system that pipes in revolutionary music; washrooms fitted with the best in vitreous china, each designated for one or other of the sexes; kitchens with running water and stoves; a telephone system; and simple medical clinics.

For the time being, the entire web is connected to the main power grid, but eventually a separate power system will be installed underground. Together with a network of pump wells, and underground food shelters, this will provide the means for sustaining life for extended periods — provided the ventilation problems can be solved.

The idea of tunnels as a protection against nuclear attack seems so far-fetched to the Western mind that it is tempting to think of the tunnels as a political response to China's fears of the Soviet Union. Could it be that the Chinese leaders ordered the system built to stiffen popular animosity toward the Kremlin, and to boost morale — realizing the tunnels would be little good if the worse came to the worst?

Obviously, a project that engages the labor of tens of millions of people is bound to accentuate the Soviet threat in the workers' eyes, but it is difficult to walk through the tunnels without concluding that the Chinese leaders could have found a cheaper means of propagandizing the people if that had been their objective.

In the end perhaps the best approach for the layman is to ask himself the question: how would the tunnels look to me, if I were given six minutes' warning of a nuclear attack? After seeing the tunnels, my answer is: very good.

For five days in August, Burns watched several thousand shirt-sleeved delegates arriving and departing from the Great Hall of the People. Following their usual practice, Peking newspapers said nothing about the massive gathering while it was in progress, and Chinese by-standers solemnly told Burns they had no idea what was going on. Then — to the usual cacophony of drums, gongs and cymbals — tens of thousands took to the streets to hail the official announcement that the Chinese Communist Party had just concluded its Tenth Congress. Apart from adopting a new Party constitution, the Congress also elected a new Party hierarchy. This was a careful (or uneasy) mix of old stalwarts and younger figures who had risen to prominence during the Cultural Revolution.

Among the latter, Mao's wife, Chiang Ching, and the Shanghai ideologue Yao Wen-yuan retained their places in the Politburo while another radical, Chang Chun-chiao, was named to the Politburo's all-important Standing Committee. But the big news was the sudden elevation of the youthful Wang Hung-men, not only to the Standing Committee but also to apparent third place in the leadership after Mao and Chou En-lai. Little was known about Wang, a handsome six-footer, except that he was a former textile worker from Shanghai, that he was also a radical and that he was somewhere in his mid-thirties. His speedy rise was seen as a deliberate indication to millions of young Chinese — who had been stirred into political activity during the Cultural Revolution — that the top ranks of the Communist Party were no longer an old-men's club. Amid the excitement over Wang, little attention was paid to another newcomer to the hierarchy, the former Party boss of Mao's native province of Hunan, one Hua Kuo-feng.

Meanwhile, the Chinese leaders continued to pursue their opening to the West. In May the veteran diplomat David Bruce had arrived in Peking to open the U.S. Liaison Office. The office was one result of the Nixon visit, and established an official American presence in China for the first time in more than 23 years. It was clearly a big step toward normal relations, although the Chinese made it evident that full diplomatic recognition was still ruled out by Washington's links with Taiwan. Then, in the autumn, French President Georges Pompidou, Canadian Prime Minister Pierre Trudeau and Australian Prime Minister Gough Whitlam made official visits to Peking as further confirmation that the days of China's diplomatic isolation were ended.

Early that winter, Burns travelled to Manchuria, China's industrial heartland in the extreme northeast of the country. In Peking, he was used to travelling in *The Globe*'s Volkswagen. But on the outskirts of Changchun he sampled the splendors of China's answer to Cadillacs and Rolls-Royces.

MOTOR CITY — I had to come to the heart of proletarian China to ride in one of the world's most expensive cars — a $25,000 behemoth hand-crafted by workers making about $6.25 a week.

My chance to be chauffeur-driven in the limousine that is used by Chairman Mao Tse-tung and Premier Chou En-lai came during a visit to the General Motors of China, a sprawling plant in the suburbs of the Manchurian city of Changchun.

The name of the suburb is Motor City, but the likeness with Detroit ends there. In fact, the differences — in worker attitudes, production techniques and the vehicles that result — are so stark as to be almost comical.

To begin with, there is the Red Flag limousine. This is the Cadillac Eldorado and Rolls-Royce Silver Cloud of China. It is a symbol of ultimate prestige that is reserved for the most privileged of foreign dignitaries and the men of utmost power in the Party. But for sheer massiveness and unsophisticated engineering it seems closer to the 1956 DeSoto.

Except for its large size, the car is not bad looking. It has clean, almost austere lines, which are enhanced by the simplicity of its paintwork — in black only. It has a spacious passenger compartment, with comfortable fabric-upholstered cushions, and one or two of the extras one would expect in a luxury car, such as twin jump-seats for extra passengers in the rear and a wind-up glass screen to separate dignitaries from the driver.

It does not, however, have a telephone, a television set or a bar. Its 150-cubic-inch, eight-cylinder engine produces a meagre 20 horsepower, its three-speed automatic transmission engages with a clunk and its suspension gives a smooth but not unimpeachably bump-free ride. It is also extremely expensive. Officials at the factory professed to be ignorant of the selling price, saying such matters are in other hands. But they estimated the production cost at about $25,000, about twice what a Chinese worker earns in a lifetime.

It would, of course, be cheaper for Chinese leaders to ride around in imported limousines — and some of them do. But dignity begins with self-reliance, and the state has chosen to invest in a do-it-yourself plant that must have the smallest output of any in the world.

Officials would not show me that part of Motor City, saying it is undergoing reconstruction after fulfilling its quota for the year. Nor would they divulge the quota, although one could make one's own calculations from the fact that the model on display — completed in November — bore the serial number 390.

However, they allowed me to take a demonstration ride.

The driver, used to more distinguished fares, seemed unamused. But he suffered in silence as I climbed aboard with a group of Canadian film-makers who are here to cover the University of British Columbia hockey team's tour, and drove us in glum silence out of the factory grounds. About a mile from the gates, he unceremoniously invited us to switch into the microbus that was following.

Workers bicycling home off their shift watched with undisguised amusement, and I must confess that the microbus was more suited to our style. We were all bundled up in the padded overcoats and pudding-basin hats that are the common man's garb in northern China at this time of year, and felt happy enough to forsake the pretensions of our lace-curtained limousine for the more modest vehicle behind.

The car ride came at the end of a tour of the Motor City truck plant, the largest in China, which produces 60,000 vehicles a year, twice the designed capacity when it opened in 1956. For a country that had no automobile industy of any kind 25 years ago, it is no mean accomplishment, but the contrasts with Detroit are still stark.

The 39,000 workers earn an average of less than seven dollars a week and the amount of labor standing around in the plant would give Henry Ford a fit. The assembly lines are dimly lit, dank and poorly co-ordinated, with hundreds of engines, chassis and drive-shafts lying outside in the weather, some of them rusting.

Despite the proximity of the Soviet Union, Burns found that officials in Manchuria seemed less concerned about the Soviet threat than they were about domestic problems, especially law and order. In Harbin, he saw several posters urging the suppression of crime and others announcing sentences handed down by the Municipal People's Court. These included life sentences and lesser terms meted out to men convicted of bribery, black-marketeering and theft. Some of these announcements gave extensive details of the crimes, presumably as a warning to others. Normally such announcements were not displayed where foreigners could read them, but no such precautions had been taken in Harbin, a city rarely visited by foreign delegations. As Burns wrote, the posters showed how unscrupulous black-marketeers could take advantage of China's tightly controlled economic system with its inevitable supply bottlenecks: "Despite the extensive police and security apparatus, the case histories of the racketeers reveal that it is still possible for a man — even one with a lengthy political record — to amass large stocks of scarce materials and squander thousands of dollars in illegal profits before the law catches up with him." Back in Peking, Burns found further evidence of a crime epidemic and linked this to another nationwide problem: the illegal return to the cities of youths assigned to labor in the countryside.

PEKING — If you take a midnight stroll in a Peking neighborhood these days, the chances are that you will be accosted by the Chinese equivalent of the bobby pounding his beat — small groups of men and women carrying menacing-looking nightsticks and flashlights, the better to combat a burgeoning wave of street crime.

It has long been known that China, for all its social discipline, has not succeeded in eliminating crime. But it is only in recent times that the problem has reached proportions that require militia patrols day and night, backed up by a poster campaign urging support for the fight against "hooliganism".

Just what the hooligans get up to is not vouchsafed by the posters, which can be seen pasted to the grey walls that line many an alleyway in the city. But there are reports that their offences range all the way from petty theft to murder, and that the incidence is enough for certain Pekingers to hesitate before walking the streets alone at night.

The problem is most apparent to foreigners in Peking, where most of us live. But visitors returning from other major cities, from Canton in the deep south to Harbin in the frozen north, report that the patrols and the posters are visible there, too — and that local officials are sometimes more forthcoming in discussing the matter than their counterparts in Peking. . . .

It is common knowledge that the biggest threat to public order is the large blocks of young drifters who have made their way back to the cities illegally from their enforced resettlement in the countryside.

These drifters, including some girls, are the deserters from a massive army of young people who have been dispatched to the countryside under a program initiated by Chairman Mao during the Cultural Revolution. According to the latest official estimate, there have been more than eight million of them in the past five years, a fair proportion of their generation.

The proclaimed purpose of the program is to purge the youngsters of bourgeois tendencies and instill in them a truly peasant outlook. But it has corollary advantages — reducing the pressure of numbers that a fast-growing population brings to bear on the cities and removing from the centre of activity a large number of young people who, as Red Guards, became accustomed to flexing their political muscles during the Cultural Revolution.

Not surprisingly, the program has run into all kinds of problems. Many of the youngsters have found it difficult to settle down in the far less comfortable circumstances of the communes, and not a few have complained that their new labors — working knee-deep in the mud and water of south China's paddy fields, or shovelling human excrement into tanks mounted atop three-wheeled bicycles and pedalling it away for use as fertilizer — are no match for their education.

If re-assignment to the countryside were for a limited period only, desertion might not have become a problem. But for most of the settlers, the only authorized way back to the cities is by admission to university — and that, of necessity, is limited to a tiny minority. As a result, defections have reached the proportions of a major problem.

There are no official figures, but one source estimates there are as many as 50,000 in Peking at the present time, out of a total of about one million youngsters that have been sent to the communes from the city. Since travelling is tightly controlled it is a mystery how they make their way back, but a fair proportion of them probably wait until they get permission to return home on holiday or to see an ailing relative — and then fail to return when their leave is up.

As outlaws, they can have no easy time in the city. Without money and the coupons that are necessary for the purchase of cotton, meat, fuel and cooking oil, the basic means of sustenance is denied to them — unless they can persuade their parents to take them in, a risky business in a society where neighbors are likely to construe it as their duty to inform the authorities.

For those without shelter at home, the temptations of crime are obvious. But even those who have a familial roof over their head may turn to theft as a means of alleviating the strain their presence places on family resources. Thus, in part, the crime wave — and the neighborhood patrols to combat it.

Apart from crime, officials in the capital were troubled by the refusal of many Chinese — young and old alike — to obey their call for frugality and plain living, as Burns reported in early 1974.

PEKING — A newcomer walking in the alleys of Peking last night could have been forgiven for thinking that a war had broken out. From dusk until late in the evening, the city resounded to what sounded like the crackle of gunfire — actually firecrackers set off by youngsters celebrating the eve of the lunar New Year.

The youngsters' hijinks marked the official beginning of a three-day annual holiday that shows every sign of being the most festive China has celebrated in years. For several days, people have been packing department stores and restaurants in the capital in a spending spree that has seen no equal since the Cultural Revolution put a stop to such pleasures seven years ago.

On the face of it this is all strangely out of temper with the times. The country is supposed to be in the grip of a major new campaign against bourgeois tendencies, and scarcely a day goes by that does not see a new front opened in the propaganda war against the backsliders. Yet people seem to be reacting by having the Spring Festival of their lives.

Presumably they are aware of the official line on the holiday, which was set forth in unequivocal terms in a front-page article in *The People's Daily*. The article, headlined "Smash the Old, Foster the New", demanded that the extravagant habits of old be eschewed in favor of the frugality appropriate to a proletarian society.

Exemplary tales of self-sacrifice and temperance in the newspapers made for an intriguing contrast with the scene in the city as the holiday approached. Stores were packed with people stocking up food and drink and picking out presents for relatives. Restaurants were doing a roaring trade in lunches and

Fishing with cormorants on a lake near Wushi.

Two young boys stare at the camera as a minority-nationality woman with a child slung on her back walks toward them.

dinners for rollicking family groups. At the main railway station, trains arrived and departed carrying thousands of travellers, almost every one of them carrying gifts in the knapsacks slung over their shoulders.

However, the spending spree was not alone as an example of the divergence between political exhortation and public behavior. Just as intriguing to an outsider were the tens of thousands of youngsters who showed up in Peking to celebrate the festival, despite repeated urgings in the press that they remain at their new homes in the countryside.

It is no secret that the youngsters committed all sorts of pranks during last year's festival, when they were permitted to travel home in large numbers for the first time since they were dispatched to the communes in the aftermath of the Cultural Revolution. This year, an effort is being made to keep them busy and entertained, if necessary by enlisting them in night security patrols by the militia. But there are still plenty of them to be seen loafing around the city to no apparent purpose.

By the spring of 1974, there were signs of a major political struggle. During the winter, a sudden shake-up of China's military leadership involved new commanders for eight of the country's 11 military regions. This implied a shift in the delicate internal power balance in favor of the central government headed by Chou En-lai. In another victory for the so-called moderates, Teng Hsiao-ping regained his seat in the Communist Party's ruling Politburo: he now ranked tenth in the hierarchy. Soon, however, there were signs of a contradictory trend, including a renewed drive to purge China of all bourgeois and reactionary influences: this took place under cumbersome slogans that called on the people to criticize both Lin Piao and the ancient sage Confucius. In an atmosphere that began to be ominously reminiscent of the Cultural Revolution, there were more mass rallies and wall posters began to appear again in major cities. Foreigners were excluded from the rallies, but by July they were permitted to read and even to photograph the posters. These charged that unnamed officials were "pouring cold water" on the anti-rightist drive and suppressing all criticism of their activities. There were also specific complaints that the critics were being arrested on trumped-up charges, brutally interrogated and falsely imprisoned. According to Burns, the critics were Cultural Revolution radicals trying to regain the initiative they had lost to leaders — such as Chou and Teng — who emphasized the need for political order, economic progress and friendly relations with the West.

By autumn, when the Chinese celebrated their twenty-fifth anniversary as a Communist state, the poster campaign had subsided, and the Party press was filled with calls for unity. But few foreigners believed that the issues had been finally settled. Adding to their apprehension was the precarious health of Chou En-lai, who was twice taken to hospital with heart trouble. During the Cultural Revolution, Chou had been a major force for conciliation; it had been expected that the 76-year-old premier would play a similar role if Mao Tse-tung died. But it now appeared that the 80-year-old Chairman might survive his colleague, and that there would be no one of Chou's stature to supervise the transition to younger leaders. Meanwhile Burns — like every *Globe* correspondent since Frederick Nossal — was engaged in the intricate game of trying to determine Mao's health and whereabouts.

PEKING — Chairman Mao is alive and passably well and living in China. But where? And does it matter? Nobody loves a good mystery better than China watchers, and the mystery of the moment centres on the whereabouts of Peking's peripatetic leader. For more than 10 weeks now he has been hiding in the provinces, giving rise to widespread speculation as to where he is and what he is doing.

Normally the 80-year-old Communist Party leader lives in a modest villa beside a willow-fringed lake in the centre of Peking. But since early September a succession of visiting foreign leaders — eight, including the South Yemini president who is here this week — have been whisked out of the capital in the utmost secrecy to meet the Chairman somewhere in the hinterland.

The most intriguing aspect of the whole thing has been the precautions the Chinese have taken to see that none of the visitors discloses the site of the rendezvous. In the early weeks even the statesman himself was not told where he was going, and though this policy has now been relaxed all subsequent visitors have been sworn to secrecy.

The procedure has raised a few eyebrows, even among diplomats accustomed to the idiosyncratic ways of Chinese protocol. Where else in the world, they ask, would a visiting leader be asked to travel without knowing his destination? And where but in China would he agree?

When they're not indulging in such pique, the diplomats are likely to be mulling over the scant evidence that is available to try to fix where Mao actually is. The tools of the game are a protractor and a map, for the most anybody has to go on is the flying time from Peking, which the visitors have variously reported as being between 30 and 90 minutes.

Working with the map and brief glimpses of scenery in television films of the meetings, diplomats have at various times had Mao in the seaside village of Peitaiho, the resort city of Hangchow and the industrial city of Wuhan. More recently some have detected a move to Changsha, capital of Mao's native province of Hunan, but neither this nor any other part of the itinerary has been confirmed by the Chinese.

Officials questioned on the matter pass it off with a smile, while interpreters who work for embassies and journalists profess to find the sleuthing pointless. "Our Chairman lives in Peking but travels to the provinces from time to time," said one young man. "This is quite normal. It is not necessary to know any more."

In the strict sense the man was right, for access to Mao is limited to a tiny group of people even when he is in Peking and they presumably know where he is. For the rest — the broad masses who have not seen Mao in public for 30 months anyway — his whereabouts can hardly be a matter for pressing concern.

Why, then, all the diplomatic fuss? Part of it is for its own sake, for the fun of playing detective, but there may also be political implications. When Mao has toured the provinces in the past, usually in secret, it has often been the prelude to dramatic events such as the Lin Piao debacle that followed on the heels of a series of talks between Mao and provincial leaders in the late summer of 1971.

He is older and more frail now and seemingly content to leave the cut and thrust of day-to-day politics to other men, but nobody is forgetting that it was during a similarly prolonged absence from Peking in 1965 that he plotted the strategy for a showdown with a group of powerful rivals who had left him

Four intriguing Chinese figures. l—r: Kang Sheng, China's Beria; Premier Chou En-Lai; Chen Po-ta, Mao's personal secretary; and Yao Wen-Yuan, Mao's son-in-law.

with more of the shadow than the reality of power. That show-down became known as the Cultural Revolution.

While the diplomats play with the more complex possibilities there is a simpler one that is in danger of being overlooked. Mao has told visitors he suffers badly from rheumatism. Could it be that he has simply fled the rigors of Peking's winter for a climate more benign?

With spring, Mao returned to Peking. He had been out of the capital for seven months, the last three of them in seclusion, before he came back in April, 1975, to greet the North Korean leader, Kim Il Sung. About the same time, Burns was reporting on a favorite pastime for many Peking residents who were not so fortunate in escaping the hardships of a northern winter.

PEKING — In China, where the state has curled its tentacles around almost every aspect of life, there are precious few ways of getting away from it all. An individual who wants solitude, a space where he can be his own man, must search for it — and finding, treasure it, for there can be no knowing when that last refuge, too, will be denied.

One such refuge lies in a small bay off the reservoir in the Valley of the Ming Tombs, 25 miles north of Peking. Here, on a winter Sunday, men gather for ice fishing, an endeavor that affords them a few hours of peace and pleasure and, when the fish are biting, a useful supplement to the bland winter diet on which Peking families survive.

From where they sit, the fishermen can gaze across the ice to the rugged mountains that tower above the tombs of the 13 emperors of the Ming Dynasty who were buried here between the fourteenth and seventeenth centuries. With the golden roofs and vermilion walls on the tombs — magnificent ruins now, with the exception of two that have been restored — there is no more exquisite setting in China.

For most of the fishermen, the day begins before dawn with breakfast in one of the numerous 24-hour restaurants in the city. There, behind windows misted over with steam, 25 cents buys them a bowl of flour fritters known as *youtiao*, a plate of meat-filled dumplings called *baotse* and a glass of *doujiang*, a milk-like liquid made from bean curd.

Girls in Tien An Men Square. Dresses are usually worn only for public celebrations or greeting foreign dignitaries.

A bus leaves for the northern suburbs around 6 a.m., and a change there gets an angler out to the reservoir around 8 a.m. It pays to start early since by 10 a.m. the ice is crowded with dozens of late-comers, men and youths, and by early afternoon the fish have all but stopped biting. Around 4 p.m. there's a bus back to town, arriving well after dark.

Out on the ice, under the clear blue sky that is characteristic of the winter weather in north China, the fisherman's first task is to penetrate the six- to eight-inch cover that comes to the reservoir in late December and persists until the break-up in mid-March. He does this with a pick that, like everything else in his gear, is home-made — usually a piece of scrap iron sharpened on a factory lathe.

The keener anglers bring two or three rods with them and cut a hole for each. In addition, to increase their catch, they drill supplementary holes 30 or 40 feet away from the first group, switching the rods from one group to the other every hour or so. Using worms for bait, the more proficient can run up a catch of 20 or 30 fish by noon.

The catch, mostly silver carp, is transferred from the hook to a shallow basin of water that the angler fashions in the ice and is left there until he transfers it to his knapsack for the journey home. None of the fish are sold, private enterprise being forbidden, but a good haul provides a surplus that can be bartered with the neighbors for scarce commodities like rice and cooking oil.

For a member of Peking's foreign community, the ice fishing provides an occasion for the sort of informal contact with Chinese that the regime often seems anxious to inhibit. Among fellow anglers, yet seated at a remove from others that precludes eavesdropping, many an angler will chat about the fishing, his family, his job — almost anything but politics, which is, naturally enough, taboo.

One man, a worker in his forties, took great pride in explaining to an onlooker how he made his rods, exquisitely crafted examples fashioned from varnished willow and finished with finely lathed brass fittings and a hand-filed steel reel. Another, a retired official in his mid-sixties, chuckled heartily as he acknowledged that the fishing is a good excuse to get out of the house — and away from his wife.

Despite continuing uncertainty over the political struggle in Peking, there were signs during the winter and spring of 1975 that China would continue its diplomatic initiatives to the West. Henry Kissinger, now secretary of state, had made his seventh visit to Peking, to be followed some time during the year by President Gerald Ford. (The Chinese press had largely ignored Watergate and the downfall of Richard Nixon.) In April, the death of Chiang Kai-shek removed a major obstacle to further rapprochement between Peking and Washington. Weeks later, the fall of Saigon led *The People's Daily* to declare that "the U.S. aggressors were swamped in a vast ocean of people's war and suffered a thorough defeat". Privately, however, Chinese officials indicated a sense of relief that Washington was now free to play a more positive role elsewhere in Asia.

Ross Munro sits atop a rampart in front of the Gate of Heavenly Peace.

CHAPTER SEVEN: 1975—1977

ROSS H. MUNRO

In the summer of 1975, Ross H. Munro became the seventh *Globe* correspondent in Peking. Munro, 34 when he took over the bureau, had joined the newspaper eight years earlier after graduate work in political science at Stanford University. After working as an education reporter, he had served as bureau chief at Queen's Park and staff correspondent in Washington. In August, he became the first *Globe* correspondent to visit Inner Mongolia.

SILINHOT — At the northern edge of the People's Republic of China, descendants of Genghis Khan's Golden Horde are still living in yurts and riding their horses across the rolling grasslands as they have for centuries.

Yet politics and progress have brought great changes to the life of the Mongolian herdsmen: they are now a minority within China's Inner Mongolia Autonomous Region, vastly outnumbered by the Han Chinese; their language and culture are protected but their Lamaist religion is almost a relic; their nomadic life has given way to permanent winter settlements; and the formation of herdsmen's groups is dictated not by kinship but by "the needs of production".

As Chimude the herdsman recounts yesterday's miseries and today's prosperity, the changes have been all to the good. He tells his story as we sit on the felt carpets of his yurt on the pastureland of the Kiringele People's Commune in the Silingol League in eastern Inner Mongolia.

To get to this isolated part of the world, we've flown into the grass landing strip at Silinhot, a frontier boomtown that serves the livestock area, and then bounced around in the back of a jeep along 60 miles of dirt road.

Now Chimude, who is a host first and an interview subject second, demands that we eat. "The more you eat," we are told, as his words are translated from Mongolian to Chinese to English, "the more your host is pleased."

Those hard squares of white cow's cheese, we are told, should be dipped first into the heavy sour cream, then into the sugar and only then into one's mouth. To wash it down there is milk tea, which is made by breaking off a small piece of tea from a rock-hard brick, brewing the tea with water and then adding milk. It is served to us in soup bowls.

At Chimude's suggestion, we drop traditional condiments such as butter and roasted millet into the bowls. It still looks and tastes like mud but as the bowls fall from our lips we manage appreciative smiles.

From the outside, Chimude's yurt is just a large tent of felt, circular in shape with straight sides and a sloping roof rising to a hole in the middle. Inside we can see it is supported by wooden lattice-work on the walls and poles on the ceiling.

Before liberation, Chimude says, his parents and their 10 children had a smaller yurt, ragged and full of holes. The children were ragged, too, and family members often had to hunt wild rabbits for food. They owned little livestock. Now his family income is the equivalent of $700 a year, which isn't so low considering that the components of an entire yurt cost little more than that and his monthly food bill is about $15. He's sufficiently affluent that he can display his watch, a radio and a clock.

Chimude, the leader of a commune brigade who has been specially chosen for this meeting with foreigners, says he and most of the herdsmen still live a semi-nomadic existence. As soon as the weather permits in the spring, they leave winter settlements and begin living in yurts, shifting the location of their yurts a couple of times during the spring, frequently during the summer and a few times during the autumn before settling back for the winter.

For Chimude's family this summer, the days start at about 4:30 a.m. The women go out to milk the cows and then return to brew tea. At 5:00 the men begin herding; they return at noon for lunch and a rest; they go back to their herding and then return at sunset. After eating supper, they cover the felt carpets with their quilts and go to sleep.

This sounds like a way of life that has gone on for centuries. But one difference is that every other night the members of the five to seven households in this cluster of yurts get together for what Chimude calls political evening school. The school has an explicitly political aim; it has also taught Chimude and members of his family how to read and write in Mongolian.

Another important change is that groupings of herdsmen like this one are only temporary, not rooted in decades of kinship or friendship. When the brigade leaders decide that certain herds of animals are to be shifted elsewhere, the households that look after those animals must also be shifted. How frequently are the herdsmen's groups reformed? "Not necessarily every year," Chimude answers.

Yet another change is permanent winter settlement. In fact, half of the nomadic herdsmen in Chimude's brigade own permanent homes of brick or mud and the hope is that soon they all will.

Change at the Kiringele People's Commune began in earnest in the early 1960s, a decade that brought profound changes to the lives of all of Inner Mongolia's herdsmen. In 1959, as elsewhere in China, communes replaced rural co-operatives. A number of second-hand reports said that many Inner Mongolian herdsmen had slaughtered their livestock rather than hand them over to the newly formed communes.

Whatever the case, it was soon after 1959, according to a Silingol League official, that there was a large influx of Han Chinese into the Kiringele commune. The purpose, he said, was to teach the nomadic herdsmen how to grow fodder, how to build permanent houses and how to set up small industries. A side effect, at least, was that the independent-minded Mongolian herdsmen were suddenly outnumbered by the Han, at Kiringele and probably many other communes on the grasslands.

The Silingol League's population today is only 25 per cent Mongolian — and this is the league once considered to be the last stronghold of Mongolian nomadic society in Inner Mongolia.

The 1960s also witnessed the destruction of the Lamaist religion. One morning just after sunrise, I went out searching for Silinhot's Bei Zi Miao, a temple and lamasery complex that had been described decades ago by travellers.

But when I found Bei Zi Miao on a hillside at the edge of

197

town, it was obvious that the Cultural Revolution had killed it. Thousands of birds flew in and out of the weather-worn main temple building. On the padlocked gate were two signs in Chinese characters reading "Not Open to Visitors" and "No Admittance".

It seemed that the wooden buildings are not being maintained and are starting to rot away: the last coat of paint was probably applied about 10 years ago, just before the beginning of the Cultural Revolution.

Historians of different political persuasions have written that the Lamaist religion — basically the same as the Tibetan brand of Buddhism — was a decadent, corrupt and exploitive force in Inner Mongolia. But they also agree that it was until recently subscribed to by almost all Mongolians. Today, officials told us, Lamaism is dead.

Back in the yurt, lunch is progressing to the main course — big plates of boiled mutton still on the bone. Our choice is to pick up a bone and gnaw away or employ a hunting knife to hack off a piece we can eat with our fingers.

There are many toasts of milk wine before we leave with a sense of good feeling and gratitude. We have not only been treated to a Mongolian feast; we have also had the privilege of probing into a man's life.

Outside the yurt, however, something is bothering me. Chimude had told us this cluster of yurts has been here for 10 days — another person said 12 days. But there are many signs that the yurts have been here for only a couple of days at most: in other words, that they've been set up for our benefit.

It's not just that they are spotless inside and out: that could be explained. But the ground between the yurts has not been worn down as it would be after 10 days and there is no mud or footprints around even though it has rained in recent days.

I put it down to the peculiar sense of hospitality the Chinese have. Like a proud housewife in the West, they want to present their guests with the best. Other clusters of yurts we saw at a distance seemed to be surrounded by muddy ground and their felt coverings were grimy. That just wouldn't be good enough for the first foreigners Chimude says he has ever met.

Besides, Chimude's words otherwise seemed to be truthful

and consistent with everything else we discovered during our stay in the grasslands. His description of the bad old days was mild compared to what many historians have written about the conditions in that region before the Communist Party won power.

Back in Peking, Munro explored the capital and discovered that its citizens were enjoying what he called the Chinese revolution's unquestionable success — food.

PEKING — Autumn is a good time of year in Peking. Dry, sunny and cool, a cherished pause between summer's humidity and winter's biting winds. Chinese women, representatives of a nation's frugality, swinging long straw brooms, sweep up the autumn leaves for next spring's compost. In the suburban communes, the peak of the harvest has passed and peasants are turning their attention to the task of reconstructing farmland — of amalgamating tiny, age-old plots into larger fields amenable to tractors and large-scale irrigation.

At the entrances of the low-lying grey-painted residences — walled off from the streets, facing on to internal courtyards — the pedicart haulers are dumping heaps of coal for winter. And householders are accumulating their piles of briquettes made with pulverized coal and some sawdust or dirt binding.

Evenings come early on the east coast of this one-time-zone country and before five o'clock the sun burns through the dusky light and the coal smoke, which is just beginning to make the nostrils twitch. In the markets are heaped piles of duck heads — cleaned of all feathers but with beaks and eyes still intact. They cost three pennies each. For hours some evenings, old people sit around a table talking with their friends in the dim light of their homes, drinking wine and beer and slowly picking clean the roasted heads.

Food, the Chinese revolution's unarguable triumph, floods the street stalls and the covered markets. The annual late-harvest glut of Chinese cabbage creates leafy green mountains on the sidewalks. Trucks and horse-drawn carts keep adding to the mountains while shoppers carry away their shares in sacks or in piles on the rear carriers of their bicycles. On the outside window-sills of apartments, you can see the cabbage heads stacked halfway up the sides of the windows. Some of the cabbage will be there until March — a hoard of vegetables for the coming winter days when leafy greens will be in short supply in the markets.

The abundance is much more than one of duck heads and cabbages. In one of Peking's large covered markets, a butcher hacks away with his cleaver at slabs of pork while jovially bantering with his waiting customers. Nearby, another butcher is meticulously stripping every last morsel of meat from the rib-cage of a sheep.

At another stall, workers dump baskets of lively crabs into white-tiled tubs and within a moment there is a long line of shoppers waiting to buy them. Crabs are one of those special items that might appear for a few days, an hour or two each day, and then disappear again for a long time. The Chinese treat these animals with an economy unknown at any North American crab feast. That yellow substance we discard they fry with onions. Then all the meat is carefully removed, not for immediate eating, but for drying so it can be stored for the next several months' soups and special dishes.

Peking's big covered markets usually have a booth at one side displaying plates of uncooked food. A typical plate might hold green beans, some noodles and cubes of red meat. The customer, apparently usually a shift worker or single person, points to the food combination he likes and the clerk scrapes the contents of the plate into some brown paper. The customer takes the package home and tosses it into a frying pan. It's China's equivalent of the TV dinner.

In December, President Gerald Ford arrived in Peking to a welcome that was only slightly less low-key than the one given to Richard Nixon nearly four years earlier. At the end of the five-day visit, there was no indication of any further improvement in relations between China and the United States. To many observers, the most interesting aspect of the visit was the prominent role played by Vice-Premier Teng Hsiao-ping. Throughout 1975, Teng had been placing his close allies in crucial Communist Party posts around the country; with the continued incapacity of Chou En-lai, he was now acting as *de facto* premier.

Then, in January, 1976, Chou died. Despite Chou's towering role in recent Chinese history and his status as a major world statesman, the government decreed that the funeral ceremonies should be subdued and circumscribed. But on the streets of Peking, Munro found that the ordinary people had different ideas. For nearly a week, he observed a remarkable outpouring of grief, as tens of thousands of Chinese braved bitter winter winds to place wreaths in Chou's honor at Tien An Men Square. Many were sobbing and moaning, and others had tears pouring down their cheeks.

It was generally assumed that Teng would be Chou's successor, and that China would continue to follow relatively moderate and pragmatic policies. But in February it was announced that the little-known Hua Kuo-feng, a younger and lower-ranking vice-premier, had been named acting premier. At the same time, wall posters in Peking and Shanghai attacked Teng as "China's Second Khrushchev". Only a month after Chou's death, the coalition he had helped to forge had fallen apart and the radicals had regained the initiative. Even *The People's Daily* admitted that the Central Committee was split, and put the blame on "the capitalist roaders within the Party who have refused to repent and reform themselves". When Chairman Mao himself was quoted as denouncing Teng, it was clear that the brusque and diminutive politician had been toppled from power for the second time in a decade. Among his many alleged offences, Teng had been scornful of Chiang Ching's "revolutionary theatre"; there were signs that Mao's wife had played a key role in his downfall.

Then — just as quickly and unexpectedly — there was a moderate backlash. In early April the Chinese celebrated Ching Ming, the time of year when they traditionally honor the dead. Once again, groups began to lay wreaths and to post poems in memory of Chou at the Monument to the People's Heroes in Tien An Men Square. This was an open challenge to the radicals; when the authorities tried to curb the demonstrators, their anger exploded into violence.

PEKING — A mob of tens of thousands of Chinese angered by a ban on further tributes to the late Premier Chou En-lai broke through police lines this morning and stormed their way to the doors of the Great Hall of the People in the centre of Peking. It was the most dramatic and politically potent defiance of authority that observers could remember in Peking since the Cultural Revolution that shook China in the late 1960s.

Cordons of unarmed soldiers, policemen and plain-clothes security officers frantically formed and reformed lines in and around Tien An Men Square in an effort to control the crowds.

But there were more than 10,000 people on the steps of the main entrance to the Great Hall alone, chanting "Open the door . . . Long Live Chairman Mao . . . Long Live Chou En-lai" and, with defiance in their voices, singing the "Internationale", the international Communist anthem.

And at the Monument to the People's Heroes in the centre of the square, youths defiantly placed three wreaths honoring the late premier as the crowd applauded.

Shortly before 1 p.m. members of the mob set fire to a jeep at the edge of the square. Flames leaped up from the jeep and thick black smoke billowed across the square as the mob stood around.

At least 15 minutes went by before two fire trucks arrived, and the jeep was destroyed. Thousands of army troops moved into the square.

The thousands of wreaths and posters honoring Chou — symbolically suggesting a moderate backlash against radical leaders and indicating support for Chou's moderate policies — had all been removed during the early hours of the morning. They were removed despite many signs left by people asking that the wreaths remain until tomorrow.

Crews removing the wreaths worked behind a cordon of hundreds of security men. About 8 a.m., however, large crowds of people began gathering at the cordon.

Witnesses then saw a scuffle, policemen's hats going up in the air and then the crowd surge forward. In a short time, the police lines were breached in a number of places and tens of thousands of people were on the square.

There was a sense of *déjà vu* for an observer who had witnessed many essentially non-violent civil-rights and anti-war demonstrations in North America. The crowd's mood was a combination of excitement, fear, curiosity and defiance.

The vast majority of the people were not violent and really didn't know what to do when they had reached the doors of the

Great Hall. They chanted, sang, applauded and surged back and forth on the steps.

Occasionally, however, violent scuffles broke out in the crowd, usually when a gang of youths attacked a single member of the crowd.

A running mob of youths hustled a young man from the Great Hall steps to the monument in the middle of the square where people shouted at him and pummelled him with their fists. Every time his face emerged from the sea of people around him, it was bloodier and more swollen. Neither his "offence" nor his ultimate fate could be determined.

Before noon, security forces had succeeded in exerting a measure of control and the crowds were thinning out. But thousands remained on the square.

Crowds of citizens cheered unidentified speakers who made thinly veiled attacks against radicals and warned against radical attempts to alter the moderate policies of Chou, who died on January 8.

Others diligently tried to decipher the shreds of posters that had been torn down, presumably because they carried provocative messages assailing unnamed "careerists", or called on the army and the police to "protect the constitution".

A few posters seen by a number of foreigners before they were torn down pointedly praised Yang Kai-hui, the wife of Chairman Mao Tse-tung who was executed by the Chinese Nationalists in 1935. Mao's present wife, Chiang Ching, is considered to be a leading force behind China's current anti-rightist campaign.

The spectacle on Tien An Men Square had been growing since early last week. At six o'clock in the cold damp morning yesterday, there were already about 2,000 people around the monument. At one point in the early afternoon there were at least 100,000 people — some estimates ran as high as 300,000 — on the square.

The riot lasted for almost 12 hours; it ended only after midnight when thousands of militia with wooden staves finally managed to clear the square, leaving behind the smoldering ruins of several cars and a small building believed to be a police headquarters. An official version of the disturbance soon emerged: according to the

Hua Kuo-feng with Mao's aide and chief bodyguard, Wang Tung-hsing.

Manual labour at a cadre school includes shovelling dirt into carts.

A young musician leaves the stage after an open-air concert.

authorities, a small group of conspirators, loyal to Teng Hsiao-ping, had engineered a counter-revolutionary incident. But foreign observers disagreed. As Munro reported, there may have been some element of organization to the wreath-laying. But most of the participants had come to the square individually, or with friends, and what was most striking was their massive enthusiasm, curiosity and excitement.

Moving with unusual speed, the Chinese authorities announced within two days of the riot that Teng had been formally deposed and that Hua Kuo-feng had been appointed premier and first vice-chairman of the Communist Party. The tall, stocky native of Shansi had thus emerged from the power struggle as the man clearly designated to be the supreme leader of China after Mao's death. Few foreigners had ever met Hua, and even most Chinese seemed to know little about him. In his mid-fifties, he had survived the Cultural Revolution in Hunan, where he had surfaced in the late 1950s as an important provincial leader. In 1975 his appointment as minister of public security — a powerful, sensitive and precarious post — showed that he was trusted by the Party elite. His new appointments were seen as a compromise, rather than a clear-cut victory for the radicals. For one thing, Hua was not identified as either a moderate or a radical; for another, he had evidently eclipsed Wang Hung-wen, the young Shanghai radical who had previously ranked just behind Mao and Chou.

Amid so many sudden changes, ordinary Chinese seemed just as baffled as the foreigners. In July, Munro described a strange mood of unease in the capital.

PEKING — A decline in public discipline. Growing tension. A sense of unease. These characteristics of China today are soft and amorphous and cannot be scientifically measured. But foreigners in China this spring and summer, in the wake of the April riot in Tien An Men Square and the leadership upheaval, have been accumulating individual experiences that add up to a developing picture of a troubled country.

The visible decline in the health of Chairman Mao Tse-tung this spring, followed by his complete withdrawal from the public eye at the end of May, has provoked widespread and worried talk among the Chinese people about how long he will continue to live. Earlier this month a look approaching panic came over the face of a young Chinese woman when she heard funeral music broadcast over the loudspeaker outside her window. When the music turned out to be a prelude to the announcement of the death of Chu Teh, chairman of the National People's Congress, the young woman was saddened but at the same time quite visibly relieved.

Two Chinese men were standing in front of a photo display case near the *People's Daily* building on Peking's main shopping street. They were looking at a newly released photograph of Chairman Mao, which Western observers unanimously believe was taken two to four years ago. This couldn't be a new photograph, one was saying, because he looks so healthy. The other man wasn't paying much attention to his friend; instead he was looking with alarm at the foreigner behind him who was listening intently. But his friend continued to rattle on, analyzing the details of the photograph just like a China-watcher, until he realized he was being overheard.

The number of night-time militia patrols on the streets of Peking appears to be increasing almost week by week. Particularly after midnight, one can see numerous small groups of militia men, and occasionally women, carrying wooden truncheons. One can see them walking three or four abreast along the roads or emerging from the shadows between office and apartment buildings.

The mounting concern over lawbreakers and "class enemies", voiced in the officially controlled press and in closed briefings for Chinese citizens, is only one explanation for the growing role of the militia. Another reason is that uniformed policemen — members of the Public Security Bureau — simply do not command as much respect as their counterparts usually do in the West. Chinese citizens often get into shouting matches with them. And in Canton last weekend a foreigner watched as a Chinese man punched away at a PSB man in uniform.

Members of the PSB, nevertheless, are not powerless. In a park in Canton, a young woman recently walked up to a wall and pasted up a wall poster. A crowd, including some uniformed

PSB officers, immediately gathered to read what turned out to be an attack on Chiang Ching, the wife of Mao Tse-tung, alleging that she is responsible for a lack of freedom in China. The PSB officers then literally picked up the young woman and carried her off, screaming and yelling.

Inside a circle of 40 to 50 youths on a narrow street in Peking, one could see two youths fiercely pummelling a third. What it's all about a foreigner will never know. After a fair amount of time on the streets during the warm weather last year, one saw maybe a couple of fights; this year one has already seen more. Last year one listened skeptically when someone claimed there are still beggars in China; this year one sees a couple of beggars who are bold enough to operate even when foreigners are around. Last year one caught glimpses of black-market activity; this year one can make purchases. Last year one saw an occasional artist in the park painting a "bourgeois" landscape; this year one sees them in greater numbers in the parks and even, in one case, boldly sitting in the middle of the road painting a romantic picture of an old-fashioned foreign-style building.

In late July an earthquake shook Peking. Lasting for almost two minutes, it rocked buildings, caused walls to collapse, broke windows and sent millions of people scurrying to the streets for safety. The epicentre of the earthquake — the worst anywhere in the world since 1964 — was at Tangshan, a highly industrialized city of one million inhabitants about 100 miles east of the capital. According to the first unofficial estimates, as many as 100,000 people might have perished, including 12,000 coal miners trapped underground. (Later estimates would go much higher.) A group of foreigners returning from Tangshan said the city had been completely destroyed, and that hardly any buildings had been left standing. In Peking the authorities imposed a general earthquake alert, hundreds of foreigners left the capital on special flights and the citizens stayed out on the streets, living and sleeping in hastily constructed shelters.

PEKING — In one of the post-earthquake shantytowns on the east side of the city a man wearing pants rolled up to his knees and a crocheted sleeveless undershirt was busy building up his family's shelter yesterday when he received an unannounced visitor.

"We are almost finished the construction," said Chang Ching-sheng, a factory worker who said he was about 40 years old. "With a little more patching of the shelter to keep out the rain we should be finished."

The shelter was like many of the hundreds of thousands of other shelters that have been built along the streets since last Wednesday's earthquake — essentially a series of beds placed right next to each other and a roof of reed matting and plastic sheets held up by poles roped together.

Even here in this primitive setting, Chang's visitor discovered, the Chinese will treat a foreign guest with the usual hospitality. As Chang continued to talk about living on the streets, two mugs of tea for the visitor and his interpreter magically appeared, thrust through the crowd of curious listeners by a man who had quietly disappeared minutes after the foreigner arrived.

A few moments later, the visitor was somewhat embarrassed when he noticed that a woman standing four feet away had begun waving her reed fan, directing a cool breeze past him through the hot lean-to.

With the traditional hospitality came the traditional caution. Chang would not be drawn into guessing about how long he and the other people of Peking would remain in their shantytowns. "It's hard to say right now. At present the time is not set," he said, sounding like an official spokesman even though he was chosen by chance for an interview. "Right now our urgent task is to take all necessary precautions against earthquakes."

Down the street three factory workers broke up their card game for a moment and said that they too didn't know how long they would have to sleep outdoors. When pressed, one of them agreed it would be between two days and two years, but he refused to be narrowed down any further.

What they were willing to talk about was what happened to them when the earthquake struck. Their stories were first-hand reinforcement of the impression foreigners had of a calm and disciplined populace in those first minutes and hours following the quake.

Like Chang, the three factory workers said that local Communist Party organizations had done educational work about earthquakes so they quickly realized what was happening and knew what to do.

"I helped my mother and father and sister to get out," the first young man said. "Then I went back in and shut off the gas and the electricity."

The second young man said he lived on one of the upper floors of his apartment block and, along with his brother, helped his parents out of the building. The third said that after helping his family get out of their ground-floor apartment, he went back and helped others to leave.

Chang and the three factory workers, who were in their late twenties, all said that since the earthquake they have been putting their shelters together with material obtained from their homes, from factories and through their local Party committees.

None of these men appeared to have used valuable building materials in any significant quantity but elsewhere in the neighborhood, and all around Peking, people are using not only bricks and cinder blocks from construction sites but even valuable steel rods used for reinforcing concrete. They are bending the rods, perhaps irretrievably, into half-circles or box shapes to form the frames for shelters they are still building.

Where all this material comes from, no foreigner can be certain, but the cost to construction projects seems to be enormous. A lot of the material appears to be distributed by official organizations but certainly not all of it. One indication of what is going on is that some wooden fences around Peking are beginning to disappear, board by board. And at some construction sites people seem to be helping themselves.

This may partly explain one slogan that was going up in the city yesterday: "Heighten vigilance and prevent damage and sabotage by class enemies."

Seventeen days after the earthquake, the Peking authorities called an end to the alert and the people began pulling down their shelters and taking their beds back home. As life in the capital returned to normal, Munro and his wife had a brief taste of the daily lot of most of China's millions.

PEKING — Chairman Mao's wife does it; office workers do it; even the foreign students in China do it. And I wanted to do it too.

I asked if I could go out to a commune and join the peasants doing physical labor. Specifically, I asked the information department of the foreign ministry whether I could help with the winter wheat harvest.

Permission was granted just as the harvest was drawing to a close. So one morning my wife and I set off for Huang Tu Kang ("Yellow Soil Dune") Commune in Peking's southern rural suburbs.

The job at hand was threshing and winnowing the already cut wheat. When we arrived at the threshing ground, I soon realized that it was going to be difficult to convince the peasants that I was willing and able to work hard.

At first, they assigned us to what is probably the easiest job on the threshing ground. With little more than a motion of his hand, a commune leader suggested we join a line of women who were carrying wicker scoops full of threshed grain over to a small winnowing machine, which blew the mixture of chaff and kernels into the air. Gravity did the rest: the lighter chaff flew free of the heavier kernels and fell to the ground in a pile separate from the chaff.

I had to admit to myself that my pride was slightly hurt when I noticed that most of the peasants on the team I was assigned to were women. A few hours later I would concede that they were probably capable of much more onerous physical labor than me.

The smiles of the women in the wicker brigade were friendly but betrayed some puzzlement about what these foreigners were doing there. The steady pace and the noise of the machines eliminated any real opportunity for conversation.

My wife and I discovered later that most of our communications with the peasants were quite similar and went like this:

They: Do you want to rest?

We: I don't want to, thank you.

They: Are you tired?

We: No, I'm not tired.

The first job was so easy that I was relieved when they transferred me to pushing a big metal cart used for carrying piles of chaff across the threshing ground to be stored for compost. I repeatedly wheeled the heavy cart to the temporary compost heap and then trotted back with the cart for another load until, after less than 30 minutes, I was beginning to work up a sweat. Whether it was coincidence or not, the moment my exertions became evident to the people in charge, they called out that it was time for a rest.

As the break dragged on and on and my wife and I made small talk with some of the peasants, it began to sink in that the old combination of hospitality and caution with which the Chinese usually treat foreigners was going to prevent me from doing anything like the full day's work for which I had volunteered.

After the break, I got my only chance to do some really hard work. I was given a pitchfork and motioned into a double line — again, nearly all women — strung out along one end of a simple threshing machine. Our job was to toss the wheat down along the line as it came out of the threshing machine, repeatedly lifting the wheat through the air so that kernels of wheat would fall onto the ground where they could later be collected. We had to work fast and the wheat seemed to become gradually heavier.

The Chinese have an expression which, loosely translated, goes "Take part in productive labor and thereby reform one's thoughts". This brief spate of work did not provide me with a Marxist-Leninist prism through which to view reality, but it nevertheless was sufficient to spark some second thoughts about a few things about which I had previously no first-hand knowledge.

As I kept swinging my pitchfork, for instance, I realized that what I was doing was so primitive that it was almost silly; it would be so easy, I thought, to replace the 12 or so of us on the pitchfork brigade with a very simple sifting and conveying machine. I had had a similar thought while pushing the handcart: why was I pushing around a 200-pound metal cart, filled with only 25 pounds of wheat chaff, when a light cart built mainly with plastic could do the job?

The point is that these are exactly the kind of reactions to physical labor Chairman Mao Tse-tung had in mind when he said that one of the reasons for sending those millions of high-school graduates to the countryside is that they can help transform rural life. Or, to put it in other words, it is Chairman Mao's hope that young people with a basic grasp of logic and the scientific method will help jolt the peasants of China out of their traditional work habits.

I had read about this, in the abstract, countless times. But it was only when I felt a mild, but undeniable, ache in my back muscles that I really understood it.

I didn't have much more time then to dwell on my new insight because our work was again cut short and we were hustled off for lunch at commune headquarters. The dishes arrived one after another; the food was simple but very tasty. Even though my wife and I went back to the threshing ground after lunch for a bit more work, we ate a lot more food that day than we helped produce.

It was one thing to exchange a few words with some peasants during an officially approved visit to a commune. As Munro also reported, it was quite another thing for foreigners to attempt any more meaningful contact with the Chinese all around them.

PEKING — The romance of a young Australian woman and a Chinese man who wish to be married has been cut short by Chinese officials who have separated the couple and forbidden them to marry.

Susan Day, an Australian English teacher in her mid-twenties, made an appeal through visiting Australian Prime Minister Malcolm Fraser to Premier Hua Kuo-feng this June for permission to marry the man and remain with him in China.

The response of the Chinese authorities was to forbid the marriage. And the young man, who was an official at the Sian Foreign Languages Institute, has been transferred to another institution away from the city of Sian.

The story of Miss Day's plight was publicized by a Hong Kong magazine yesterday even though she had told friends she did not want publicity because she did not believe it would help in any way to persuade the Chinese to change their minds. Miss Day has not seen her friend since he was removed from the institute earlier this year.

Miss Day, described by those who have met her as tall, dark-haired and attractive, went to Sian in central China in April, 1975, after signing a two-year contract to teach English at the Foreign Languages Institute there. Despite the romance the institute has reportedly asked her to remain until her contract expires and she has reportedly agreed to do so.

Chinese authorities told her there is no general regulation forbidding Chinese citizens to marry foreigners but, in this particular case, there is a special regulation that does forbid the marriage of Miss Day and the Chinese man, who is also thought to be in his twenties. It is believed, although this could not be confirmed, that the Chinese said the man could not marry a foreigner because his father is a member of the People's Liberation Army.

This is the first case foreigners in Peking could recall of a Chinese citizen and a foreigner seeking to marry each other since the Cultural Revolution of the early 1960s. That a romance was able to blossom at all between Miss Day and her friend may be due partly to the fact that they were in Sian, far removed from Peking where officials have much experience in keeping relations between Chinese and foreigners distant and correct.

In Peking at least, social relations between Chinese and resident foreigners, even if they are of the same sex, nearly always follow a set of unwritten but quite rigid and restrictive rules. Chinese officials, for instance, will occasionally accept invitations for dinner at the homes of diplomats and journalists with whom they deal officially. But the Chinese almost invariably come in groups of two or more and leave early — and at the same time.

Foreign students are allowed to have Chinese roommates but they quickly discover that their roommates will not go to restaurants or other off-campus locations with them unless it is an organized event sanctioned by the educational institution.

"When the Chinese talk about friendship between Chinese and foreigners," said one foreigner who is outspokenly sympathetic to the Chinese revolution, "they are not talking about the sort of friendship we have in the West where two people trust each other and are open and candid together. They are talking about a political kind of friendship, which furthers China's relations with the rest of the world."

The citizens of Peking are reportedly strongly discouraged, in intermittent briefings, from exchanging anything more than a friendly "ni hao" (hello) with foreigners. One Chinese woman visiting Peking from Outer Mongolia and apparently unaware of the rules engaged in a friendly chat with the wife of a Western journalist on the street. After a few moments the two women said good-bye to each other but, as the journalist's wife was walking away, she looked back and saw and heard a police officer scolding the woman.

More recently three Canadians in the Foreign Languages Bookstore began exchanging some friendly small talk with a uniformed PLA soldier. After three or four minutes the bookstore clerk, a middle-aged woman who had been watching and listening from behind her counter, approached the soldier. "What do you want to buy?" she asked the soldier in a cool voice. The soldier mumbled something and hastily said goodbye to his new acquaintances.

Experiences such as these are cumulatively very inhibiting. Foreigners begin to realize that any Chinese stranger who is sufficiently friendly or naive to enter into a conversation might get into trouble. So, with time, most foreigners stop trying to engage people in small talk unless they are the waiters, elevator operators and staff members whose jobs bring them into regular contact with foreigners. And these people are well versed in the proper limits of social conversation.

Foreigners who hunger after normal contacts with the Chinese people find there is one area where they can enjoy some latitude. Short chats with children, including those who are with adults, are considered sufficiently innocent. But even here there can be problems.

A journalist and his wife who were recently photographing the harvest scenes near Peking came upon a boy of about three and a girl of about six standing by the roadside. They were too cute to ignore so the foreign couple asked them to pose for their Polaroid camera and then gave the two children their instant portraits. The children were intrigued and delighted as they watched their images develop.

But suddenly a woman across the road shouted at them: "Show me what you've got there!" The little girl's face clouded with panic and she ran across the road and nervously showed the pictures to the woman. The woman turned out to be quite pleased. The little girl was so relieved that she literally danced down the road in happiness.

On September 9, 1976, Mao Tse-tung died at the age of 82. Although long-expected, the death of their great leader capped a year of ominous misfortune for the Chinese, since it followed the death of Chou En-lai, the Tien An Men riot and the devastating earthquake. Throughout this time, China had been divided by a power struggle that now promised to become deeper and even more divisive. Across the vast nation, millions of people put on black arm-bands and the ubiquitous portraits of the Chairman were everywhere draped in black crepe. In Peking thousands of grief-stricken Chinese — from Politburo members to ordinary workers and peasants — paid their respects to Mao as his body lay in state in the Great Hall of the People. Many of the mourners were shaking and wailing with sorrow. After 10 days, the official mourning period ended with a massive and sombre rally.

PEKING — Close to a million Chinese gathered in the centre of China's ancient capital Saturday afternoon to mourn the late Chairman Mao Tse-tung at a brief and austere rally that ended in a wave of sobs.

Premier Hua Kuo-feng read a memorial speech from a specially built rostrum immediately in front of Tien An Men (the Gate of Heavenly Peace) where a triumphant Chairman Mao had declared the founding of the People's Republic of China almost 27 years ago.

Premier Hua, now the most senior Communist Party leader in China, called on the Communist Party, the army and the people of China to "carry on the cause left behind by Chairman Mao" in an address that was the Chinese equivalent of a funeral oration.

After the speech, many of the officially estimated one million people standing in Tien An Men Square and along the Avenue of Eternal Peace for a mile in each direction began to cry and moan quietly. It was controlled rather than hysterical, but the sound reached the upper stories of the Peking Hotel where some foreigners were watching.

The rally began at 3 p.m. with everyone standing for three minutes in silent tribute to Chairman Mao. Everyone in China had been asked to do the same. Throughout Peking, the wailing of sirens and factory whistles filled the air. The whole city seemed to stand still. The only visible movement was that of smoke rising from factory chimneys where workers were able to interrupt their chores only momentarily.

Earlier in the afternoon throughout Peking, in scenes certain to have been duplicated everywhere in China, small knots of people gathered outside their homes to listen to the radio and await the three minutes of tribute. Larger, organized groups sat in front of television sets, which were set up outdoors by neighborhood committees, or marched solemnly to smaller memorial rallies at schools and work places.

On television, the scene at Tien An Men Square was one of calm, order and decorum. On the magenta-colored rostrum, decorated and surrounded by evergreen branches, flowers, wreaths and funeral bunting, stood virtually the entire Chinese leadership.

Arrayed in the square in front of the leaders were massive blocks of organized mourners — long rectangles of army men in green tunics, school children in white shirts and workers and peasants in blue shirts.

Chiang Ching, Mao Tse-tung's widow, was wearing black and had a black kerchief. She seemed grief-stricken although she maintained the composure she has displayed all week. Some of the oldest leaders were so frail they required assistance in standing throughout the 30-minute rally. Soong Ching-ling, the 86-year-old U.S.-educated widow of China's first Republican president, Sun Yat-sen, sat in a chair leaning on a cane.

As Premier Hua delivered the memorial speech in his thick Shansi accent, the picture Chinese television viewers saw on their screens was of two men — Premier Hua and Wang Hung-wen, the second-ranking member of the Communist Party, known for his radical Shanghai background, who stood beside and just behind the premier, silently and intently following the text of the speech the premier was reading aloud.

For the future, the underlying message of Premier Hua's

speech seemed to be one of continuity in the ideological line that has emerged during the past several months. He explicitly called for a continuation in the criticism of Teng Hsiao-ping but he also issued a plea for an end to factionalism.

Then the premier led the people in three bows to the black-and-white photographic portrait of the late Chairman which stood at the centre of the Gate of Heavenly Peace. As Wang Hung-wen called out the timing of the bows, everyone in the area bent from the waist in unison.

Then, with the playing of "The East Is Red", which has become the anthem of Chinese Communism, people began crying. A moment or two later, they were told they could rest and, as they sat down, many buried their faces in their arms.

Within 30 minutes, groups of mourners were being marched away to the assembly points beyond the cordoned-off area where trucks and buses awaited them. Some marched, some ran, but the scene was quiet and orderly.

On October 1, when the Chinese celebrated their twenty-seventh National Day — and their first without Mao — the radicals were still in strident voice. An editorial in *The People's Daily* emphasized Mao's most provocative legacy: his contention that the Communist Party still sheltered many anti-Communists who should be purged at frequent intervals. As Munro reported, however, diplomats in the capital were doubtful that the radicals could transform this attitude into political action. Then — just one month after Mao's death — came the startling news that his widow and the three other leading radicals had been toppled from power.

Apart from Chiang Ching, the victims were the so-called Shanghai Radicals: Wang Hung-wen, the young worker who had stood second in the Party after Hua Kuo-feng, the fourth-ranking Chang Chun-chiao and the sixth-ranking Yao Wen-yuan. Although there was no official confirmation for two more weeks, it was soon known that the four had been arrested in their homes on October 7 by plain-clothes security men backed by a crack PLA unit. Soon wall posters attacking them appeared in Shanghai, where demonstrators jeered at huge caricatures of the radicals with nooses around their necks. Next, tens of thousands of Chinese streamed into Peking's Tien An Men Square to shout denunciations of the four, enthusiastically following the promptings of their cheerleaders. Finally, on October 22, the official media broke their silence to announce that Chiang, Wang, Chang and Yao had been "liquidated" after their plot to seize power was crushed by Premier Hua (whose appointment as Communist Party chairman was also now confirmed). Later, an official spokesman stated that the four radicals were still alive but indicated they would be incarcerated for the rest of their lives. They were now being called the Gang of Four.

At a mass rally in the capital, about one million people heard speakers denounce the purged radicals as "conspirators, forgers and counter-revolutionaries who are filthy and contemptible like dog's dung". Although it was generally believed that the Gang, especially Madame Mao, were close to Chairman Mao during his last years and relied on him for protection and legitimacy, the same speakers made great efforts to portray a gulf between him and the four.

By December, Munro was reporting that thousands of officials had been dismissed from their posts as attacks on real or alleged supporters of the Gang continued in every province. In some areas these attacks became so disorderly and indiscriminate that army units were sent into factories, schools and government offices to restore order. In early 1977, wall posters in Peking were demanding that Teng Hsiao-ping be restored to public office. These were part of a remarkable outpouring of political sentiment in the capital.

PEKING — The political-poster campaign in Peking's Tien An Men Square has become a "go" signal for a host of frustrated poets, essay writers, calligraphers, craftsmen and even graffiti freaks.

Once it became clear that the new set of posters had secret high-level backing, creative people with similarly anti-leftist viewpoints knew they had a short-term licence to do their thing.

The result has been an outpouring of creativity and expresion that one rarely sees in a Communist system where culture usually must adhere to narrow guidelines and thus is sterile and dull.

Many of the hundreds of thousands of people who have come to Tien An Men Square during the past week to read posters are looking for clues about how strongly the political winds from the right are blowing. But many also come to admire the quality of the posters and the displays.

A poster with well-executed Chinese characters always pulls a crowd, even if it simply repeats sentiments expressed by many other posters, because calligraphy is still admired in China. A few posters, in fact, seem to have been put up by some unappreciated calligraphers anxious to display their work to the public even if they can't risk signing their own names.

On many posters are intricate poems written in the classic Chinese style. Basically they express political sentiments similar to those in the first posters put up with high-level backing but, again, this is secondary. The important thing is that frustrated poets, particularly those who won't write the doggerel that often appears in *The People's Daily*, have a brief opportunity to anonymously show their stuff before the curtain comes down again.

The other night, a Western diplomat who is well versed in Chinese literature walked along the fence at Tien An Men reading the latest classical-style poems and pronouncing a few of them "superb".

The appearance of a large collection of poems, collected during the anti-radical demonstrations last April, raises the possibility that there are underground presses operating in Peking. The poems are mimeographed or printed in folio form, that is, as pages for a book.

Not all the poems are art nor are all the poster essays elegant. There are artistic and political bores in China too and some of the essays are maudlin, imitative, cliché-ridden and just plain dull.

One often observes Chinese people at the square glancing briefly at a poster essay that lacks political interest and artistic verve and then remarking to their friends, "That one's not interesting, let's read the next one."

Other posters — arrayed along the wooden hoarding in front of the construction work for Mao's mausoleum — attract crowds of intense Chinese who copy every character down in their notebooks. The temperature hasn't risen above 20 degrees Fahrenheit in recent days and, with a strong wind blowing, members of the notebook brigade can be heard saying to their friends, "My hand is too cold to write any more; here, it's your turn."

Among the notebook-wielders one often sees people in their twenties whose fine facial features immediately set them apart from the rougher hewn majority. They possess the aristocratic jaw and cheekbones that betray the survivors and descendants of Peking's centuries-old upper class of bureaucrats, scholars and artists.

All this is not to suggest that the scene at Tien An Men is just one of high culture and conspiratorial politics. One Westerner says he watched a group of Chinese engaged in what amounted to a spitting contest, the target being a drawing of the radical Gang of Four.

And then there are the graffiti written on the margins of other people's posters. One item reflected a certain peasant wisdom: "Teng Hsiao-ping is a heroic eagle; people like Wu Teh [Peking's mayor and an outspoken critic of Teng] are nothing but mother hens in the back yard of socialism." Other graffiti are a lot ruder than that.

The behind-the-scenes organizers of the anti-radical poster campaign seem to have enlisted skilled craftsmen to put together displays that will draw large crowds. Effigies of the four radicals on Peking's main street last weekend reflected the work of a highly skilled puppet-maker: the papier mâché faces were immediately recognizable and small items such as eyeglasses and shoes were meticulously detailed.

On the north side of Tien An Men Square, a twice-life-size and realistically done hardboard figure of a waving Chou En-lai is the biggest attraction. Young people jostle all day long for a position beside it so they can pose for their parents' and friends' cameras.

Spinning nearby is a globe, perhaps seven feet high, covered with white paper flowers. With the hundreds of colorful, tinsel-covered wreaths brought to honor Chou, the carnival-cum-Christmas atmosphere is complete on the north end of the square.

At night the scene changes. The children go home and most of the action is again over by the construction fence. Often clusters of 50 or 100 people listen while a man or woman buried in the crowd and wielding a flashlight reads out the contents of a poster. The overall impression sometimes is of a series of small political meetings strung out along the fence.

This happens less during the day and not just because it is easier to read the posters. During daylight there are too many men around with cameras taking photographs of people in the crowd. The cameramen are neither journalists nor amateur photographers: they are agents, but exactly for whom in faction-ridden China, it's impossible to tell.

Every government ministry, every Party faction, as well as the police agencies, have their agents on the square. They take photographs, make meticulous notes on the posters and just keep watch, reporting back to their offices on the latest developments on the square.

Under the cover of darkness, people can be freer with their opinions. When a young man the other night read out, "Teng Hsiao-ping is a good comrade," the crowd of 40 listeners chanted back, "Good, good."

By February it was evident that Teng Hsiao-ping's long-expected return to power had been inexplicably delayed. At the same time, the anti-radical campaign showed signs of faltering due to cynicism and apathy among ordinary people and officials who had endured so many political twists and turns in recent years. It was also clear that the top leadership was failing to provide a firm sense of political direction because it was split on some basic issues. Amid the continuing uncertainty, Munro reported from Wuhan that law and order were being restored in one of China's largest and most politically volatile cities.

WUHAN — In this industrial city in the Chinese heartland, the current efforts of China's new leaders to re-establish public order have reached from the execution grounds to the local bus stops.

Foreigners visiting Wuhan have reported seeing official wall posters announcing the execution of criminals and political prisoners. Others have seen men, their heads bent over signs announcing their crimes, being paraded around the streets in trucks.

The behave-yourself-or-else message in these displays seems

to have already had the intended effect. Just a few months ago, according to one of the few foreigners then allowed to visit here, beggars were operating much more openly than they do elsewhere in China. But now a visitor can walk for hours in the city streets and not see a single beggar.

Foreign visitors also often complained about being the object of rude or hostile remarks and gestures by citizens of Wuhan. But while a foreigner today can sometimes still look around and find dozens or even hundreds of Chinese following him, now the crowds seem curious and friendly and certainly not hostile.

It is at the bus stops, however, that the public order campaign is most obvious to the casual visitor. Teenaged militia members or traffic wardens are stationed at every bus stop in the city just to keep order. In the central commercial districts, there are usually four people keeping order; in the outskirts there may be only two.

The bus stops are all festooned with slogans urging waiting passengers to be courteous and not jump the line. To further get the point across, the authorities have put up ropes between the sidewalk and the street to discourage people from rushing the buses when they pull up at the stops.

These measures might strike the foreigner as a little overdone until he happens upon a bus stop that for some reason — a negative example perhaps — has been left without the benefit of teenagers, ropes and slogans.

A bus pulls up to this particular stop and a minimob of about 25 people rush toward the door as it begins to open. The people already on board who want to get off look at the crush of people, plead for an opening and, when they don't get it, simply let themselves fall, one by one, into the mob blocking their exit. As they make their way to the safety of the sidewalk, the pushing and shoving among those trying to get on the bus intensifies.

This isn't a riot. There is pushing and shoving but no punching or swinging of elbows; grunts and groans but no shouts or cries. The crush, however, is so intense that some people are quite literally lifted off their feet and for several seconds are held airborne by the pressure of the crowd. This sort of scene is now the exception in Wuhan; people who were here a couple of months ago said it was the rule.

At least hundreds, and perhaps thousands, of militia mem-

Yis, some in costume, are among students at the Yunnan Institute for Nationalities in Kunming.

Water splashing is a tradition at the spring festival in southwestern China.

One million people turned out at Tien An Men Square to mourn the passing of Mao Tse-tung.

bers are on duty on the streets of Wuhan even during daylight hours. It seems there is a new militia just recently organized by city officials. The militia members seen here are almost all young and act as if they're new on the job. What's more, they all wear brand-new militia badges on their chests.

It's likely that Wuhan is one of those cities where the radicals established at least a beachhead within the militia. Now that the radicals are being purged, the city officials have been able to disband the old and politically unreliable militia that they were probably unwilling to put on the streets.

The only visible deviation from the straight and narrow — except at that one bus stop — is a small amount of black-market activity. In a scene that belongs in one of the poorer neighborhoods in ultra-capitalist Hong Kong, an old man is selling pants and shirts from a cart. He good-naturedly harangues those who stop to look at his merchandise. He picks up a pair of pants and crumples the fabric in his fist. "Look," he seems to be saying, "they're really good quality — they don't crease."

The pants are indeed well made — good wool, good stitching and tailored much more slimly than any pants sold in any Chinese store. Chances are the pants are either from a private workshop or were made for export and somehow diverted. When a foreigner tries to photograph the scene, the man angrily waves him away.

That summer — during a train journey to the coast — Munro caught some vivid glimpses of Tangshan, the city devastated during the previous year's earthquake. The destruction has been compared to the nuclear bombing of Hiroshima.

TANGSHAN — Many miles before you arrive in this rubble heap that used to be a city of one million people, you notice all the new burial mounds.

The countless clusters of traditional conical mounds, still a common sight in rural China, cover the bodies of only a relative few of the hundreds of thousands of people who died in the Tangshan earthquake 11 months ago. Most of those who died in the city itself are rumored to have been buried in large common graves.

It was just last July 28, at 3:42 a.m., that the earthquake levelled this city and within a few seconds claimed enough lives here and in the surrounding countryside to make its mark as one of the greatest disasters in the history of man.

The best estimate of the number who died comes from what is alleged to be a restricted Chinese provincial government document that puts the toll at 655,000. Scientists recently told a visiting Mexican seismologist that it was the worst earthquake in China since 1556 when 830,000 died.

For 40 miles either side of Tangshan, every village has been or is being rebuilt. New rail bridges replace the crumbled originals and huge stores of bricks and cement line the track.

Evidence of the intensity of the shock abounds. Normally level fields are heaved into mounds and craters. The way surface earth subsided into the Kailuan coal mines, north of Tangshan, is clearly visible.

Three of the pit heads appear to be working, but nearby coal trucks and twisted rails are scattered like toys down a hillside.

Foreign seismologists were told recently by Chinese experts in Peking that the shock was like a huge jolt from below that knocked people up against their ceilings and left those outdoors clinging desperately to swinging trees as the earth shook.

In the centre of Tangshan, 100 miles from Peking, the survivors are still living amid the rubble. They're sleeping in tiny houses made of mud along with bricks, pieces of wood and maybe some sheet metal salvaged from the debris.

The roads between these shanties are really paths along which cyclists and horse carts negotiate their way, often overshadowed by piles of rubble on each side. The dirt and dust blown about by the wind complete the scruffy picture.

There is no sign, however, that permament new housing is being built. Some say the Chinese want to wait until after the last of the major after-shocks — the most recent occurring only last month — before they invest in housing. Others point to indications that the Chinese plan to abandon Tangshan and build a new town, perhaps north of the original site.

For more than 10 months, Chinese authorities have ignored requests from foreign journalists to visit here and see for themselves. But yesterday a group of Peking-based correspondents became the first journalists to view the area in daylight by taking a train to the seaside resort of Peitaiho. This report is based

227

on what could be seen from a train moving relatively slowly through the Tangshan area and what could be seen from the Tangshan railway station during a 20-minute stopover.

From an elevated pedestrian walkway at the station, where a policeman tried to prevent photographs being taken, it was impossible to see anything even resembling an old building that has remained intact. As the first reports said, Tangshan was almost levelled. Now the shantytown has at least temporarily taken its place.

Just south of the station is the badly twisted and tangled steel skeleton of a factory otherwise destroyed by the earthquake, which measured 8.2 on the Richter scale.

The station's terminal building has almost disappeared; the brick walls rise only two or four feet to the point where they were sheared off by the earthquake. On a now-useless set of tracks are two railway cars, buckled at the centre where the old station building presumably fell on them. The cars were also gutted by fire, which burned hot enough to peel off the exterior paint.

In July, Munro was back in Peking for the long-awaited announcement that Teng Hsiao-ping had regained all his key posts in the political hierarchy. Rehabilitated for the second time in four years, the 73-year-old Teng was once again a Communist Party vice-chairman and a government vice-premier, as well as vice-chairman of the military commission and army chief of staff. In theory he now ranked third behind the 57-year-old Hua Kuo-feng and the 80-year-old Yeh Chien-ying, an old ally of Teng's who was also a Party vice-chairman. In practice, according to Munro, Teng was expected to wield tremendous and perhaps decisive power.

There was further confirmation of the new moderate trend in August, when the eleventh Congress of the Chinese Communist Party formally inaugurated the post-Mao era. Meeting in Peking, the 1,510 delegates adopted a new Party constitution that aimed at achieving tighter discipline and more centralized control, as well as making China a modern industrial, agricultural and military power by the year 2000. Dozens of leftists were dropped from the Central Committee, to be replaced by veteran officials who had lost their posts during the 1960s. In his key-note speech, Chairman Hua formally declared an end to the Cultural Revolution; while refraining from any criticism of Mao, he made clear that his predecessor's radical inclinations would no longer prevail. When Mao's mausoleum in Tien An Men Square was opened in September, on the first anniversary of his death, editorials heaped lavish praise on the former Chairman, but strongly implied that his policies were not automatically relevant to present-day China.

Although foreign observers had been labelling the contending Chinese factions as "moderates" and "radicals", they had no illusions that the victory of the moderates would lead to any significant relaxation of political controls, or that the new leaders harbored secret yearnings for Western-style democracy. From the time of Frederick Nossal, every *Globe* correspondent had reported on the way that ordinary Chinese were subject to relentless regulation in their daily lives, and to unceasing demands for political and social conformity. Now, in a series of six articles, Munro investigated the whole panorama of human rights (or the lack of them) in China. Filled with explicit examples, his detailed articles were based on his own contacts and observations, as well as material from the Chinese press, briefings and interviews, wall posters and official court notices. These were his major points:

● China, in many ways, is the most tightly controlled nation on earth. . . . Today, Communism has combined the conformist and anti-individualist tradition of the Chinese past with the techniques and organization of modern totalitarianism to create a unique system for controlling people's lives.

● Everybody in China is affiliated to a "unit" that is based on the work place and that is often an integrated living and working community. People have little freedom to choose — or leave — their unit. Life within the unit is strictly regulated, often to the point of deciding who can own a bicycle or even which couples can conceive a child.

● People can travel in China only with official permission, and the cities are filled with innumerable people from rural areas who have reached them illegally, and who lead marginal existences because they can obtain neither regular housing nor the ration coupons necessary to buy rice and clothing. At the same time, the state has arbitrarily sent millions of young people out of the cities to the countryside.

Two faces: a minority-nationality woman and a majority-nationality man.

● No Chinese can choose his own job. Those who are fortunate enough to become cadres, or officials, pay for their privileges by being subjected to controls on their lives that are even more extensive than those over ordinary workers and peasants.

● Chinese are still executed solely for their political beliefs and for such political crimes as "intention to distribute counter-revolutionary pamphlets" and "shamelessly supporting the Gang of Four".

● China lacks a written code of law or any concept of an independent judiciary. Offences — real or imagined — are often handled within the "unit", leading to frequent miscarriages of justice.

● At least thirty million Chinese suffer open and systematic discrimination — including economic deprivation and social and political isolation — because of their "bad class backgrounds".

Widely published in other Western newspapers, Munro's articles stirred great controversy, especially among foreigners sympathetic to the Communist regime. They were also read with chagrin by Chinese officials: in a letter to *The Globe and Mail*, the Chinese embassy in Ottawa said that Munro's visa, dated to expire on December 23, would not be renewed "due to obvious reasons". In effect, Munro was being expelled. But he was preparing to return to Canada anyway — as the Chinese were aware — and his successor, John Fraser, was already on his way to Peking.

John Fraser and friends in Peking. Composer Huang Anlun is second from left.

CHAPTER EIGHT: 1977–1979

JOHN FRASER

Munro turned over the Peking bureau to Fraser just before Christmas. Fraser, 32, was born in Montreal and educated in Ontario, Newfoundland and England. He had started in the newspaper business at 16, working as a copy boy on the Toronto *Telegram* during summer holidays. More recently he had been *The Globe and Mail*'s dance critic and then its theatre critic, winning a National Newspaper Award in each capacity. He was accompanied to Peking by his wife, the writer and photographer Elizabeth MacCallum.

In early 1978, Fraser was reporting that a mood of relaxation was evident in many areas of Chinese life. Education was continuing to recover from the ravages of the Cultural Revolution and the Gang of Four, and learning from foreign sources was all the rage. Traditional operas were again being staged, and artists were being allowed to express more individuality. There were also signs that the authorities were preparing to receive a record number of foreign tourists. This moderate trend was confirmed when the Fifth National People's Congress (China's nominal legislature) met in Peking. There were no startling changes in the top leadership, and a new constitution was adopted that made some tentative gestures in the area of human rights.

In April there was further evidence of the new relaxation when the entire Peking press corps was taken on a week-long tour of Szechwan, China's most populous province. For decades, Szechwan had been visited only by a handful of favored foreigners. No *Globe* corrrespondent had been permitted to see the remote Western province and its major cities of Chengtu and Chungking, where Chiang Kai-shek established his government after the Japanese invasion and where contending factions fought bloody pitched battles during the Cultural Revolution. The trip marked a more open response by the Chinese authorities to foreign curiosity about China's most persistent problems. In the past, *Globe* correspondents had been generally restricted to visiting communes and factories that were show places, or where standards were at least above the national average. Now, as an official told Fraser: "Perhaps if you can see first-hand some of the things we are very far behind in, you will understand our determination to improve matters and this will put a new light on our successful communes and industries." At any rate, no attempts were made to shield the visitors from the backwardness of Szechwan.

CHUNKING — . . . After six days, the immediate impressions have been the ones that endured. The countryside, of course, is famous for its unique beauty. Every square inch of soil seems to have a specific function, even if it is on a 70-degree precipitous incline.

One of the great sights in the world is an enormous terraced hill in Szechwan with the wild array of contrasting colors that comes from crops of yellow rapeseed, watery rice paddies, innumerable varieties of vegetables, alfalfa and clover — all tended by the industrious Szechwanese, many in broad-rimmed straw hats, who fuss over their irrigated fields with loving, inspiring care.

People here work very, very hard to make a living, even if that living is now guaranteed by the state. Many of the ninety million inhabitants do their work under ancient and by now unacceptably primitive conditions, even for China. The most startling irony of the trip came during a visit to a local arts-and-crafts institute where we saw painfully realistic, life-sized sculptures depicting in lurid detail the lives and hard times of peasants in pre-Liberation China. The most striking of all was of a teenager straining at his shoulder harness, which was hitched up to a monstrously heavy load of bricks.

Yet in Chengtu, the capital of Szechwan, such sights are everywhere. We saw just such a youth hauling just such a load and he was bent over so far by the strain that he was virtually on all fours. You don't see this sort of thing in Peking or its rural environs any more, but you do throughout Szechwan. China has other areas where the revolution has so far failed to make significant differences in the material well-being of the people. The wonder is that this province, with its evident agricultural bounty, should have progressed so slowly.

There is a context to be understood. I saw no one who looked seriously underfed, least of all starving. People were adequately clothed. Homes, however primitive, were in a good state of repair. There is considerable, although far from complete, rural electrification, and there has been an impressive effort to establish light industry in urban areas. Because the Szechwanese are so close to the source of so much food, it is not surprising to learn, for example, that they have twice as ample meat rations as the people in neighboring Hupeh Province.

Provincial officials, many of whom are not native to Szechwan (the price, presumably, of so much Cultural Revolution anarchy), freely admit to an over-all backwardness in development, although they do cite light industry as one area that is up to nationally acceptable levels — levels that they admit with equal candor are well behind Western standards. Certainly in the plants we were taken to there seemed to be sensible and intelligent management. Pay incentives are about to be re-established and there was less waste and sloth than many foreign observers have noted in other parts of the country. . . .

The feeling from this trip is that Szechwan really is in for better times. At the moment, walking through Chengtu or driving around the countryside, you get the distinct and not unattractive impression that you are seeing China much as it was 25 or for that matter 250 years ago. It is a picturesqueness observed from a distance, however, and one has ample reason to suspect that it hides some heavy burdens on the people, despite their infectious enthusiasm for life, warm friendships and gloriously hot, spicy food.

Yet there is also a distinct mood of optimism, and not just from the earthy, colorful officials. Walking around Chungking, I stopped on a high terrace overlooking the harbor below on the Yangtze River. A small crowd immediately gathered (you don't get a chance to examine a hairy, white foreigner every day in Chungking), which included a marvellously beautiful old woman with her four-year-old grandson. I blurted out some nonsense about being a Canadian and visiting Szechwan with many other foreigners and how much I liked her city. She put the boy down and gave me the kind of knowing smile that seemed to instantly sum up 60 or 70 years of hard-won experience. "Xianzai hao," she said quietly, keeping a careful eye on her grandson. "Now things are good."

At the end of their tour, the journalists were given another rare opportunity as they took the legendary boat ride down the breathtaking Yangtze River, then known to Westerners more through imagination than experience.

ABOARD THE EAST IS RED #32 — The moment we stepped onto this amiable, vintage vessel in Chungking, it was obvious that this was going to be a remarkable voyage, a trip of a lifetime along the fabled Yangtze River and deep into China's past.

To approach the docks of Chungking, you have to work your way down a precipice and across a stretch of muddy flats. All around us in the early, misty morning, thousands of Chinese were scurrying about on some aspect of river business — many of them weighed down with heavy loads perched precariously at the ends of those ubiquitous bamboo shoulder poles.

The atmosphere of excitement and adventure among the fortunate foreigners who are, at long last, about to embark on this famous voyage — so long forbidden to outsiders — is everywhere evident. To enhance the mood, the dockside PA system is blaring out "Sailing the Seas Depends upon the Helmsman", a jaunty, martial air that for once seems appropriate.

Three days on the Yangtze! About 800 miles by water from Chungking in Szechwan Province to Wuhan in neighboring Hupeh along a waterway that is still a principal thoroughfare for passengers and cargo in central China as it was two millenia ago. A private berth on a colorful steamer. First-class spicy Szechwanese food from dawn to dusk. A full day to pass through the Three Gorges, one of the world's great geological sights.

It sounds like a travel agent's exaggerated dream brochure, but in this case it is all turning out to be true. The fact that so many foreign journalists have been invited to make this trip probably means that tourists will be able to sign up soon. At the moment the cost of the three-day trip is cheap beyond recognition. For $60 you can get a private room and all the food you could possibly eat. That's first-class. For $16 you can ride fifth-class on a lounge chair. When the tourists do come, though, there will probably be an increase as the Chinese are learning very quickly these days that tourism is a handy way to raise needed foreign capital.

Although our ship was built only 20 years ago in Shanghai, it seems much older because it was modelled on pre-war designs. It is not a luxurious boat — nothing in China could be described as that except the limousines senior officials ride around in — but it is more than comfortable, at least for foreigners and Chinese with good jobs. On the fourth-class deck below us, ordinary Chinese share long, narrow cabins containing 22 bunks each.

More than 20 steamers like *The East Is Red #32* cruise along the river, all but two having been built in China. (Those others were pre-Liberation boats made in Canada which still provide reliable service.) In a crunch, she can accommodate 800 passengers. Our captain, a 58-year-old mariner named Hsiung Chung-pei, has had 30 years of experience along the Yangtze.

He is obviously pleased with his vessel, even when he dutifully recites its shortcomings, and his proudest moment came eight years ago when the late Premier Chou En-lai took the trip. Captain Hsiung says he has seen a lot of changes along the Yangtze since Liberation, of which the two greatest are the dredging of the channel through the hazardous Three Gorges and the start of 24-hour navigation in 1962.

Throughout Chinese recorded history, the stretch of the Yangtze going past the gorges has been notorious. For one thing, the current is exceedingly swift. Our downriver trip will take three days, for example, but the same distance on the return takes five. There are fierce rapids along the way and wild lurches in the course of the river. At the west entrance to the Chutang, or first gorge, the Yangtze is less than 100 yards wide. All this has meant that there were more wrecks piled up than there were along the Spanish Main.

In comparison, things are pretty tame now. Channel markers line either side of the river for the full length of the route. The steamers are outfitted with powerful engines and can traverse fast water with ease, and even the trickiest parts of the gorges are now safe for night sailing. Still, the Chinese are not taking any chances and through this stretch there is only alternating one-way traffic.

We had been told that the first and last days would be relatively uneventful, with the scenic glories all piled up on the second day as we passed through the gorges. Consequently, nobody was really prepared for that first day, which struck the Chinese accompanying us as ho-hum stuff while we were wide-eyed with wonder. From the moment we left the outskirts of Chungking, we found ourselves floating through a China nobody had realized still existed.

Isolated, beautiful pagodas on the peaks of the surrounding hills were the first hint. Then we saw a large sampan being rowed along close to the bank. Two rows of men, six to a side, were straining at long oars from their standing positions. A thirteenth man held the tiller while a tattered sail shifted listlessly in what little wind there was.

We were to see many such sampans on the way to the gorges and not one motorized vessel except our own. In Szechwan, sampans remain the principal river vessel and they are an extraordinary sight. The physical exertion required just to get them moving in the first place must be equally extraordinary. Sometimes we heard lusty rowing songs echoing down the vast canyon made from the steep hills on either side.

We came across only two distinct signs of modern China during this stretch. Both were slogans painted in white on the rockface. The first was a famous quotation of Chairman Mao Tse-tung: "Be prepared for war. Be prepared against natural disaster. Do everything for the people." Later on, we saw another sign that struck a less lofty note: "Tow the boat for the revolution."

We saw this last one shortly after observing exactly what it meant. It's one thing to row a boat with the help of a fast current, even cutting across that current. It's quite another thing to get the same boat back home. For that, the crew has to get off the sampan and bring a long tow rope to shore. Then it's just a matter of pulling. The load is so heavy that the front men are almost on all fours straining at the line. Watching the men grunting and groaning, I wondered, perhaps a little cynically, if it was "the revolution" that was foremost in their minds.

This sort of scene you just glide effortlessly past and concern for the well-being of the workers can become a trifle suspect in the plushy confines of the first-class deck. Also, things have to be seen in some sort of context, for while the backwardness of Szechwan has its price in human labor, it also has its rewards in another area — independence.

River people live all along here in their isolated but sturdy-looking thatched cottages. There are no roads and little electricity. Each habitation seems to be built beside small hill streams and there are picturesque terraced fields with crops growing and animals grazing at the side. Some minimal form of collectivization probably exists, but there is simply no way the full authority of a modern Communist state — or any kind of state — could be brought to bear on such residents.

Watching children exploring river caves while their fathers fished or were working on the sampans was a wonderful sight. These people lead among the most independent lives in China today and were the source of some envy from all decks of our ship.

The gorges themselves were almost an anti-climax after all this. Almost, but not quite. They are famous in Chinese mythology and many of the rock formations have been immortalized in poetry and painting. Their beauty comes not so much from their grandeur as in their unpredictability. Because the river weaves all over the place, a new spectacle awaits you at each corner and anticipation is half the fun. The cliffs are so high (more than 3,000 feet) that you see the sun only at high noon.

Beyond the gorges, the river widens markedly and becomes tranquil while the land is flat and boring in comparison. Here is the new China, with extensive modern shipping, heavy industry belching out black and grey smoke from huge, ugly stacks. The contrast is so remarkable you can scarcely believe you saw all the things you did in another time and another world.

From the old to the new. After their Yangtze trip, the journalists were shown the giant steel mill in Wuhan. Again the Chinese authorities made no attempt to hide some striking evidence of their industrial backwardness.

WUHAN — China's second-largest steel mill, in this sprawling tri-city (comprising Wuchang, Hankow and Hanyang) in Hupeh Province, provides a handy and graphic picture of the best and worst of things in Chinese industry today. Since the worst is at the forefront in this enterprise at the moment — and clearly so — it is to the credit of the Chinese authorities that they permitted foreign journalists to see it all close up.

Wuhan Iron and Steel Company, despite production gains from the years of anarchy during the Cultural Revolution, is plagued by worker sloth, poor production standards, dreadful pollution, a woeful lack of anything beyond rudimentary safety precautions and make-shift management that would appear to be slow in accepting the reality of these problems.

But it is also an immense and impressive operation employing more than 90,000 people who work in mines (two for coal and four for iron ore), four blast furnaces, eight open-hearth mills, a coking plant, three heavy-steel and blooming mills, a steel-plate mill, sinter-crushing works and all the subsidiary enterprises that go with such a vast business.

It is a crucially important supplier for Chinese industry, producing more than 7,000 metric tonnes of steel and 8,000 tonnes of iron every day, a 3.8 per cent increase over average daily output last year, according to a spokesman for the company's revolutionary committee, which acts as management.

Obviously then, real work is being done here, but even the quickest of tours — and we stretched ours out for as long as we could get away with — brings one into direct contact with all the problems Chinese industry is having such persistent difficulty in correcting. The following observations came in the order they were made on this visit, each one followed by the response made by Sun Chen-mao, vice-chairman of the Wuhan Iron and Steel Company Revolutionary Committee, when he was questioned later.

POLLUTION. Everywhere we went, the filth was overwhelming, even making allowance for the kind of work going on. The air is colored a sickly grey and orange; although it was a bright day, the sun is visible in the vicinity of the plant only as a vague haze. When people sneeze, their phlegm is filled with tiny bits of metal and soot. Eyes regularly water from sharp, stinging sensations.

"Our smokey environment is our most backward aspect. Conditions here are not so good yet. But we have fine workers who are striving to promote production because they know that if production develops well there will be better conditions. . . . We have been planting trees to improve the air and we have rest houses to provide afflicted workers with protective treatment."

SLOTH.   At a rough but excessively fair estimate, I would say that up to 30 per cent of the workers we saw in the mills were doing no work at all. They sat around gossiping, played cards, stretched out in a quiet corner for a nap, leaned against the wall. Nobody could accuse them of having been briefed to look busy for a foreigner's inspection.

"We are about to apply new incentives for our workers. The most important incentive will be moral or spiritual [worker certificates of commendation] supplemented by material benefits."

ACCIDENTS.   An extraordinary sight awaited us in the steel mill itself. This was in a section where huge cauldrons of molten metal, resting on cradles atop a railway flatcar, are brought. The cauldrons are manipulated by overhead cranes and the molten metal is poured into molds. A short time ago there must have been a terrific accident with one of the cauldrons flipping off the flatcar and smashing through an entire concrete block wall. Railway track is curled up from the molten metal and the whole corner of the building, perhaps a half-acre in size, is in a terrible mess still.

"We have a number of accidents here, no matter how hard we try to prevent them. I'm not aware of the one you are referring to."

WASTAGE. In the yards around the mills and inside the buildings themselves, unbelievable amounts of unused equipment and products lie around gathering dust and rust. In places, the company's premises resemble a scrap-iron heap.

WORKER SAFETY.   Out on the tracks of rolling, red-hot steel there was another extraordinary sight. A female worker, clad in ordinary blue working pants, cotton shirt and cotton shoes, decided on the spur of the moment to take a shortcut to the other side of the tracks. Easy enough. She jumped up from the gangway and proceeded to simply walk across. In the middle she had to stop because in front and behind her the bars of red-hot steel were whizzing by at considerable speeds. She looked for all the world like an animal caught in the middle of a busy freeway not knowing which way to turn. There was a momentary lull in activity and with about seven seconds to spare she scampered across.

Most people here work without benefit of safety helmets, safety boots, proper eye protection or inhalation safeguards (other than surgical gauze masks, which are few and far between).

"We have a program of safety education for the workers and those who work nearest open fires have clothing that has been soaked in fire-retarding solutions."

Mr. Sun turned out to be a remarkably complacent man, although he obviously got rattled a bit under persistent and increasingly hostile questioning from more than 30 foreign journalists who decided his emporium was not a very nice place to work. When it was put to him that in any Western country such appalling conditions would have caused a major strike years ago, he simply said:

"Our workers do not work for themselves but for the country and the people. They know conditions need to be improved and they also know the harder they work and the more they increase production, the sooner those conditions will be improved."

The Wuhan Iron and Steel Company has never had a happy time of it. It was to have been one of the great Sino-Soviet friendship enterprises, but before the entire plant was completed the Russian advisers were withdrawn in 1960 and it took China five years to figure out how to complete the place, including creating equipment on their own.

The fact that they are producing so much steel today is a testimony to endurance, and whatever problems do exist, they do not include defeatism. It is rumored that in the large package of agreements recently concluded between China and Japan, a total facelift for the Wuhan complex is in the works.

Also, in a short time the last major remnant of the Cultural Revolution — the revolutionary committee — will be disbanded and a proper management installed.

Back in Peking, Fraser began to report on major Chinese foreign-policy initiatives that involved a further widening of the gap between China and the Soviet Union and its satellites, as well as more openings to the non-Communist world. That summer the Chinese became locked in a bitter propaganda battle with their former Vietnamese allies. Charging that Hanoi was treating its large Chinese population with brutal cruelty, Peking cancelled part of its aid program and ordered the Vietnamese to close three consulates. Then it became known that the Chinese were planning to send at least 10,000 of their brightest young people to study in several Western nations, including the United States.

By late summer, the new-look foreign policy moved into high gear. First, Peking signed a peace-and-friendship treaty with Japan, which included a controversial "anti-hegemony" clause that was clearly designed to infuriate the Soviet Union. Next, Chairman Hua Kuo-feng took a historic trip to Romania, Yugoslavia and Iran during which he exploited Moscow's paranoia toward China with veiled attacks on Moscow's alleged expansionist designs. Then, in September, Chinese sources told Fraser that the leadership had relaxed the restrictions against unofficial contacts with foreign residents. But as foreign tourists began to arrive in sizeable numbers, Fraser reported that there were some areas where the cultural gap might never be bridged.

PEKING — The best traveller's tale so far this year comes from a young French woman who was staying in the Peace Hotel in Shanghai last July. After a long, wearying day, she took a bath and afterward went to get dressed in the adjoining bedroom. No sooner had she emerged from the bathroom than the floor boy walked right into her room with no warning. He had come to change the hot water in her Thermos bottles, a standard procedure here throughout the day.

It is impossible to lock your hotel room anywhere in China and staff barge in all the time and without notice. There is simply no Western conception of privacy in this land where communal necessities traditionally outweigh individual considerations. The French woman was stark naked and they were both so startled at each other's presence they stared in mute horror for a few seconds before beating a retreat in either direction.

A half hour later, one of the managers and some of the staff appeared at her room and asked the woman to join them downstairs for a discussion. She followed them and was ushered into

Mass Tai Chi exercises in a Peking park at 6:30 a.m.

A bridal couple in Shanghai poses in rented gown and western jacket.

a large room and offered some tea.

"There has been an incident," said the manager in a very serious voice. Pointing to the young floor boy, who stood somewhat abashed off to the side, he added: "He walked into your room when you were naked."

The woman, who was full of enthusiasm for China, at this point, immediately rose to the floor boy's defence. "It wasn't his fault," she said. "No one has ever trained him to knock at the door. I haven't made any complaint. Nothing happened and he didn't do anything wrong."

Deathly silence.

"Of course he didn't do anything wrong," said the manager finally. "It is you who did something wrong. It is not permitted to walk around naked in this hotel. It is not decent. It is only permitted to be naked in the bathroom. You have seriously upset this boy and he will have to go home to recover." There was another 10 minutes of constructive criticism before she managed to extricate herself. She left the room a humbled and chastened woman.

After a tour of Vietnam, Fraser was back in Peking in November, just as large numbers of wall posters began to appear around the capital for the first time in a year. Most of these posters praised Teng Hsiao-ping and the late Chou En-lai; some were critical of Mao Tse-tung's role during the Cultural Revolution, and others called for the protection of democratic and human rights. As the campaign continued, Fraser and the other journalists realized they were witnessing an unprecedented outpouring of protest; to their amazement, they found that ordinary Chinese were now prepared to discuss their demands quite openly with foreigners.

PEKING — For the first time since 1949, when Chairman Mao Tse-tung proclaimed the founding of the People's Republic of China, foreign journalists and diplomats have had a chance to talk directly and spontaneously to thousands of ordinary Chinese people and listen to their frustrations, grievances and aspirations. It turns out that the Chinese — or at least the citizens of Peking — have been burning to speak their minds for years.

It all began late Saturday afternoon on Chang An Avenue near the intersection of Hsi Tan Street, the site of a long brick wall where big-character posters, or *dazibao*, on major political issues have been appearing for a week. Foreigners making a daily check on the area suddenly found themselves surrounded and besieged with questions.

Yesterday it was the same story, only more so. Sunday crowds swelled by workers resulted in a vast assembly that may have exceeded 10,000 at one point. It was a good-natured crowd, but the atmosphere was electric. Encouraged perhaps by mutual curiosity as well as the protection afforded by sheer numbers, citizens once again surrounded foreigners and blitzed them with questions and requests for information.

My own experience was different only in detail, not kind, from that of other journalists or diplomats, all of whom have been profoundly affected by the experience that has pulled aside a thick veil of secrecy that had until this weekend seemed unmoveable.

Shortly after 6 p.m., I arrived at the Hsi Tan area accompanied by Robert Novak, the syndicated political columnist from Washington who is visiting China at the moment. Within minutes we were surrounded and people demanded to know who we were. With my rudimentary Chinese, I got across that I was a resident correspondent from Canada and that Mr. Novak was a visiting journalist from the United States. In under a minute, a crowd of perhaps 100 swelled to well over 1,000.

My wife, who finally managed to join us in the centre, said that the crowd was at least 15 deep all around. People climbed trees in the distance, others stood on some of the nearby cars. The first few minutes were very confused with everyone pushing for a closer look at the foreign faces. Somehow, someone started to bring a rough order to the proceedings and before we knew it people in the front five rows were squatting and sitting while the others stood behind.

Introductions are very important to the Chinese. It took at least five minutes for our names to be circulated and to work out the difference between my resident status and Mr. Novak's visit. By this time it was clear that neither my wife's nor my own Chinese was up to this occasion, so there was a call for someone in the crowd who spoke English to help us. After a bit of jostling, a young woman appeared who spoke basic English very well, but her voice was weak. No problem. A young man with a voice like a bullhorn stood up and said that he couldn't speak English but he had a strong voice and would shout out questions and answers.

And so the dialogue began, under a darkening Peking sky with a cold wind whipping up the dust all around us in regular gusts. When we started there were at least two other groups like our own at other sections of Chang An. We have all been busy piecing our various experiences together ever since.

The consensus is that the questions were profoundly difficult for journalists and diplomats alike, who suddenly found themselves thrust into a political meeting that might be interpreted as a provocation by the authorities. The crowds asked many of us if we were afraid to talk to them. We said no, but were they afraid to talk to us? Most foreigners got the same response — an enormous shout of "meiyou pa" or "we aren't frightened".

The instant and somewhat uncomfortable pundits tried to explain how the system of government worked in their own country. Our particular situation became more complicated when the crowd learned that Mr. Novak might have the chance to interview Vice-Premier Teng Hsiao-ping. A huge roar of approval went up and we were deluged with written questions that might be put to him, including the request to visit the Hsi Tan posters.

There was enormous interest in how Western countries handled elections. One person was very insistent that we understand the situation in China, and he received warm and loudly enthusiastic support from the crowd.

"Why is it that in our factory workshop, the people have the right to choose their leader, but we have no say about the people who run the country? This is not right."

We all had our own questions for them, of course. People were asked who they would vote for if they had an election for the post of premier (currently held by Chairman Hua Kuofeng). The shout of "Teng" went up at once. Who would they vote for as Chairman? "Hua," went up a similarly vociferous shout. But what about Chairman Hua's role in the Tien An Men incident of 1976?

"Chairman Hua's role in the Tien An Men affair is still unclear," said one. "But the Chinese people are very grateful to him for overturning the Gang of Four and he is a good leader."

Among the surprising things we learned this weekend was the fact that many Chinese know the names of resident foreign journalists, particularly the agency journalists of Reuter and Agence France Presse. Those who can speak English also listen regularly to the news broadcasts of the BBC and the Voice of America — which were banned throughout the Cultural Revolution. People even expressed a preference for the Voice of America broadcasts because they were delivered in "special English" — VOA news readers speak at a speed about half that of normal conversation.

It is not clear at the moment where all this is heading, how far it will be allowed to go and how long it will last. The vast majority of people who took part in the impromptu discussions were young workers, all of whom have grown up under Chinese Communism. Their questions show both naivete and an astonishingly clear understanding of what constitutes freedom of expression. They were all supporters of Chinese socialism and fans of Vice-Premier Teng, although I heard only support for Chairman Hua.

In the frenzied atmosphere that has overtaken Peking, rumor-mongering is rife. Among the most difficult problems is separating the truth from some of the "black information" that is pouring forth from Soviet and Eastern-bloc journalists and diplomats. As far as I have been able to determine, stories of fighting breaking out at Hsi Tan and open bickering about Chairman Hua can be traced back to such sources.

What is certain now is that this weekend Chinese people spoke openly and bluntly to Westerners in a way they have never done before. By doing so, they have ended any nonsense or illusion about Chinese not understanding what freedom of speech is all about.

They know and they want it.

Fraser would win a National Newspaper Award for this report — his third such award and also the third for a *Globe and Mail* Peking correspondent. On the following evening, he returned to the Hsi Tan wall where he was the main actor in an even more remarkable drama. That afternoon, the visiting American columnist Robert Novak had his expected interview with Teng Hsiao-ping; later, Novak authorized Fraser to pass on some of Teng's remarks.

In an unprecedented occurrence, the Canadian journalist addressed a crowd of more than 5,000 in the heart of China's capital and told them what their vice-premier thought of their protests and demands.

PEKING — . . . Shortly before 7 p.m. my wife and I arrived at the Hsi Tan site where the crowd had assembled. All the foreign correspondents in Peking were there, along with numerous observers. I learned later that before our arrival, crowd leaders had been shouting to the people that they must be orderly and disciplined because many foreign friends would be present. "If we do not conduct the meeting properly," said one, "no one will believe we are ready for democracy."

Being at the centre of all this was possibly the worst place to report on what was going on inside the ranks of people. It took at least 15 minutes to bring the meeting to order and several times excitement overwhelmed some people so much that the crowd surged forward from all directions. At one point I found myself being hoisted up on two sturdy sets of Chinese shoulders so people in the back could see me and calm down.

Quite frankly, all I wanted to do at this point was read the information I had from Mr. Novak and clear out. Unfortunately, it first required a volunteer interpreter from the crowd and several sturdy-voiced men to pass on the word. When that finally got organized, I read out this short report:

"The American journalist Robert Novak met with Vice-Premier Teng Hsiao-ping this afternoon in the Great Hall of the People. Journalist Novak said I could tell you the following.

"He told Mr. Teng that he had spoken to a large crowd of people at Hsi Tan Democracy Wall and that the people had some questions to ask.

"Vice-Premier Teng said that he thought the Hsi Tan Democracy Wall was a fine thing. Vice-Premier Teng also said he thought some of the things the masses were saying there were incorrect. For example, he said that he did not agree with the 70-30 evaluation of Chairman Mao. He said Chairman Mao was better than that. [This refers to several wall posters that said Mao was 70 per cent good and 30 per cent incorrect.]

"Vice-Premier Teng indicated to journalist Novak that it was possible that [former defence minister] Peng Teh-huai would be rehabilitated shortly.

"Journalist Novak told Vice-Premier Teng that whenever the vice-premier's name was mentioned, the people cheered their support. Vice-Premier Teng said he did not approve of this because he was only 60-40. He said Peng Teh-huai was also only 60-40. When journalist Novak asked him about the rehabilitation of [former head of state] Liu Shao-chi, Vice-Premier Teng made no response to this question.

"This is the information given to me by journalist Novak and I have fulfilled my promise to you to return and make a report. Now I would like to leave because my job is done and I have nothing else to say."

With that I made a remarkably easy exit at the thinnest point of the crowd, a crowd — I should point out — that was extraordinarily well-disciplined despite periodic moments of confusion. There was a surging effect 15 minutes later when it dispersed and some people, including a couple of foreigners, received superficial injuries. As far as I have been able to discover, no one was seriously injured — Chinese or foreigners.

The crowd then proceeded across the broad expanse of Chang An Avenue after someone suggested they go to Tien An Men Square to continue the discussion. They grouped in an informal phalanx of about 20 to 25 people wide and proceeded toward the famous heart of Peking where so much of recent Chinese history has been played out. They linked arms as they walked and sang the "Internationale" and the Chinese national anthem.

After arriving in Tien An Men, one of those things happened that astounds foreigners not fully aware of how disciplined a society China has become since 1949. With hardly any words spoken, this large group (which had dwindled by now to around 2,000) broke into three main sections and for about 10 minutes they discussed what to do. Eventually most decided to go to the Martyrs Monument in the centre. Other smaller groups, with foreigners in the middle, dallied to continue lively discussions on journalism, law, elections, human rights and the present world situation.

At the monument, my report on Mr. Teng was repeatedly read out, interspersed by various statements and speeches from several people. Someone talked about learning from the Yugoslavian experience. Another said that in the United States, there was a bourgeois democracy and the Chinese people did not

251

want that. They wanted, he said, a proletarian democracy, but this did not mean there wasn't anything to learn from bourgeois democracy. He particularly pointed out the importance of separating the executive, legislative and judiciary powers.

As on Sunday night, the various group discussions were on a wide variety of subjects. I got involved with the correspondent of the Australian Broadcasting Corporation, Richard Thwaites, in a discussion on journalism. We asked people if the evening's events would be reported in *The People's Daily* and a huge, spontaneous laugh went up.

"No," said one very articulate young man, "*The People's Daily* reflects only the views and perspective of the leaders. It does not represent the true feelings of ordinary readers. We would like to see *The People's Daily* report what the masses really feel as well as what the leaders think and in this way it would be a truly great newspaper."

We then moved on to a discussion of *Reference News,* the extraordinary daily newspaper circulated to more than fifteen million trusted Chinese (all the way down to middle school) that publishes the reports of Western journalists. This was a good thing, we were told, but more people should be allowed to read it. There was also a more privileged version of *Reference News* available only to very senior people and this was wrong.

Still another group, joined by British journalists, had a discussion on the arts. The Chinese here said they wanted to see more foreign films, read more foreign books and they also wanted to have big dances in order to socialize in a friendly but organized manner. They would like foreigners to be able to attend these dances.

And there was still more. Another group, accompanied by a British and a French journalist, had a discussion on Soviet dissidents, led by several young people who were completely up-to-date on the major figures in the movement there. The talk went on to include contradictions in U.S. foreign policy over human rights and the question was put to the journalists: "Why is there so little reflection of human-rights problems in China from the Western press?"

Another group discussion went into the various economies of Asian countries. A British diplomat was asked to list the most prosperous Asian countries and there was immediate agreement and recognition when Taiwan was mentioned. "But Taiwan also has serious human-rights problems," said someone.

If all of this makes mind-boggling reading, it has been no less of an amazement to the resident journalists who have been overwhelmed by the deluge of new, specific information on what young Chinese people are thinking. (The vast majority of people were in their early twenties and are either students or workers.)

Throughout the remaining weeks of 1978, there were more rallies at Democracy Wall, and fresh posters calling for a wide range of democratic reforms. There were also demonstrations against unemployment in both Peking and Shanghai; the demonstrators demanded fair treatment for young people who had returned illegally from the countryside to the cities where they were denied jobs and ration coupons. At the same time, newspaper articles and editorials indicated that the authorities had begun a discreet campaign to control the explosion of public protest: Fraser also noted growing numbers of plain-clothes security men at the Hsi Tan Wall. In late December, the Central Committee of the Chinese Communist Party ended a five-day plenary session with a long communiqué that held out some hope for the increased use of democratic procedures — while making clear that any reforms would take place within the framework of a one-party system.

In the first days of 1979, posters in Peking announced the formation of a new democratic movement, the Human Rights Alliance; for the first time, the authors signed these posters with their real names. As Fraser was discovering, the young activists were also showing no hesitation in openly visiting foreign homes. His own new friends included journalism students, a doctor, a composer, a former PLA soldier who now had a good factory job and a brilliant young bureaucrat. While they all accepted the impossibility of a multi-party system in China, they wanted to institutionalize opposition within the Communist Party and government. "They believe China has an alert population that is responsive to changes for the better and will work to attain them. They are serious about their involvement in change and I have not run across a group like them anywhere else."

Apart from the young activists, another group of quite different demonstrators appeared on the streets in January. These were

253

several thousand poor peasants who had come from various parts of the nation to protest against past injustices and present living conditions. Despite freezing weather, their numbers continued to swell and the authorities permitted them to build a crude shantytown in the heart of the capital, while acknowledging that they had nearly all suffered mistreatment and promising that their cases would be investigated. During an official banquet at the Great Hall of the People, about 150 of the bolder peasants gathered outside with banners reading: "In the name of Chairman Hua and Chairman Mao, we want equality" and "We want to eat" and "We want clothes".

In January, the Chinese government launched the next stage in its overall plan to transform the Chinese language into a romanized system. Beginning that month, all Chinese publications in any romanized language adopted the official Chinese spelling known as "Pinyin". In several ways, this was significantly different from the Wade-Giles system generally used by Western publications, including *The Globe and Mail*. Attempting to condition his readers to the change, Fraser warned them that the Pinyin alphabet used four letters that might give them trouble. "These letters are *c, q, x* and *z* and their respective sounds are *ts, ch, sh* and *dz*. Other changes in letters make familiar words look strange, but they make sense to Western eyes. Thus the Hsi Tan Democracy Wall has two changes, but only one represents a real problem. With Pinyin spelling the wall becomes *Xidan*.

"With these changes, there will also be a style change in Chinese proper names. The Chinese family name still comes first, but the two familiar names that follow will now no longer be hyphenated. Thus, Chairman Mao Tse-tung becomes Mao Zedong and Vice-Premier Teng Hsiao-ping becomes Deng Xiaoping.

"Most major Western news agencies have begun to adopt this system and the new spellings will begin to appear on all maps issued by the United Nations. There will be some exceptions with extremely well-known place names and certain historical figures. Thus, Mao Tsetung and Chou Enlai will remain in the familiar form, although without the usual hyphen. Peking and Canton will also be unchanged. *The Globe and Mail* is making the change to the new system. The chairman of the People's Republic is no longer Hua Kuo-feng but Hua Guofeng."

At the end of January, Vice-Premier Deng Xiaoping left Peking on the first state visit to the United States by any Chinese Communist leader. This followed the announcement in December by Chairman Hua and President Jimmy Carter that their two countries had taken the historic decision to normalize their relations. Deng's trip was striking confirmation of China's new "opening to the West"; as Fraser reported, people in China's major cities were already showing a distinct taste for Western art and entertainment.

PEKING — Western culture has started returning to China in a very big way during the past few weeks. Mostly banned for more than a decade, Western films, drama, ballet, literature, television programs, opera and even a bit of hard rock have been surfacing for some time but are now getting a concentrated push.

Productions in Chinese of Shakespeare's *Othello* and Brecht's *Galileo* will be mounted in Peking and Shanghai shortly, while both cities presented gigantic rallies recently to celebrate, among other things, Walt Whitman and Puccini. Charlie Chaplin is being introduced to a wildly enthusiastic new generation of Chinese, while a humane and sensitive Japanese film on the life of a prostitute has got a rip-roaring debate going thanks to a few nude scenes.

The banning of Western culture for the broad masses of the Chinese people during the Cultural Revolution was one of the monumental hypocrisies of the century. The architect of the plan was chairman Mao Tsetung's wife, Jiang Qing (Chiang Ching).

A former actress who once played Nora in Ibsen's *The Doll's House* during her Shanghai days, Madame Mao subjected the Chinese to her mind-numbing conception of revolutionary art while she held regular private screenings of her favorite Greta Garbo films.

The frightful legacy of Jiang Qing seemed far away recently when 20,000 people jammed Peking's Workers Gymnasium for an evening of Western poetry and song. It was the kind of occasion that could only have been conjured up in China. The masses had come to hear Shakespeare, Pushkin, Tagore, Hugo, Gorky and Mayakovsky read to them by poets and actors who had been in disgrace since 1966.

Perhaps the most emotional moment came when Xie Bingxin (Hsieh Ping-hsin) made her dramatic appearance. One of China's most beloved novelists, Madame Xie is nearly 80 now and was one of those stalwarts who refused to mend her "counter-revolutionary" ways during the Cultural Revolution. She hadn't been heard of for more than a decade and her popular books on the Chinese family facing both tragedy and gaiety are only now returning to library shelves and bookstores.

She is a tiny speck of a person and that night was dressed in black peasant pants and jacket as she shuffled proudly toward the centre of the vast amphitheatre. A traditionally chatty Chinese audience fell into a profound silence as she opened a book of poetry by Tagore and began reading a love poem in English. Most people there couldn't have understood what she was saying, but how they loved her for the simplicity of her bearing and the record of her courage. Since respect for old age is still strong in China, the combination of all this was quite electrifying.

The poetry readings were followed by operatic selections and song cycles (including a somewhat lurid rendition of Gordon Lightfoot's "In the Early Morning Rain" adorned with Verdi-like embellishments). The acoustics were dreadful but the occasion was wonderful and it was an extraordinary experience to walk out afterward into the cold Peking night in the midst of an obviously excited and exuberant crowd.

Shortly after Deng Xiaoping's return from the United States in February, China's punitive invasion of Vietnam was further evidence of the steadily deteriorating relations within the Communist world. As the Chinese eventually withdrew their troops — and entered into drawn-out negotiations with their adversaries — the foreign journalists in Peking began to report a growing crackdown on the democracy movement. In April, *The People's Daily* announced that "human rights is not a proletarian slogan". This was followed by strict new guidelines to limit criticism and dissent. Within days, the spirit of the Xidan Wall had died, as its posters and cartoons became bland and sycophantic. Fraser estimated that about 15 of the leading activists had been arrested; several of his Chinese contacts told him that they felt betrayed. The crackdown was one indication of a major debate among the leadership over the future direction of the country. Apart from differences over the democracy movement, the debate was fueled by the inconclusive results of the war with Vietnam, as well as economic setbacks. In May, a series of newspaper articles indicated that China's ambitious modernization program had been significantly revamped only one year after it was publicly launched by Chairman Hua. For the hundreds of Western businessmen who had flocked to Peking, hopes of an instant bonanza quickly began to fade.

The crackdown on the democracy movement continued in June, as municipal officials in Peking issued an edict prohibiting all but officially approved contacts with foreigners. It was now forbidden to have meals with foreigners in restaurants, join them at the theatre, attend dance parties or visit them in their homes. As Fraser also reported: "And trickling down a reliable grapevine this week came the news that I and my wife, along with a few other foreign journalists, students and diplomats who established numerous Chinese contacts six months ago, have been informally labelled 'international spies' by the Peking Public Security Bureau. It is nonsense, but it preys on the mind and certain biases do arise."

Despite this disfavor, the Chinese authorities made no attempt to stop Fraser from visiting Taiwan. It was the first time a resident journalist accredited in Peking had travelled to the Nationalist stronghold and then returned to the Communist capital. ("Although some discretion was necessary with Communist officials, the new propaganda line simply meant that I was visiting 'another province of China' and no complications were put in my way.") During two weeks on the island, Fraser reported in detail on Taiwan's economic progress and high standards of living. Despite Peking's new advocacy of peaceful and gradual reunification, he found that not only Premier Sun Yuan-suan and other officials, but also ordinary Taiwanese, had no desire to risk their future with the Communists.

Back in Peking, Fraser reported that another session of the National People's Congress had taken some cautious steps toward a more open and democratic society. It now seemed that the spring crackdown on the democracy movement had not been the signal for widespread repression. Instead, the Congress approved plans to introduce an element of real choice in elections at the local level. It also announced that China would soon have its first comprehensive criminal code in thousands of years of recorded history, with safeguards against arbitrary arrest and political persecution. In his key-note speech to the 3,000 delegates, Chairman Hua reiterated his government's moderate economic policies — including unprecedented incentives to both peasants and urban workers. Also, the Chinese issued the first group of significant statistics on production and earning power since the early 1950s. As Fraser concluded: "It is never safe to predict very far with China, but it is clear that this session of the National People's Congress has gone a long way to clear up a number of major doubts and grievances held by many people. The theoretical direction is positive and progressive; it now remains to be seen if the words are backed by actions."

In July, Fraser and his Peking colleagues were taken to Tibet. This was a remarkable occurrence: even more than Sichuan (Szechwan), Tibet had long been barred to all but a handful of foreign sympathizers who always painted glowing pictures of steady progress under benign Chinese rule. As Fraser reported, the reality of Tibet was quite different.

LHASA — Few places in the world have been so shrouded in mystery as Tibet, particularly during the past two decades when the Chinese government was busy consolidating its rule after religious and national groups loyal to the Dalai Lama staged a valiant but vain rebellion against the Peking authorities.

The entire foreign press corps resident in Peking has been invited to visit this extraordinary place where so few foreigners have ever been. However, unlike the strenuously controlled trips made by official delegations, so-called Friends of China and a few Western journalists being rewarded for good behavior during their Peking postings, we have been allowed unprecedented access not just to the people of Lhasa, but to the nomads and herdsmen of the interior as well.

Some of the things we saw showed a genuine effort by the Communists to improve the quality of life for ordinary Tibetans, but many other things pointed up the contrast between the reality and the official propaganda from Peking as well as the random reports of sympathetic but biased observers.

● Despite official and fulsome invitations to the exiled Dalai Lama in India to return and play "a patriotic role" in the future of China and Tibet, the Communists will never allow him to officially retain his role as spiritual leader of Tibet. In unofficial interviews with a number of Tibetans, including lamas who were forced to become workers, it soon became clear that the Dalai Lama wields more power over the hearts and minds of his people in exile than he ever would as a token figurehead inside China. Official interviews indicated he would not be allowed to set up residence in Lhasa.

● The city of Lhasa itself has been gradually transformed from the capital of Tibet and symbol of Tibetan nationality to a sort of colonial Chinese outpost where the Han (Chinese) population now outnumbers the native Tibetans by 70,000 to 50,000. This does not include the large number of military personnel from the People's Liberation Army, almost none of whom is Tibetan and for which officials refused to supply figures.

● Despite official propaganda, Tibetan independence forces still exist in what is now called "the autonomous region of Tibet", and although muted, these forces are sufficient to keep Tibet under strong military rule. One Chinese official we spoke to literally did not understand what was meant by the word "election" even though he said he was democratically elected.

● The Cultural Revolution as well as official Communist policy on the suppression of religion — the policy is in the Chinese constitution under the heading of freedom of religion — has resulted in the closure or destruction of more than 2,500 monasteries. As well, more than 100,000 monks and nuns have been persuaded, by one means or another, to give up their religious habits and homes. These figures were provided by officials in Tibet.

● Despite some good efforts in public health, much of the Tibetan population is still plagued by tuberculosis and serious skin diseases. Many of the children in Lhasa we saw had open sores on the visible parts of their skins (faces, hands, arms and legs) and any efforts at conducting a hygiene-education program were not in evidence. The contrast between Chinese and Tibetan children in this regard is notable.

● One lower-level official originally from Sichuan Province who had been in Tibet for 20 years and had married a Tibetan woman — a very rare occurrence — told me privately that "many Chinese people resent the posting, despise the Tibetans and make no effort whatsoever to correct local problems and grievances." Some aspects of his criticism were later confirmed by a senior Tibetan official at a press conference.

• Despite the resentment of a Tibet posting, all Chinese who are sent to Tibet receive extra stipends and special concessions for accepting a job in a hardship area.

• Road-building, electrification and agricultural reform have been carried out by the Chinese in a conscientious way and while life for the average Tibetan peasant has become more circumspect and dull, his material well-being has improved from what he would have known under the theocratic government before 1951.

• Public education and official policy toward "minority people" is being used to undermine a genuine sense of the Tibetan people as a unique entity. Lamaism and the Buddhist church, which formed much of the substance of Tibetan nationality, has in effect been eradicated from normal approved life. Where it is officially allowed, it is made to seem backward and silly. Whatever vestiges of distinctive culture that do officially remain have been prettified and served up unctuously as examples of Chinese concern for curious minority customs. One possibly trivial example: it is not possible to purchase a record of traditional Tibetan music in all of Lhasa, but they can be easily obtained in Peking under the category of "minority music".

• Although China's right to rule Tibet has been formally agreed to by the present Dalai Lama in 1951 and generally recognized by all governments, the Communist authorities remain clearly paranoid about any suggestion that Tibet has a right to independence. Throughout our trip, we have been bombarded with various historic and contemporary facts that are designed to prove China's right to rule. Nevertheless, for many Tibetans, China's sovereignty remains *de facto* and exists only because it is backed by so many soldiers and civilians.

Ironically, many of these details of the Tibetan situation have become possible to observe only because of the increasing openness and candor of the Chinese government. Its Tibetan representatives are clearly confused by this new liberalism, but they got the word that the foreign journalists were to be given far more than usual access and this often led to embarrassing but revealing incidents.

By reasserting a pre-Cultural Revolution policy of allowing controlled religious activities, the authorities may have been surprised to discover how strong Tibet's distinctive form of Buddhism has been. Two years ago, people like the author Han Suyin reported that religion had all but died out in Tibet. In her book *Lhasa, The Open City* she wrote that she saw only one person wielding a prayer wheel.

What we saw was just the opposite. Not only was Lhasa abounding with prayer wheels and beads, but on the three mornings of the week that the faithful are allowed to go into their temples we counted hundreds of people pouring in of whom the vast majority were well under 40. Although they were being charged an entrance fee to see "a cultural relic", they very quickly set about traditional prostrations while chanting centuries-old prayer liturgies that have obviously been passed on by both lamas and parents.

As for the socialist revolution, it would be hard to find a more capitalist corner of China than the older quarter of Lhasa where some of the few foreigners who were allowed into Tibet in the past were physically prevented by officials from entering. Nearly 500 Nepalese still live here and ply the merchant trade alongside Tibetan free enterprisers and state emporiums. It is from private dealers that one can purchase the old and intricately beautiful Tibetan carpets. The state shops sell the new variety, which mostly feature lurid Chinese designs and use synthetic dyes.

Over this whole scene sits the brooding Potala Palace, home of the exiled Dalai Lama. It is more than just a symbol. The previous power and traditions of the Dalai Lama mean the Potala is Buckingham Palace, Westminster Abbey and the Houses of Parliament all put together on a jutting mountaintop soaring toward heaven. At the top of its seven storeys, the Potala is nearly 12,000 feet above sea level, and there's not much higher you can go on earth.

Try as they might, the Chinese have been unable to make the Tibetan people accept the Potala as a "cultural relic". It can be seen everywhere on the vast plain Lhasa is built upon. Although it has often been a source of autocratic and feudal despotism in the past, it is such a resolute and undeniable source of Tibetan national feeling that it mocks every new Chinese structure around it. On two nights, I walked its full perimeter and each time I met dozens of Tibetans who used either sign language or simple Chinese to signify their pride in this glorious manifestation of human will and devotion. As often as not, they were clutching prayer beads and with a furtive and cautious look over their shoulder, they would inquire if we knew when the Dalai Lama was coming home.

The Chinese are anxious for the Dalai Lama to come home, too, but not to rule from the Potala as he was allowed to do between 1951 and 1959 under Chinese suzerainty. The Chinese want to end what they consider a chapter of history and they recognize that so long as the Dalai Lama remains abroad his power is potent — so his stubbornness is annoying and frustrating to them.

In the meantime, Tibet is enjoying a kind of peace and stability it has not known since the mid-1950s. Domestic rebellion started in 1956, followed by its massive suppression in 1959. In quick succession came the Sino-Indian border war, the Cultural Revolution and the reign of the Gang of Four. (Officials are noticeably quiet on the subject of the Gang in Tibet since they are still pushing hard at the evils of the Dalai Lama's regime.)

Tibetans are a marvellous race. They seem perfectly equipped to accept the better deal they are getting from China today, while at the same time holding out for their own distinctiveness. And they have this quality that separates them from the average rural Chinese. On seeing a foreigner for the first time they do not stare with mute disbelief at some strange animal escaped from a zoo — they smile with mild surprise at a fellow pilgrim through this world of wonders and sadness still untold.

On the same trip, Fraser drove deep into the Tibetan interior — where he encountered several herdsmen — and many more yaks.

YALAN, Tibet — A visit to a yak ranch in the interior of this mountainous wonderland is not one of your every-day experiences, so there was an expectant air when our group from Peking was trundled out of bed at 5 a.m. to prepare for a punishing four-and-a-half-hour bus trip to the Qinghai Plateau — the highest flatlands in the world.

We headed northeast of Lhasa in three old vehicles that may

have done service in the revolutionary wars 30 years ago. Here are the Chamdo and Napchu districts of Tibet from which derive the sources of two great rivers of Asia — the Yangtze and the Mekong.

None of us has interviewed a yak before. We don't even know what to call his female mate. (She is known as a *dri*, we learned later from a herdsman.) So there is a bit of confusion and amiable banter in the bus as we bump and grind our way along a road that is often just two tracks in the plain and sometimes not even that.

Fortunately, the calamitous state of both bus and road requires numerous stops. Sometimes the radiator boils over and sometimes the mud ditches cannot be navigated by the bus.

The unscheduled stops are usually glorious moments. Journalists with camera bags around their necks go running off in all directions, toward the yak-wool tent of a herdsman or toward small earthen and brick cottages. It is a chance to see the real life of real Tibetans before we get to the model commune and the model peasants.

Once, as the bus was seething and gasping in the far distance, I stuck my head into such a tent to find an ancient fellow brewing himself some yak-milk tea. He had one tooth left and somewhere along the line he also had had his left eye gouged out. I don't think it is fanciful to suppose that I was the first fair-skinned Caucasian foreigner on whom he had set his remaining eye.

His face broke into a grin of delight. With hardly a moment's hesitation, he motioned for me to sit down on one of the numerous and beautiful saddle carpets and began pouring out a bowl of his pungent brew. The small stove, fuelled by dried dung patties, was in the middle of the tent with a precarious tin chimney poking through the tent roof.

Another journalist poked his nose through the tent flap and I snarled sufficiently to send him packing. "Find your own story," I bellowed. High altitude, one is told, causes extreme irritability. Anyway, I had ten minutes alone with my venerable herdsman. Sign language, smiles and mutual observation were the means of communication. But they seemed to suffice.

Journalists are not as insensitive as they usually appear in groups. Our crowd wanted to get the genuine flavor of rural

263

Tibet but most of us were not without a certain amount of guilt for snapping away at gentle, warm people who may not have understood what a camera is all about. Consequently, when there is the remotest chance of effecting a genuine exchange, we jump at it.

An opportunity came when we returned to our bus, which had once again girded its sagging loins for an assault on the road. A herdsman with two small children walking in our direction saw a rare opportunity to grab a lift. We were delighted and ushered them into the bus with considerable ceremony. The children were shy but sensed that they were surrounded by spontaneous and genuine affection and curiosity, which was instantly reciprocated.

Sadly, we hadn't calculated on the reaction of our official Chinese hosts who were appalled at this unplanned happening. The Tibetans were ordered off the bus in arrogant and peremptory tones. We protested volubly; I have never seen my colleagues so angry, although this kind of thing happens often in China.

Finally, the Tibetans were physically pulled off the bus and the mood was bloody. One of the Chinese said the Tibetans were trying to go to Lhasa, although we could see that they were walking in the direction we were heading. After five more minutes of shouting, the officials agreed that we could proceed and then pick up this family, which by now was several hundred feet ahead of us. We sat down somewhat mollified and off we went. As we approached the family, however, the bus speeded up and when we shouted for it to stop, the senior official at the back motioned to the driver to proceed. This was the kind of arrogant and summary behavior we were to see often from Chinese officials in Tibet. We could only guess its effect on Tibetans.

We were not amused several hours later when the same official made an unctuous and flamboyant offer to a model Tibetan herdsman at the model commune to drive about 400 yards with us to his model living quarters.

Fortunately, model Tibetans are still people of the land and however well-prepared for this weird visit by strange people with one-eyed machines perpetually held up to their faces, their own natural curiosity revealed itself.

This gesture toward Tibetan identity is more than balanced by strong Chinese cultural intrusions.

Girls reading posters at Xidan Democracy Wall in Peking.

Emancipation Commune was set up in 1970 and is organized around six production teams, which represent the efforts of 158 families. (The total population is just under 1,000.)

Unlike the one-eyed herdsman I had met earlier, who was bundled up in a threadbare yak-hair blanket to fend off the morning cold, the commune's citizens were well-dressed, well-housed and their commune offers them an unprecedented opportunity to expand gradually the size of their own private animal holdings after they have fulfilled state quotas. Commerce is still primitive and the price of commodities is valued in terms of animals.

Thus, one yak equals 12 goats or six sheep, while a good horse can fetch 24 goats.

As for the yaks, who were the primary reason for this expedition, I can report that the living is good. A yak is a very long-haired ox, unique to Tibet and its surrounding areas. Before you set eyes on this sturdy beast, you come to appreciate its importance in the Tibetan way of things.

Butter, cheese and milk from his mate nourish the population. The butter also provides fuel to light the altars of Buddha and quite a few tents. Yak wool is sturdy and tough and can be turned into anything from tents and clothing to twine and carpets. Because the wool is oily, it keeps out water and the smell is something you get used to after a short time. A yak gets angry if teased but its presiding nature is benign, perhaps because Tibetans love all animals and care diligently for them.

One journalist asked if the commune's herdsmen have investigated the possibilities of artificial insemination of the *dri*. A recent New China News Agency report said that experiments had been started at certain places in Tibet.

"No," a spokesman said. "Our yaks do things naturally. Sometimes they do need a bit of encouragement so we have a special brew of mountain herbs to feed them that seems to do the job."

Back in Peking in August, Fraser discovered that the on-again, off-again Democracy Movement had come alive once more with a new spate of outspoken posters at the Xidan Wall. The most remarkable poster was spread over nearly 200 pages: in great detail it claimed that 67,400 people had met unnecessary and violent deaths during and after the Cultural Revolution in one area of China alone — Guanxi Autonomous Region, which borders on Vietnam. There were also demonstrations by poor peasants. Police and soldiers prevented foreign journalists from approaching the protesters, but Fraser reported that they seemed even more undernourished and impoverished than the peasants who had made similar demonstrations during the previous winter.

Later that month, Fraser travelled through Shandong (Shantung) Province, and became one of the first foreign journalists in several years to reach the major coastal city of Qingdao (Tsingtao). Here he found further evidence of the privileges enjoyed by senior officials despite the old Maoist rhetoric that called for equality and frugality.

QINGDAO — This is China's holiday town. For those who think they know everything there is to be known in this country, Qingdao provides a scenario that makes you think you are in a dream.

This city of one million on the Shandong coast did not exist before 1898, when German entrepreneurs decided they wanted to move into the lucrative Chinese concession business in a big way. Aided by a bit of Prussian military might, industrialists established themselves here to take advantage of cheap labor, natural resources and a deep all-weather port.

They built a city of sturdy spacious houses, a vast cathedral with twin spires, a smart shopping district and grand Wilhelmian state buildings. They gave Qingdao the air of a prosperous, middle-class Bavarian burg.

In time, the Revolution and the reckoning came. Qingdao — or at least the original German city — has remained much as it was in 1949. On the perimeter, however, the Chinese have expanded the industrial base so that it is the most important such centre in Shandong Province.

The natural setting of Qingdao is appealing. Sandy beaches abound and the mountainous outer islands provide a backdrop of stupendous beauty.

Nearby is Laoshan, a small but wondrous mountain whose principal river provides the water for China's best beer, soft drinks and famous sparkling bottled water.

But the real action is down on the beach and along the old

German shopping district. Because Qingdao is also a manufacturing centre, which sends vast quantities of clothing around the world, the shops are stocked with far better-quality goods than normally are found in China. In Qingdao, chic is proper and the result produces a strange reversal of reality in China — foreigners stand around gawking at smart young Chinese couples in disbelief. Can this be China?

Down on the main city beach, in front of a spanking new 17-storey hotel and 10-storey trade centre, the incessant buzz of Sea Fleas and motorboats pulling daredevil water-skiers provides an unprecedented sight of the Chinese at play.

A lot of this activity is for the benefit of the Chinese elite. Also, there is a large naval establishment that appears to enjoy its perks with enthusiasm. Part of the charm of Qingdao is that it is a real Chinese city, unlike the unreal antics at Beidaiko (Peitaiho) on the North China Sea, which is a showpiece holiday town where the few local residents lie low as Party cadres and fancy foreigners take over.

In Qingdao, students and workers flock to the beaches in such numbers that it is impossible sometimes to see a square inch of sand or water. In summer, the atmosphere of the city is light-hearted and amiable. It is possible to strike up an interesting, useful and friendly conversation with ordinary Chinese in a way unthinkable in most other Chinese cities.

There is another side to Qingdao. The industrial growth, which is impressive in its size and output, has unfortunately ringed the city with some of the darkest satanic mills to be found anywhere. The planning has been haphazard and the living conditions for the workers in the suburbs — just judging from the pollution — must be grotesque.

And, despite all the goodwill in the world, this depressing aspect must be compared to Qingdao's secret residential area where high Party cadres frolic and rest in a fashion alarmingly similar to their predecessors in the Kuomintang and German business circles.

Neither foreigners nor members of the masses are encouraged to tour the neighborhood, to put it politely. Armed guards of the People's Liberation Army perform a function remarkably similar to those paid "protection personnel" at Florida housing compounds.

Chinese elite retreats are pretty tame. The major advantages they offer to top officials are space, quiet and better living conditions. The German mansions seem well maintained from the outside, with clipped hedges and neat front yards. Shanghai sedans and the occasional Red Flag limousine grace the driveways and children romp about.

In China, space and perks like access to a car, a good holiday home and a quiet beach define the difference between the leaders and the led. None of this would be sinister except for two things: the public are not permitted to see it; and it illustrates the degree of hypocrisy that surrounds the propaganda of socialism in China.

By Western standards, the Qingdao officials' neighborhood is not unduly extravagant. By Chinese standards, it is Shangri-la. The reason the masses are not allowed to see it is that some might get the wrong idea and think the officials actually enjoy living in such conditions, or even wheel and deal so they can get access to them.

As numerous conversations proved, the citizens of Qingdao want the good life for themselves and their families too. They condone the fancy neighborhood, one expects, because they can envisage it being expanded to include themselves.

Fraser was now preparing to hand over the *Globe and Mail* bureau to his successor on October 1 when the Chinese Communists would celebrate their thirtieth anniversary in power. To the end, he reported on further demonstrations in the capital by democracy advocates, poor peasants and railway workers protesting against unemployment and bad living conditions. In a final series, which looked back on the tumultuous events of his two-year posting, Fraser praised the human-rights activists for their bravery, their self-sacrifice and their dedication to a more open and democratic China.

PEKING —. . . They are all children of Chairman Mao Tsetung's China. If some of them had parents who pined wistfully for the old days, then these were the kids who gave those same parents the hardest time. They believed they were fighting for a kind of democracy and freedom the world had never known, free of a litany of curses that had afflicted the Chinese people for thousands of years.

They deified Mao as only a young teenager can deify a living human being, and then they were betrayed, put down and shipped out to the countryside.

Even this they accepted willingly at first. It was for the good of the revolution. Ultimately, though, they were faced with lies they could not avoid. They discovered the lies of government propaganda about the happy life of the peasants; they discovered the lie of the selfless official working for "the good of the people" and they discovered the lie about equality and justice guaranteed in the constitution.

Cheated of a formal education, they learned logic and ethics while digging cabbages and planting rice. They reached maturity against a backdrop of privation and suffering unknown to their peers in the West. They were witnesses to the vicious power plays and purges of Mao's dotage.

It was from this vantage point that they studied and dreamed of alternatives: there is nothing theoretical about their struggle. When they found a crack in the wall of oppression last November, they rushed to make it a vast gap.

Other characteristics observed: they have no sense of materialism, at least as we know it. Of the activists who visited foreign apartments, I know of none who paid the least attention to record players or antique Chinese furniture or warm rooms. For some, these things might have been obtained through advancement in the state, but they eschewed that course.

Because their lives have been anonymous and their short-lived writings in wall posters have the fleeting effect of a ballet performance, they will never penetrate international consciousness the way the great dissidents from the Soviet Union have.

Indeed, there is much disagreement over the word "dissident". In China, patriotism runs hard and deep and these activists have rarely spurned the state, in the traditional manner of dissidents. There was nothing underground about their activities: everything was opened to view — by foreigners, the people and the police. They did not feel alien from the state but sought to change the state from alienating the people.

So convinced were two of the groups that they were working for a common purpose with the Communist Party of China that they formally petitioned the government to make their publications official. This strikes us as naive, perhaps even silly. That is a common perception of Chinese revolutionaries by Westerners and goes right back to Sun Yatsen.

Three of those arrested were known to me, two of them fleetingly. I saw Fu Yuehua in action twice. She helped give the poor peasants who came to Peking early this year some expression and direction.

They had come from all over China asking justice for ancient wrongs but once they arrived they didn't know what to do. Miss Fu showed the way and led them to the gates behind which the government operates in total secrecy.

Shortly before Vice-Premier Deng Xiaoping went to the United States, the police picked her up and nothing has been heard of her since. She has a natural empathy for poor people and I once saw her wrap a young child in her arms for warmth on a bitterly cold day. For me, that action came to symbolize the absurdity of her apprehended threat to the state.

Wei Jingsheng, 29, the unlikeliest zoo electrician one could imagine, was something else again. There are not many searing essayists who have a chance to be heard from in Communist China, so there may be better writers than Wei around, but no one knows.

As it stands, he is the finest political polemicist China had produced since Lu Xun (who died in the 1930s) and his style owes much to his illustrious predecessor whom George Bernard Shaw admired.

Wei and his followers ran *Explorations Magazine* and they were the most extreme of all the activists. They rejected Marxism-Leninism, at least as it was practised in China, and they had serious and penetrating criticisms to make about the Maoist legacy.

Wei's own past was as fiery as his present and he was a member of one of the most famous Red Guard groups of all. Reading over the collected works of *Explorations* today makes staggering reading: the audacity is amazing.

And yet, at his most critical, Wei seemed to be after one objective alone — to engage the Communist Party in a debate, not warfare. It was his firm belief that China's ambitious Four Modernizations program was impossible without a fifth modernization, democracy.

His arguments were too impressive and persuasive to stand unchallenged, but instead of debate, he received the mailed fist of the state and was labelled "counter-revolutionary".

If the government thinks it can re-educate Wei into accepting the "correct line", it is in for a rude awakening. It will have to be careful with the people sent in to do the job because they may get contaminated by one of the most precise and articulate sensibilities anywhere.

I really saw those two only from afar and these judgments are based as much on what they did and wrote as anything I was able to learn directly.

With Ren Wanding it was something different. He is not an image to me, but flesh and blood. The head of the China Human Rights Alliance was, at 35, one of the oldest and most reluctant of the activists. Kindly, gentle and with a wry sense of humor, he was forever tying to put the best and most optimistic interpretation on things, even when they seemed utterly black.

For most of his adult life, he had had to live with an "anti-rightist" label that was only removed a few months before the events of Xidan. A victim of persecution, he had no persecution complex. He was painfully shy.

The lens on the right eye of his glasses had broken two years ago but he didn't have the money for a new one. Ren also had what might be described as an imperfect understanding about human rights and a naive faith in the ultimate goodness of the Communist Party.

And yet his honesty gives him a nobility that still awes me. When the government started spreading slanders that "under-ground groups" were seeking to undermine the state, it was Ren who first had the courage to sign his own name to a wall poster and to state that he would return to debate the issue with any-one interested.

Although he thought that protection of human rights would be a good thing for China and the government replied that human rights was an alien, bourgeois concept, he stumbled along — literally stumbled, because his eyesight was bad — in the firm conviction that he was on the right path.

The night before he was arrested at Xidan Democracy Wall, we spoke for a long time. He told me he was going to put up a poster protesting against the recent arrests of Wei and the others. I think I had one of my small-l liberal worried looks on my face and I asked him why he was going to take the risk. "It's a trap they've set for you," I said in a rare prediction that, alas, came true.

He refused to accept this. The crackdown is a temporary business, he said. "The constitution of a country carries more weight than some silly civic ordinance on public safety."

Off he went into the night with his papers falling out of his pockets. He would reach down to pick them up while others fell out of another place. The improbability of this decent and compassionately disorganized man being considered a threat to the state reassured me for that night. By 10:30 the next morning, the Public Security Bureau had arrested him.

Things may yet turn out right for China. The only safe thing to predict in this country is that anything can happen. If they do turn out right, somewhere along the line people like Ren and Wei and Miss Fu will gain entrance to the real pantheon of revolutionary heroes.

Bryan Johnson goes down on his knees during a hockey game with Chinese players in Peking.

BRYAN JOHNSON

In the autumn of 1979, the Peking bureau entered its third decade as Fraser was succeeded by Bryan Johnson. Born in Newmarket, Ontario, the 30-year-old Johnson had been a reporter on the *London Free Press*, a free-lance writer in Europe and the sports editor of the *Peterborough Examiner*; he had also spent eight months in India researching a documentary film. He joined *The Globe and Mail* in 1975 and had been its theatre critic for the previous two years.

Johnson arrived in time to describe the final repression of the democracy movement. In late October, Wei Jingsheng, the most outspoken of the activists, was put on trial and sentenced to 15 years for "counter-revolutionary agitation" and "supplying intelligence to foreigners". As Johnson wrote, if it was a harsh blow to Wei and his supporters, "it may have been equally harsh to China's much-heralded new legal system. The so-called public trial — held before an invited audience while activists and foreign journalists stood outside — gave all appearances of being a sham." As the official press bristled with denunciations of Wei, Johnson had a direct experience of the growing repression.

PEKING — Spontaneous contact between foreigners and Chinese is rare enough here at any time. But during the past week, in the wake of activist Wei Jingsheng's sentence for "supplying intelligence to foreigners", it has become almost non-existent.

So when the young man in the grey jacket slipped in beside me Sunday and said, "Do you understand what these poems are about?" I was almost too surprised to answer.

The occasion was an outdoor poetry reading, sponsored by

five democracy activist groups in defiance of the apparent government crackdown. There were more than 500 people in a little park, and the place was crawling with undercover Public Security Bureau agents.

I explained that I had a few of the poems partly translated, but was hard-pressed to understand whether they were strongly political. "I think that most of these have some political content, either obvious or perhaps more subtle," he said. He was just in the middle of explaining how he spoke such good English when a small, squat woman began asking him questions in Chinese.

I asked what she wanted. "Oh," he replied, "she's just curious. Most people are curious about foreigners. But of course, also, she is paid to be curious." He smiled and stared at the woman, whom he obviously took to be a PSB officer.

We stood listening to the poetry for a few moments, while I wondered if I dare ask something about the Wei trial without frightening him off. Finally I mentioned casually that I had been reading the local newspapers and understood most people thought the 15-year jail sentence was a fair one.

"Pardon?" he asked.

The 15-year sentence, I repeated.

"A good thing?"

Yes, I said.

"Perhaps you should ask some people privately for their opinion," he replied at last. "That is best. They may be afraid to tell you publicly . . . uh, precisely how they feel."

I told him that seemed a good idea, and assured him I certainly wouldn't ask for *his* opinion in public.

"No," he said, then added incongruously: "I am studying the American Revolution at the moment. Life, liberty, and the pursuit of happiness. . . ."

I had no idea how to answer.

"We hold these truths to be self-evident . . ." he continued.

Well, I said finally, do the people of China hold these truths to be self-evident?

"No," he answered.

He slipped back into the crowd before I could get his name or give him mine. The little squat lady, I am glad to report, stayed with me.

The crackdown continued with more arrests at Xidan Wall. Then, in December, the Wall itself was officially outlawed: a few days later, a new government-approved poster wall opened for business a mile away. But everyone with a poster was required to register his name, and every poster was examined before it was put up. Nearly all of these dealt with personal problems or legal grievances; Johnson concluded that "the exciting Xidan era is over." There was further confirmation of this when Fu Yehua, the woman activist who had helped to organize the poor peasants when they arrived in Peking during the previous winter, was sentenced to two years for violating public order. To complete the crackdown, security officers began ordering certain Chinese to end their friendships with foreigners. Finally, at year end, the authorities moved against one of the more pathetic remnants of the capital's brief fling with liberalism.

PEKING — It surprised no one that authorities finally rounded up the prostitutes at Peking's Peace Café. The question is why they waited so long.

For weeks now, ever since the final crackdown on Xidan Democracy Wall, observers here have been wondering when the bizarre little café would be reined in.

Now that it has been stripped of its painted ladies (some wore lipstick, a sure sign of immorality here), the Peace Café remains an enigma, a little haven of decadence in a determinedly upright society.

Word of the prostitution ring being run from the café had been circulating for about three months, first as an unlikely rumor, then as an obvious fact of life. In a country as puritanical and tightly controlled as China, they seemed an astonishing aberration. And their demise was always certain.

The puzzle was how they had been organized — and how, in a place crawling with blatant undercover security men, they were allowed to operate.

Finally last week, they simply disappeared. And inevitably the *Peking Daily* reported a few days later that 16 prostitutes and their agents had been duly arrested.

"This gang of male and female hooligans who corrupted the reputation of China since September of this year, dressed seductively, have been hanging out at the Peace Café doing mischief," the report said. "The broad masses of people demanded that they be punished to maintain the state dignity."

The article claimed that "two men seduced female hooligans into hanging around with foreigners, making profit out of it, thus creating a very bad effect on the fame of our country.

"Hard-faced youths, coats slung over their shoulders and cigarettes dangling from their mouths, use the café for arranging dates for their rouged and lipsticked girl friends with foreign students and diplomats from Third World countries."

In fact, it had always been my impression that the girls' main customers were Overseas Chinese tourists, who could easily smuggle them back to rooms in the hotels reserved for Overseas Chinese here. But it is probably true that both students and Third World diplomats occasionally made use of them.

In any case, the careful reference to Third World customers seems calculated to disgust and outrage the average race-conscious Chinese citizen. And it is quite probable that the mention of hard-faced hooligans is a prelude to a greater clampdown on the Peace Café, or even its eventual closing.

The café is a grimy little boxcar of a place, located down an unlit alleyway off the city's main shopping street. It opened as an adjunct to the Peace Hotel last winter, but only became Peking's notorious hot spot when people realized it was a place foreigners and Chinese could mix freely over a bottle of beer or a dish of ice cream.

As hot spots go, it is something less than Studio 54. Originally, its closing time was 10 p.m., but when gangs of drunken young Chinese staged a couple of wild fights there — complete with bottle tossing and overturned tables — that was changed to 9 p.m.

Still, the anti-foreigner campaign that accompanied last month's closing of Xidan Wall seemed to have little effect on the Peace Café. The number of undercover agents, making themselves obvious enough to scare off the faint-hearted, may have increased slightly.

But, if anything, young Chinese seemed to flock there even more desperately, as a kind of last refuge of international sophistication.

The café's young clients have little relation to the core of democracy activists involved with Xidan. Indeed, *The People's*

Daily described many of them accurately with its stories of dangling cigarettes and hard looks. The only item needed to complete the newspaper's picture is the ubiquitous Hong Kong sunglasses affected at all hours of the day and night.

The prostitutes at the Peace Café were never particularly obvious, partly because all Chinese girls who go there seem to make an attempt to look unusual. In a city where pigtails and baggy blue dungarees are the norm, patrons of the Peace usually wear some kind of makeup or have permanent waves.

Some even sport sleek overcoats with fur trim, and others go so far as to wear Western-style (that is, Hong Kong-style) clothes. Most of these, however, are apparently the children of top Party cadres — although there's speculation that even a few of those were occasionally prostitutes.

The majority of the arrested girls are believed to be people dispatched to the countryside during the Cultural Revolution, many of whom have returned to the city illegally.

For the intrepid foreign resident, it was still possible to mingle with ordinary Chinese in a more innocent manner, as Johnson discovered when he unpacked his skates.

PEKING — The ice is an odd shade of brownish-grey, because when the wind whips in from Mongolia it brings part of the Gobi Desert with it. Old men sit on stools to watch, so every slapshot carries the risk of mass homicide.

Pucks disappear into holes in the ice. Pretty girls giggle at the players. And sometimes the defencemen wear speedskates.

It's not exactly a Canadian postcard scene, but it's hockey. And in a lot of ways it's hockey the way many of us remember it, before it stopped being fun and took up its sombre status as the "Canadian specific".

It may be true, as the analysts say, that hockey is the key to our culture. But that doesn't matter here. For a foreigner trying to break into Chinese society, the game is a different kind of key altogether.

In a country of locked doors and high walls, hockey is one way of breaking down the barriers. Anyone is welcome on the ice, particularly if he is a 20-year veteran of exuberant shinny games just like these. And after four months in Peking it is hockey that has provided my first real link to home.

The games seem to go on continually, in all parts of the city. And it's one of the happy accidents of Peking that most of the best ponds are in the most beautiful areas.

That lake at the exquisite Summer Palace, where people row away the stifling summer hours, becomes a breathtaking open-air arena in January. Drive out there on a weekday afternoon, just on the off chance of finding a few skaters, and you'll discover hundreds of people gliding and stumbling around in the sun.

In the middle of them, furiously ignoring the pleasure skaters, are a dozen guys swatting at a puck.

Right near the Temple of Heaven there's another superb lake, the shinny-hockey heart of the city. There the son of a high cadre — completely outfitted in Canadian CCM gear, right down to the helmet and faceguard — flits around the ice like a spider while mere mortals try to catch him.

Day in and day out, the same players are there, most of them with battered Chinese sticks and no equipment at all. A couple of rocks serve for a goal, and they weave in and out of spectators on an end-to-end rush. The players greet you cheerfully when you arrive, chase you like madmen for an hour and go on skating after you've limped home in total exhaustion.

Hockey isn't the main attraction at the little lake near Bei Hai Park (the old imperial Winter Palace), where loudspeakers play Western music and shy Chinese couples pay five cents each to skate around with each other without holding hands. But even here, a special rink has been set aside for the game, cordoned off with wire and straw matting.

And when a dozen Canadians from the embassy drop the puck there on Saturday afternoons — it's intramural now that games with the Soviets are banned — the crowds come over to shake their heads and mutter about the strange *weiguoren* — the outside-country people.

It was the embassy games that first got me interested in Chinese hockey, but I soon discovered it was better to show up alone at the rink than with a busload of round-eyes.

Still, there are certain perils involved in going solo. I bought a new pair of skates just before leaving Canada, the modern type with plastic blades and nylon uppers. And I have yet to lace them up before an audience of less than two dozen. The Chinese crowd around in amazement, all asking questions at once, and trying to figure out why anyone would try to skate on plastic.

But once the game begins, the curiosity is all mine. Even though I haven't played much hockey since my teens, I find the Chinese style of play endlessly interesting and am forever trying out Canadian tricks on the Chinese to see how they'll react.

There is some organized hockey in China. The national team is occasionally reported to be playing somebody, and inevitably seems to lose by lopsided scores. But few of the pond players have ever seen even that level of play, never mind the NHL or top international hockey. Their game is totally improvised.

By and large, they skate like the wind, sometimes leaping gracefully in the air to avoid a stick or streaking around a body check. But few have mastered such fundamentals as giving and receiving a flat pass, the backhand shot or the slapshot. And all the standard "dekes" and moves of the NHL game seem to leave them totally bewildered.

The physical side of the game is also foreign to them, although the northern Chinese by no means conform to the stereotype of small lightweights. At only 170 pounds, I find it easy to push even the biggest players off the puck, but once they get over the surprise of being manhandled a bit they seem to immensely enjoy that kind of give-and-take.

In fact, they enjoy everything about the game in a way that would stir up nostalgia in most Canadians. Mostly factory workers and students in their late teens and early twenties, they play all-day shinny like 10-year-olds on the prairies.

In March, a major shake-up of the Chinese leadership consolidated the powers of Vice-Chairman Deng Xiaoping. Two of Deng's protegees, Hu Yaobang and Zhao Ziyang, were elevated to the ruling Politburo, and several Maoists were dropped from senior posts. At the same time, the late head of state Liu Shaoqi (Liu Shao-chi), Deng's former ally and a fellow victim of the Cultural Revolution, was given a posthumous rehabilitation: an official communiqué said that Liu — once condemned as a "renegade, traitor and scab" — had suffered "the biggest frame-up our Party has ever known."

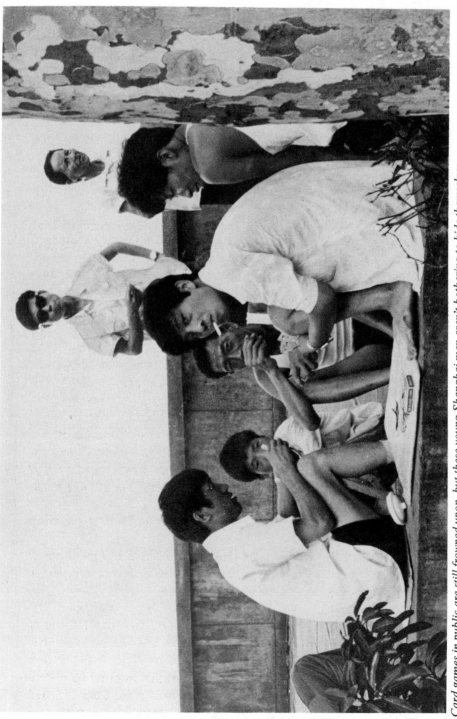

Card games in public are still frowned upon, but these young Shanghai men aren't bothering to hide themselves.

Both Hu Yaobang and Zhao Ziyang were economic specialists in their sixties: in Chinese terms, they were relative youngsters. As Johnson reported, the 76-year-old Deng had been frustrated by the cautious attitude of senior officials and believed that only a more vigorous group of technocrats could fulfil the tough goals he had set for China's modernization. Soon there were further signs of economic pragmatism: an official declaration that competition was a "good thing", and another announcement that China was abandoning its policy of full state employment for all citizens and was shifting to a system in which millions of Chinese would find — or create — their own jobs.

But there was no solace for the genuine youngsters who had been in the forefront of the Democracy Movement. Another communiqué bluntly abolished the Four Great Freedoms — the rights to "speak out freely, air views fully, hold great debates and write big-character posters". However briefly, these freedoms had formed the cornerstone of China's constitutional human-rights guarantees: observers saw their abolition as a further victory for Deng, who had argued that they "upset stability and unity". As Johnson wrote, the illusion of democratic reform had been completely shattered: "Anyone who reports on this country now stares daily into the maw of a naked and awesome totalitarianism."

Like all his *Globe and Mail* predecessors, Johnson was finding it difficult to penetrate beyond these political and economic events for glimpses into the lives of ordinary Chinese. In July, however, he became one of the relatively few foreigners ever permitted to attend that most basic forum of human passions — a divorce trial.

PEKING — Yao Yitian looked up helplessly at the dais, pleading with the three judges.

"In my deepest pain," he told them, "I had the most pessimistic view of life. I even thought of suicide. I must tell you, I feel pain every time I hear my wife's voice."

It was the most poignant moment in a sad, rather nasty divorce case. And it followed three hours of conflicting testimony about exactly who beat whom most viciously and who was guilty of the most callous abuse.

But the audience packed into the Peking Intermediate People's Court had an odd reaction to Yao's plea: they laughed aloud. It began as a titter at the back, grew into a wave and drowned the next few moments of testimony.

The triumvirate of judges, intent on restoring marital harmony, didn't even glance up.

This cavalier, almost carefree mood was demonstrated often during yesterday's hearing — opened to foreign reporters who have been pestering the authorities for a first-hand look at Chinese justice. And the repeated guffaws caught the outsiders off-guard.

The People's Republic has many virtues, but a gay, carnival atmosphere is seldom among them. This is a country where cheering fans at football matches are instructed over loudspeakers to quieten down. So reporters hardly went to the grey, forbidding court — scene of Wei Jingsheng's celebrated trial last October — looking for live theatre.

But that's often what we found.

Things got off to a slow start when Yao, a 52-year-old editor seeking divorce from his wife of 18 years, recited a long litany of her offences. The crowd was titillated when he accused her of throwing boiling water on him, but they merely oohed and aahed a little. And the allegation that she had pulled a knife on him left the spectators unmoved.

Things changed immediately, however, when it came time for 50-year-old Chen Zhengyu to defend herself.

Contesting the divorce vehemently, she began gunning her husband down with a barrage of accusations, all delivered in a high-pitched, shrewish whine.

She had been talking for only a few moments when the gallery began nudging each other appreciatively. And within two minutes or so she had brought on the first explosion of laughter.

"He said he wanted to beat me," she shouted. "He said he had the right to beat me. But since this is a socialist country, how can he say that?"

It says a good deal about real attitudes in this Communist country that everyone in the room immediately broke up at that line. But there was more to come.

A few minutes later, Yao quoted his wife as saying: "I just want to make trouble for you. With eight hundred million people, how can we make progress if we don't struggle?"

This is a bizarre usage of an axiom often repeated by Mao Tsetung, and it simply brought down the house. Surprisingly, however, the trio of judges waited patiently for things to quieten without any admonition to the audience, and even seemed rather to enjoy the irony.

But the trial did have its serious side, quite apart from the devastated marriage under examination.

For one thing, it did much to reveal why China's divorce rate is so astonishingly low: a mere two per cent of all marriages. Even to get to this stage, it was revealed, the husband had to repeatedly petition his unit to look into his case and endure round after round of what seems to have been a kind of enforced reconciliation.

Eventually, the couple were taken before the district court in their neighborhood in eastern Peking. That court seems also to have recommended a reconciliation, but the determined husband managed to force yesterday's higher session — a very serious step under the Chinese legal system.

Yet even the damaging evidence heard yesterday (including separate living quarters in a one-room dwelling, accomplished by partitioning it in half) is no assurance the divorce will be granted.

The tribunal, which included two women and one male chairman, suggested that the two try to "compromise" and "correct your thinking". The judges then decided they would "investigate further in your neighborhood" before reaching any decision.

In September, Johnson reported an extraordinary event: the first peaceful transition of power in Chinese Communist history. In a direct, unemotional speech to 3,200 delegates at the National People's Congress, Hua Guofeng resigned as China's premier. As had been widely predicted, his replacement was Zhao Ziyang, the 61-year-old vice-premier who had entered the government only five months earlier under the aegis of Deng Xiaoping. Hua would continue as Party chairman, but as Johnson noted, "His power there has been largely circumscribed by the Deng faction and he seems likely to depart the Communist hierarchy within the next year."

Ironically, it was Hua who was given the task of telling the delegates that China was scrapping its ambitious 10-year economic plan in favor of more cautious goals. These would be the responsibility of his successor, the "wizard of Sichuan". After he took charge of China's most populous province in 1975, Zhao introduced a raft of liberal reforms, including bonuses to workers and self-management for selected factories. As a result, Sichuan had boosted its industrial output by 81 per cent in only three years. As Johnson wrote, however: "Cynics wonder how much credit for the turnabout belongs to the Party propaganda department. They note that what is hailed as brilliant innovation in China is little more than common sense to a Western economist."

Amid these heavy events, the Communist leadership was still concerned about the attitude of many young Chinese, especially in the larger cities. That autumn, a skeptical Johnson encountered some of these "decadent youth".

PEKING — The newspapers have made it dead easy to identify China's young "bad elements" if you happen to run across them. They'll be the ones shaking their legs in a "disgusting manner", listening to "obscene foreign music" on tape recorders, dressed in outlandish clothes, sporting Hong Kong sunglasses, cigarettes drooping from their mouths. Little subversive monsters, apparently, these "male and female hooligans . . . cuddling licentiously in tight-fitting clothes".

Still, after months of reporting on the villains, I have to admit to having doubts whether they actually existed outside the fervid imaginations of Party propagandists. My visits to the parks are quite regular and I had never seen anything more outlandish than a pair of young lovers who seemed to be removing some article of clothing. In other words: normal, healthy behavior.

Finally, however, I've had my first encounter with a half-dozen of the dreaded leg-shakers and licentious cuddlers — found dancing up a storm one afternoon beside the Temple of the Azure Clouds in Peking's gorgeous Western Hills. They fit the newspaper description so perfectly that, at first glance, I thought they might be a group of actors playing the part we've all read about so much.

In fact, they turned out to be the real article, right down to the Teresa Teng tapes from Taiwan, the Hong Kong label on their sunglasses and a pair of bell-bottom corduroy jeans. But it is only fair to report that China's "bad element youth" really are just a creation of the media.

Unlike the usual situation here, getting to talk to them was no problem at all. I was visiting the temple with a lovely Chinese-Canadian woman who speaks fluent Mandarin and who, more important, has a penchant for the briefest of jogging shorts. We were mobbed by the decadent dancers and immediately found ourselves holding lighted cigarettes, although neither of us smokes.

(It was a grey, overcast day, but I had a fleeting impresson one of the gang would produce two pairs of Hong Kong sunglasses and slip them on our noses, too. Sunglasses have become the sine qua non of being modern in today's China.)

The conversation started out the way all such meetings do here: the girls slipped shyly to the back, eyes averted, and resisted all attempts to ask them a direct question; the boys came confidently forward, trying out their few phrases of English, asking how old we were and laughing delightedly as we guessed they were five years younger than their real age.

The four boys turned out to be in their late twenties — not "boys" at all in our terms, but acting so much like North American teenagers that it is impossible not to think of them that way. The girls were only a couple of years younger, but could easily have passed for 16-year-olds in appearance and demeanor.

All six worked at the same factory in the northern suburbs of Peking, putting together radio parts in an assembly line. The oldest, at 29, has been there 13 years and his seniority has given him the very high salary for a worker of 72 yuan (about $58 Canadian) per month.

One was dressed in an elaborate brocade jacket and bell-bottoms — a daring display of color in a land where the blue-cotton work uniform is still the norm — and kept breaking off the discussion to do some spirited leg shaking with another male friend. The girls, apparently, were too shy to dance in front of strangers. A few yards away, some others of the "restless youth" broke up a card game behind a discreet stone fence to peer over at the foreigners.

All in all, a typical display of the "youth problem" that so concerns China's newspaper commentators. But are they bad elements? A few excerpts from our conversation cast some pretty strong doubts on the label.

We asked why, for example, none of the dancers was married, although they had all reached the permitted age.

"Oh," answered the oldest, "right now we are devoting all our energies to the Four Modernizations. Our country needs us to work hard. Later on we will marry."

What about dressing up wildly and coming to the park to dance? Do they do it often?

"No, no," answered another. "This is only for relaxation on our day off. The rest of the week is taken up by working for the prosperity of our country."

The young "hooligan" took a drag on his cigarette, his friends nodded in earnest agreement and the intrepid foreign correspondent just stared at them blankly. This, I couldn't help thinking . . . this is what passes for "decadence" in China.

By now Johnson had completed his first year in Peking. As the first dust storms blew in from the Gobi Desert, he reported on how the citizens of the capital were preparing for another arduous winter.

PEKING — It is 3 a.m. on an icy November morning when a reporter approaches an old man standing in the line to buy cabbages. And the feisty Peking gentleman is in no mood to hide his disgruntlement at the way things are going.

"I had to get up at midnight to come here and stand in line," he moans. "And this is the sixth day in a row. Even then, I am not sure that I will get any. Buying these cabbages has really been too difficult for me."

Obviously, the man hadn't just dropped in to pick up a few vegetables for lunch. It is the time of year when Peking goes a little mad — or perhaps squirrely is a better word. The capital becomes a city of six million squirrels, frantically hoarding provisions for the winter.

They queue, often in shifts, for armloads of vegetables; they haul coal on the backs of bicycles; paper over their windows; haggle over coats and quilts and boots; and most of all, they wrap themselves in layer upon layer of thick, long underwear until they resemble a city of Michelin tire mascots.

There is an intensity about these preparations that mystifies a Westerner the first time around. My own experience of getting set for winter never amounted to more than an engine tune-up, a new hockey stick and a full tank of fuel oil. So when it all began last year, I viewed it with detached amusement.

One taste of Peking's brutal winter, however, is enough to knock the smirk off anyone's face. And a visit to an average Chinese home in the dead of January drives home the urgency of these November line-ups.

A tiny, round coal stove, perhaps a foot in diameter, provides both heat and cooking in temperatures that average –10 or –15 degrees Celsius. And the pile of dirty round coal briquets becomes a virtual lifeline. By January or February there are virtually no fresh vegetables in the markets. So the cabbages, peppers and onions that are stacked against a wall or buried in huge pits are the only variation in a diet of rice and a minuscule meat ration.

That kind of stark necessity, and the endless line-ups, gives China's "squirrel time" a vastly different look than our own idea of autumn harvest cornucopias.

It is not unusual to see men sweating under huge loads of coal on their tricycle-wagons: three-wheeled cycles with a flat board across the back. The other day, I saw one toppled over in the middle of a main street with a knot of spectators standing around and the driver wondering what to do with 300 pounds of broken briquets.

Finally, black with coal dust, he began sifting through the rubble in a desultory search for whole pieces.

The markets are full this time of year, but they offer little choice. The long, green-and-white Chinese cabbage is the dominant commodity, and the trucks unload them right on the sidewalk or on the ground, often in piles five feet high and the same width across. For two weeks the city is simply buried in cabbage. Half the bicycles have huge bundles of the stuff strapped across their back carriers. The rest of the city, apparently, is lined up night and day trying to buy their share.

This year, however, the situation is far worse than usual. The

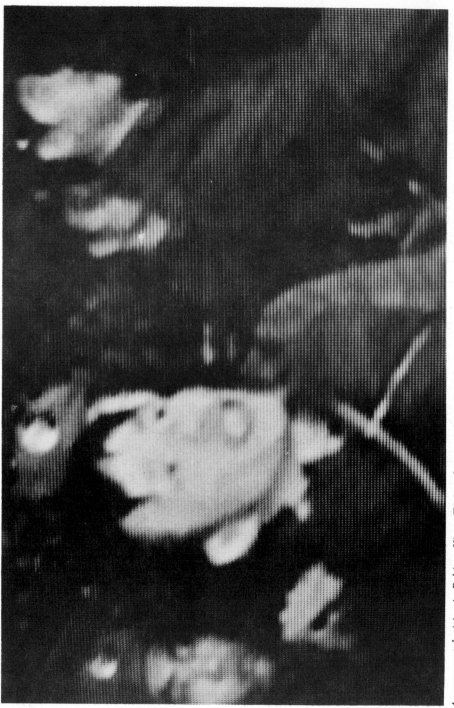

As seen on television in Peking, Xiong Ziping shouts at the judge after receiving his death sentence.

Xiong Ziping is shown forced to his knees outside the court building.

Xiong Ziping lies in a heap on the ground after being shot.

distribution of cabbage has hit a terrible snag, and people are up in arms about it — all but literally; the letters-to-the-editor columns of the newspapers are dominated by the "cabbage crisis". And the ensuing scrap has been immensely revealing about daily life here.

The problem centres around the "number-one cabbages" — the best, leafiest grade, which sells for about two cents a pound. This grade has been rationed in the past, but people were so nonchalant about picking up their share that thousands of pounds were destroyed last year in an early frost. This year authorities have declared an open market but, despite a reported bumper harvest, there are no "number ones" to be had anywhere. As you can tell from the following letter, Peking citizens are both outraged . . . and suspicious.

"My friend Granny Zhou from the eastern district got to the vegetable stall at 2 a.m. and found herself thirty-ninth in line," one irate letter writer told the *Peking Daily*. "She and her son and daughter took turns standing in the cold for five hours, but the line stopped short, sold out after only 20 people had been served.

"In my whole office, only eight people managed to buy even Grade Two cabbages, and they weren't as good as Grade Three in past years. The only people benefitting from the free market are those who can go through the back door" — that is, people with connections.

The old man in the cabbage line at 3 a.m. echoed this view exactly. "We must stop this evil wind of slipping through the back door to buy cabbages," he said, roughly translated. "And any of these people who try to use this chance to put up the price of vegetables really have to be dealt with severely."

Winter in China, obviously, is very serious business; and woe betide the bureaucrat who comes between the masses and their cabbage.

For everyone in Peking — foreigners and Chinese alike — there was one major diversion that winter: the long-awaited trial of the Gang of Four. In late November, Mao's widow Jiang Qing and her three colleagues — Zhang Chungquiao, Wang Hongwen and Yao Wenyuan — appeared in a cavernous Peking courtroom before more than 800 carefully chosen spectators. Like other foreign reporters, Johnson was excluded from the trial, but watched edited versions every evening on television. According to Johnson, Jiang looked calm, dignified and defiant as she listened to a 20,000-word indictment that listed 48 charges against the Gang and another group of six aged generals and bureaucrats associated with the late Lin Biao (Lin Piao). These included attempting to kill Mao, staging an armed uprising in Shanghai and trying to overthrow state power. Although not implicated in the attempt on her husband, the 67-year-old Jiang was accused of leading the "frame-up" of Liu Shaoqui, persecuting thousands of Communist cadres during the Cultural Revolution and slandering Deng Xiaoping.

As the trial unfolded over the next several weeks, Wang Hong-wen, the young Shanghai worker who had enjoyed such a spectacular rise to power, emerged as a virtual witness for the prosecution, readily blaming his colleagues. At the other extreme, Jiang was totally contemptuous of the battery of prosecutors and judges. While this was evident to the television audience, both television and news-agency reports avoided the details of her testimony, fuelling speculation that Mao's widow was invoking the name of her late husband in her defence. Soon, however, the television audience would see Jiang being dragged out of the courtroom by two armed female guards after a tumultuous shouting match with her judges.

Well in advance of any verdicts, the Chinese press was busy condemning all the defendants. Soon Johnson was speculating that their fate was being decided — not in the courtroom but at a tense and continuing meeting of the Communist Party's Central Committee. Citing well-placed sources, Johnson said the meeting was a "bloody battleground" in which Deng Xiaoping was trying to eliminate the last remnants of Maoism: ". . . both Jiang Qing and Chairman Hua Guofeng have become pawns in this struggle, which revolves around a sharp difference on the policies of Mao. Aside from Jiang's life and Hua's career, the future of China's liberal economic policies is also thought to be riding on the outcome."

Finally — in late January, 1981 — Jiang was dragged from the courtroom for the last time. She had just been sentenced to death, but granted a stay of execution for two years. The same sentence was imposed on Zhang Chungquiao, the former Shanghai mayor who was regarded as the brains of the Gang and who had remained virtually silent throughout the trial. According to Johnson, their two-year reprieves were seen as a virtual guarantee that they would never be executed. At the same time, the special court gave the compliant Wang Hongwen a life term, while the critic and polemicist Yao Wenyuan was sentenced to 20 years in prison. The six members of the "Lin Biao Clique" received sentences ranging from 16 to 18 years.

Chinese officials made no attempt to explain why Jiang — labelled as "the greatest persecutor of the twentieth century" — had been granted a reprieve. But Johnson speculated that Deng, after weeks of top-level in-fighting, had feared making her a martyr and an immediate rallying point for millions of disaffected leftists.

As Deng and his supporters consolidated their power, they were also tackling the problem of dealing with the thousands of foreigners — tourists, businessmen and Overseas Chinese — who were flocking to China in growing numbers. Here, at least, a tentative liberalism was permitted, as Johnson discovered on a visit to China's most cosmopolitan city.

SHANGHAI — The Greek sailors at the far end of the bar are drinking too much and talking far too loud. A young Chinese waiter glides by them with a tray full of gin-and-tonics.

And as an elegant Japanese couple get up to dance, the seven-piece jazz band starts in with a muted, sultry version of "Smoke Gets In Your Eyes".

No, this is not 1931 in the classiest hotel in the wildest city on earth. It is 50 years later in the same hotel and same city — under the benevolent dictatorship of the proletariat.

Shanghai, home of the Gang of Four and once the hotbed of revolutionary Maoism, is no longer the fabled Paris of the Orient. But as China's leadership mellows and the country again opens up to the West, this city has at least regained its status as China's New York.

And there are few better symbols of the resuscitation than the no-name jazz band in the Bar of what was once the elegant Cathay Hotel, now the Peace Hotel.

The band is playing tunes from an age that has vanished in the West. Benny Goodman's "Sing, Sing, Sing" . . . "The

294

Trumpet Rhumba" . . . "In the Mood" . . . "Summertime".

They're all songs, as the bass player admits, "which we learned from watching American movies before liberation. We haven't even heard the records, really."

Like Shanghai itself, the band would rather keep its decadent existence a secret from the rest of China. When a foreign correspondent tries to interview trumpet player Chou Wangyung, he is politely rebuffed with the answer that "it is not a good thing, not a good idea".

Pressed for some explanation, Chou laughs in embarrassment and shakes his head. But after a couple of minutes, he offers the halting opinion that "it is not good to talk about us, because we are the only band of this kind in China. It is . . . Western . . . just for Western people."

Indeed it is. And in case any of the locals feel otherwise, the following instructions have been placed in both Chinese and English at every table in the marble-walled bar:

"This room is specially for the foreigners and the Overseas Chinese. In order to meet their needs, the following rule is made. Customers must be granted permission before they bring in their relatives and friends living in Shanghai. Co-operation is expected."

Such restrictions are a normal part of the Chinese strategy for isolating foreigners from chance encounters with "the masses". But the unusual strictness and prominence of these rules are apparently related to the nightly jazz concert.

All Western music, from Beethoven to Bob Dylan, was outlawed as decadent during the Cultural Revolution. And even now, Chinese newspapers regularly rail against the contamination of syrupy Hong Kong love songs that are smuggled in on cassette tapes.

The current political status of Western jazz has never been defined by China's cultural overlords. And that ambiguity, it seems, is the reason my request for an interview is treated like a political time bomb by everyone involved.

The bar's maitre d' informs me that any interviews must be approved by the manager and asks me to wait. Ten minutes later, a large, dour man named Kan Aiquong arrives to present the Peace Hotel's official position on the jazz band.

"Our foreign guests like the music and need it," the bar

manager says gravely. "So we provide the music . . . the old music . . . it is mostly 40 years old."

Two of the musicians nod vigorously as their boss makes this last point — as if it somehow clears the enterprise of any modern contamination.

Eventually, the musicians are allowed to speak, and the whole exchange is translated for Mr. Kan. The double-bass player explains in perfect English that he is Harold Wu, a former student at Shanghai's famous Saint John's Christian School in pre-revolutionary days.

He used to come to the Cathay Hotel to watch the foreign jazz band in an eighth-floor spot called the Towe Club, he says, and got hooked on the music.

In genuine surprise, I remark that I had no idea Chinese were allowed in Western bars in those days — then quickly realize the embarrassing irony of my comment.

"Oh, we didn't come often." Mr. Wu shrugs amiably. "You had to dress up and everything."

All seven of the Chinese musicians have formal musical training, although they modestly dismiss themselves as amateurs. They were recruited to entertain foreigners at Christmas last year and have been kept on, first playing twice a week and now doing a nightly three-hour show that ends at 11.

"We play everything from the orchestrations," Mr. Wu explains. "We haven't really practised very much. We just went over everything once or twice by ourselves. That's enough.

"We are all over 50 and heard the music before — at the motion pictures. My heroes were Harry James and Louis Armstrong . . . Satchmo, is that right, Satchmo?"

Yes, the name is Satchmo. But what about his music? Is it still considered decadent in China? Can the Chinese be contaminated by a visit to the Peace Hotel?

The question seems too hot for Mr. Wu, who joins in long, embarrassed laughter with Mr. Chou. Mr. Kan doesn't laugh, nor does he offer any answer. I decide to wait in silence until one is forthcoming, but Mr. Wu casually deflects my ploy.

"We just play for foreign guests," he says with another smile. "It is not decadent for them." He looks at his watch and excuses himself.

"Show time," he says.

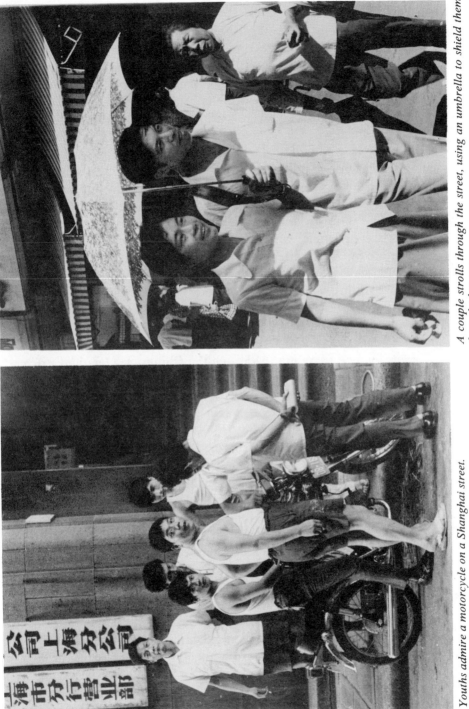

A couple strolls through the street, using an umbrella to shield them from the hot sun.

Youths admire a motorcycle on a Shanghai street.

In late June, Deng Xiaoping finally completed the rout of his Maoist adversaries. After a two-day plenum of senior leaders, Hua Guofeng was dropped as chairman of China's Communist Party. The designated successor of Mao Tsetung, Hua was given the face-saving position of Party vice-chairman, but an official commentary said he had been severely criticized for his "leftist errors". His replacement was Hu Yaobang, who had already been running the party as its general secretary, and who was once denounced for being Deng's bridge partner. As Johnson recalled, the 66-year-old Hu had moved in virtual lockstep with Deng since the outbreak of the Cultural Revolution — when Red Guards charged that he was flown into Peking from Shaanxi Province expressly to play "the bourgeois card game" with his mentor. Both were among those rehabilitated in 1972; after the Tienanmen incident in 1976, both were sent back into political limbo. Both had returned to power after the overthrow of the Gang of Four: "Since then, the diminutive pair — Hu is probably two inches shorter than the five-foot three-inch Deng — have become the most powerful one-two punch in Chinese politics."

It was the end of an era. Although the Chinese leaders had still to deliver their final verdict on Mao Tsetung, everything and everyone connected with him — his policies, his disciples, even his widow — were in disgrace. It was a generation since Mao had proclaimed the founding of the Chinese People's Republic from the Gate of Heavenly Peace, and more than 20 years since Frederick Nossal had arrived in Peking to find the Communists celebrating their first decade in power with a display of pride and confidence. Now the mood was much more sombre and tentative. If China was still an oppressive, totalitarian state — which it clearly *was* — its rulers were less bound by dogma and more ready to admit their past mistakes and current problems.

Over the years, *Globe and Mail* correspondents had avoided the folly of making rash predictions about China's future. There were always too many imponderables. As Johnson prepared to end his two-year posting, he again turned his attention to the biggest question mark of all: the six hundred million Chinese who had been born since 1949. They were a generation in crisis, Johnson wrote. "The authorities have admitted for more than a year that young people are experiencing a 'crisis of confidence', showing a marked indifference to Marxism and 'blindly worshipping anything foreign'. But only recently has the full extent of the problem begun to surface."

In a series of articles, Johnson described the apathy and cynicism he had found in his Chinese friends — students, factory workers and former Red Guards. Many longed for greater political freedom; most were just as disaffected by the regime's puritanical strictures on sexual relations and material goods. Others criticized the inadequacies and rigidity of China's schools and colleges. As Johnson noted, more than twenty million urban youths were unemployed, with the inevitable result that crime and random violence were on the rise. Despite attempts to reform the Communist Party, corruption and nepotism were still widely prevalent: this, too, encouraged disaffection. Most serious of all for the regime, opinion surveys had shown that nearly a third of Chinese university students doubted the oft-touted "superiority of socialism", while only 10 per cent believed that Deng Xiaoping could achieve his ambitious program to modernize the nation.

From Peking, Deng and Hu Yaobang were presiding over the advent of a new era in China's history. But they were old men, and six hundred million Chinese under the age of 30 would be just as crucial in giving that era its distinctive stamp.

Stanley Oziewicz is getting some curious looks from the descendants of Confucius in Qufu, the sage's birthplace.

CHAPTER TEN: 1981—1983

STANLEY OZIEWICZ

As China continued its policy of openness to the outside world, and the Communist leadership that was seeking to guide the country's destiny through to the twenty-first century solidified its position, the pattern of coverage by Western reporters changed. Much more information became available; many more places were opened to outside scrutiny. *The Globe and Mail*'s tenth correspondent, Stanley Oziewicz, who arrived in Peking during the fall of 1981, took advantage of the political calm to travel more extensively in China than any of his predecessors.

Oziewicz, who was 29 when he took up residence in China, joined the newspaper in 1976 after graduating from the journalism school at Toronto's Ryerson Polytechnical Institute. He also studied at York University and the University of Bordeaux. After a stint as general reporter, he worked at both the Quebec City and Queen's Park (Toronto) bureaus.

His very first dispatch was a troublesome one for the Chinese authorities because it dealt with the plight of a young Chinese dissident in a labor-reform camp.

PEKING — A prominent Chinese dissident now languishing in a reform-through-labor camp says he was beaten until his "whole body was blue and covered with wounds" for refusing to assume a submissive posture.

Liu Qing's description of his ordeal in China's little-known "gulag" is contained in a 200-page document reportedly smuggled out of prison. It has now come into the hands of some journalists here.

Liu, 38, was co-editor of the *April Fifth Forum*, a magazine that took hold during the democracy movement of 1978-79. It gained prominence for its reporting of the trial of dissident Wei Jingsheng. Wei was sentenced to 15 years in jail.

Defiantly, the magazine posted transcripts of Wei's testimony on the Xidan Wall in Peking and later published a special pamphlet edition of his defence.

On November 11, 1979, Liu went to the wall to sell some of the mimeographed transcripts. But the attempt was violently stifled by a swift police raid in which wall posters were torn down and some buyers and vendors arrested.

Liu then walked to Public Security Bureau headquarters claiming full responsibility for the transcripts and demanded the release of the arrested people.

For his trouble, he himself was arrested and held for months without charges or trial, with word finally leaking out that he had been sent to a labor-reform camp called Lianhua Temple in Shaanxi province.

Until last April 10 his colleague Xu Wenli was not given any trouble. Then, suddenly, he too was seized.

All along, Xu believed he and his partner had not committed any crimes. Xu said he was fighting for a socialist democracy and trusted China's constitution.

According to one translation of Liu's smuggled tract, Liu also maintained to his interrogators that what he was doing was legal.

"My insistence on the law and on legality enraged the PSB interrogators. Finally one of them said angrily: 'Now that you are here, you don't have to answer our questions. But as long as you refuse to answer our questions, you'll never be allowed to leave.' I reminded them that detaining me without proper papers was illegal, and that I had no intention of submitting to illegal detention.

"Their reply: 'This is the office of the dictatorship'."

Called "a dispirited recollection and observations; I lodge my complaint before the court of society," Liu's account of a Chinese prison camp is one of the few to reach the West in recent years.

Held in solitary confinement for more than five months, Liu began to lose his hair, his feet became swollen and his near-sightedness worsened.

Refusing to cower before his interrogators led to a beating. He says: "I was sent to a small cell. I was beaten until my whole body was blue and covered with wounds. My head was covered with a gas mask, which made it difficult to breathe. My hands were cuffed behind me and the metal bonds were piercing my flesh."

Liu asks for a public trial, saying that the Chinese judicial system won't help him.

"So I place my hope in the resolution of this case to society," he says. Another translation quotes him as saying, "I want the people to know the truth of this matter."

During his period in solitary confinement, Liu says he talked to himself and had intense debates with an imagined opponent. "I thought a lot about my mother and the grief I brought her in her last years. I felt very guilty."

A university graduate whose father worked in the old U.S. embassy, Liu wrote his account on paper, intended for self-criticism.

Although much of the account deals with the helplessness that Liu feels in face of the "unbridled authority of the dictatorial machinery," he sticks to the belief that the Democracy Wall was "at the front line of thinking of this generation".

In one cynical aside, he asks why the security bureau doesn't just turn the whole country into a reform-through-labor camp.

"I believe in genuine freedom of speech. Before the 1949 liberation Marxists and Communists said free speech meant the right to speak out against the class in power. . . . When they had no freedom of speech, they struggled to achieve it. After they secured freedom of speech they deny their own citizens the right of free speech."

Deng Xiaoping's government last year withdrew the "constitutional right" to publish and paste up wall posters.

Liu's document calls the jailing of Wei "a public mockery of China's implementation of a legal system. It is an attack on democracy and the rule of law." He adds: "If one sees unfairness or inaccuracy but does not have the courage to point it out, closing one's eyes or looking the other way, progress cannot be achieved."

On the Chinese political system, Liu said, "I do not agree with this principle of the dictatorship of the proletariat, nor with the use of the concepts of revolution and counter-revolution in our present society.

"These kind of frightening things have no benefit for our society and state and are harmful."

The official reaction to this and similar stories in other Western newspapers was swift and angry. Liu Qing's document, said a foreign ministry official, was "sheer fabrication" and "full of vicious attacks". The foreign ministry then went on to warn all foreign journalists that they risked their accreditation in China if they "defied the provisional regulations" the government had passed to govern their activities. In the warning was an echo that sounded back a quarter century to the days of the very first *Globe and Mail* correspondent.

As Oziewicz took stock of the political and social situation in China, it became clear to him that there would be no major news story in the immediate future, barring the death of Deng Xiaoping. His challenge, therefore, was to take advantage of the increased travel in the country and a more accessible citizenry. He even found an occasion to look back into China's past in an interview with one of the last living eunuchs of the Imperial Court.

PEKING — Sun Yaoting is 80 now, severely bow-legged and feeble but possessed of a quiet humor and serene dignity. Attendants support his arm as he walks with his cane over to a stool. Before he sits down, a pillow is placed on the seat.

When he feels up to it, Sun receives visitors. Those ministering to his needs politely but firmly remind them when it's time for Sun to rest. That done, he can tend the garden in the tranquil courtyard and perhaps reminisce with a dear friend, Ma Deqing, also 80.

Only blocks from the shadow of the Drum Tower, near where the two venerable gentlemen live, lies the Forbidden City. It was there, as eunuchs to the last imperial court, that they did the bidding of others as dutiful feudal servants.

No one knows how many eunuchs, archaic reminders of a varlet class noted for cunning and often unscrupulous palace machinations and despised for their "injury", still survive. At most, there is a handful.

It is said that nearly all major Chinese dynasties were charac-

Sun Yaoting, now in his mid-eighties, is one of the two remaining imperial court eunuchs.

Two workers repair the base of the statue of a martial-arts warrior protecting the Shaolin monastery in Henan province.

terized by the usurpation of power by scheming eunuchs who had risen from their base estate of looking after imperial harems.

Sometimes they numbered in the hundreds, at other times in the thousands. In the thirteenth century a eunuch secret service was formed, which later developed into an organization for terrorism.

But by 1916, when Sun entered the palace, the dominance of eunuchs had waned. The dowager empress had been dead for eight years, and her favorite eunuch, Li Lianying, nicknamed "Cobbler's Wax Li", died three years later.

Li, it is said, had castrated himself with a cobbler's knife after puberty, having been tempted by the glamor and riches of the imperial court. He was not disappointed. "The Old Buddha", as the empress was known, regarded Li highly, bestowing upon him a peacock's feather and a ruby button. By the time he died, Li had amassed a personal fortune.

Such was not the romantic and intriguing lot of Sun or of Ma, who was not able to attend the interview because of poor health. Both were on the lower rungs in the eunuch ranks.

In a sunny room in the compound for the Bureau for Preservation of Temples and Monasteries where he now lives, Sun laughs quietly when asked what he liked and disliked most about serving empress Wan Rong, the teenage wife of emperor Pu Yi.

"I didn't have any feelings like that," he says, leaning forward and grasping his cane. "I just felt lucky to serve the empress. She was very kind to me and never abused me."

About her own age, Sun used to satisfy her most petty whim, pour her tea, provide her with tobacco and sweets. And when the empress fancied playing games, Sun and the other 19 eunuchs who waited on her joined to play hide-and-seek and drop-the-handkerchief.

Castration was an official punishment in China for many centuries until it was apparently abolished in the sixth century. Thereafter, the needs of the court were supplied in large measure by young boys captured in the south.

But Sun's castration, at the age of 10, was voluntary, or so he says. He admits that it was done "without any clear idea". Even worse, once castrated, he and his family had no guarantee that he would be accepted at the court.

And it was not Little Knife Li, the official court castrator, who performed the humiliating operation, but Sun's own father. The young boy fainted during the operation and the wound took two months to heal.

Sun was born near Tianjin in Jinghai county. His family, miserably poor, occupied a two-room mud house and farmed a pitiful plot.

"There was no other way out," Sun recalled. "We were a very poor family. We wanted a way out. Becoming a eunuch was a way up to help the family."

But the wait was long. To pay for a tutor, his mother cooked for a landowner while his father tilled his land. After six years, some eunuchs in a nearby village helped Sun get accepted at the imperial court. Immediately, he had to suffer another indignity. A master eunuch probed to check whether the young boy had been properly and fully castrated.

When he first entered the Forbidden City, Sun had to learn his duties and the court etiquette. For a time, he reported to a master eunuch, learning to load water pipes and the proper way to subjugate himself before superiors. Before the emperor, for example, he was required to genuflect three times and perform nine kow-tows.

The cardinal sin was the clapping of hands, taboo because it was associated with the mourning for an emperor.

Having served his apprenticeship, Sun worked for the chief eunuch in the accounting office of the palace, increasing his pay by six taels of silver with the promotion. His salary jumped to 20 taels a month when he was told to serve the empress Wan Rong.

He has fond memories of the empress, but remembers that her teenage son could be cruel and callous.

"Although he was an emperor he was childish and bad-tempered."

Sun recalls the time Emperor Pu Yi ordered him to ride a bicycle (imported from England).

Sun didn't have the faintest idea how to go about it. But Pu Yi forced him to get on, pushed him, terrified and cowering, along and laughed uproariously when eunuch and bicycle crashed into the dirt.

"It was very embarrassing and the emperor was obviously very pleased."

Sun worked at the Forbidden City for eight years, until the teenage emperor, his family and the palace eunuchs were expelled in 1924.

Having been relatively secure and comfortable within the walls of the Imperial City, Sun and the other eunuchs were left to fend for themselves in a society that regarded them as pariahs.

Abused and taunted, some of the eunuchs banded together, bound by the castration they endured and their new lowly status.

"We were looked down upon," Sun remembers sadly. "It was difficult for us to go to the public toilets. We found it impossible to go to the men's and we couldn't really use the women's either."

In China, public toilets are truly public.

At first, they lived in the Green Dragon Monastery on the savings they had accumulated. Soon, their money was exhausted. Sun became a peddler, selling boiled peanuts and pears and scrounging coal dust and orange peel.

Outcast and neglected for 25 years, Sun and his companions found times changed again with the proclamation of the People's Republic of China in 1949. With it came political classes and state control of monasteries, churches and temples.

Relics of China's imperial past, the few remaining eunuchs became dependants of the new order and were given menial jobs. Conditions did not really improve for Sun until 1953 when he joined the Bureau for the Preservation of Temples and Monasteries.

"Now my life doesn't have any difficulties," he sighs.

One of the most fascinating developments in the post-Mao era is the flirtation with modified forms of capitalism. Communist orthodoxy requires this be called something else — "a transitionary stage in socialist development" — but there was no denying the enthusiasm of peasants and city dwellers for whatever it was called. Communes were dismantled, free markets opened up, cooperatives encouraged to garner and keep portions of their profits and itinerant entrepreneurs became, once again, a feature of street life. Nowhere was this change more dramatic than in the "special economic zone" created near the arch-capitalist British Crown colony of Hong Kong. When Oziewicz travelled to Shenzhen, the key community in the new zone, he found a scene that old China hands could never have imagined possible even five years before.

SHENZHEN — Until just recently the crass, bustling modernity of capitalistic Hong Kong ended abruptly at this southern Chinese frontier post.

Across the small steel-and-wood bridge was a quaint peasant village, complete with bullocks ruminating in the paddy fields. You didn't have to be told you had entered China.

Today you might scratch your head a bit. Soldiers wearing the baggy green uniforms of the People's Liberation Army still greet visitors at the customs checkpoint. But outside Lo Wu railway station is a town undergoing a startling transformation.

In the past 18 months Shenzhen has developed into a Western-style industrial boom town with a decidedly saucy imprint. And that's just how the new generation of innovators in Peking wants it — at least in a few carefully restricted areas.

Shenzhen is the largest and most advanced of China's "special economic zones", which have been set up on the southeast coast to attract foreign investors to build factories producing mostly export goods. The aim is to acquire Western technology, train skilled workers and reap foreign exchange to speed China's modernization.

Chinese leaders have acknowledged that to prosper, these zones must be allowed a healthy dose of capitalism. So the experiment is restricted to four areas, three in Guangdong province bordering Hong Kong and the other in Fujian province to the northeast.

Some of the figures surrounding Shenzhen's progress are staggering. In three years, the zone's annual revenue has jumped five times to roughly $100 million U.S. Its population has increased fivefold to 150,000 and is still rising. By late last year there were signed agreements for 1,000 development projects totalling $1.3 billion U.S.

Once a quiet backwater known for its lichee nuts and as the gateway to China, Shenzhen now resembles a colossal construction site. Datsun taxis, minibuses and North American-style transport trucks tear through the red soil where rice formerly grew. Powerful bulldozers are digging craters for 20- to 40-storey skyscrapers.

Factories are already assembling goods ranging from elec-

An old man in Qufu contemplates his surroundings and has a smoke amid citrus trees on his cart.

Some short haul goods are still pulled by hand, as here along Liberation Avenue in Chengdu, Sichuan province.

Lunchtime at the Returned Overseas Chinese Resettlement Farm at Wenchang, Hainan Island.

tronic gadgets to designer jeans, and bottling Pepsi-Cola. As apt a symbol as any of the economic integration with Hong Kong is the transport by conveyor belt into the British colony of crushed granite from a quarry on the Chinese side.

Garish restaurants with lots of mirror and marble have been built for the swelling number of investors and for the Chinese workers, who are better paid than elsewhere in China. (One official complained during a recent visit that many common workers in Shenzhen earn more than Communist Party cadres.)

The transformation is social and cultural too. Waves of Hong Kong residents visiting relatives bring bamboo poles laden with color televisions, tape recorders, tapes of Hong Kong pop stars, electric rice cookers and stylish clothes.

In Canton, 140 kilometres up the rail line, the authorities are pulling down aerials in a campaign against Hong Kong television. But no antenna is needed in Shenzhen to receive the bourgeois broadcasts and advertisements.

In the streets and walk-up cafés of Shenzhen, it's becoming almost impossible to distinguish the *ye yu gang ke* (spare-time Hong Kongese) from the real thing. All the trappings, from Winston cigarettes to Calvin Klein jeans, are the same — and readily available at the foreign-currency shops.

There is more personal freedom here than anywhere else in China, but the authorities are beginning to question how far social control can be relaxed. For the moment, they seem to be waging a losing battle against rampant smuggling and the proliferation of pornography and even prostitution.

In one notorious recent case, local party officials and a representative of a Chinese electronics import-export corporation had smuggled 530,000 television sets and 300,000 tape recorders from Hong Kong before they were caught. Acting in collusion with Hong Kong businessmen, the officials had also illegally bought $13 million U.S. in foreign currency on the black market to finance their operations.

The extent of prostitution and drug-taking is difficult to gauge, but enough is going on to warrant the issuance of warnings about the penalties for those caught pushing drugs or pimping. Even those suffering from venereal disease are to be punished.

The English-language *Peking Review* noted recently that

special attention must be devoted to the "ideological education of people in the special zones" because their lives are bound to change and capitalist ideology is bound to increase.

The Shenzhen government has set up an Office for the Cultivation of Spiritual Civilization, whose job is to foster socialist values through cultural and educational programs and outright propaganda.

Spokesman Li Ying said the office is eager for Shenzhen to absorb advanced technology and Western management methods. "The thinking of the Western way of life will influence people. We mustn't be afraid to keep the door open. But we should take measures to protect people."

One way to protect the people from "corrosive" influence is to ban outright pornographic video tapes and discos, as the Chinese have done. For the moment, however, clothes are being overlooked by the morals team.

"We don't interfere in clothing and dress," said Li, "because the workers are working hard and try their best on behalf of the Four Modernizations. Just because a woman puts on a dress doesn't mean she doesn't love our country."

Chairman Mao's birthplace in the remote Hunan countryside had, throughout the Great Proletarian Cultural Revolution, been turned into a national shrine where millions of Chinese made a pilgrimage in much the same fashion as their ancestors went to holy mountains or the birthplace of Confucius. Oziewicz went to Shaoshan in December, 1982, and found that only on the best of days did visitors number over a couple of hundred (where once 4,000 a day was considered normal). Furthermore, the former shrine was being used as a kind of indoctrination centre for new agricultural policies of the Dengists and as a means of disabusing visitors on the subject of the Great Helmsman's previous infallibility.

In other travels within China, Oziewicz, who was fascinated by the after-effects of history, visited Kaifeng to find out what happened to the legendary community of Chinese Jews. Later he went to Hainan Island, previously closed to Western journalists, and reported on the life in the leper colony at Haikou. And an article from Taishan in Guangzhou Province (of which Canton is the provincial capital) was read avidly by many Chinese-Canadians because this was where their fathers and grandfathers had first come from.

KAIFENG — They are called followers of Tiajinjiao, or the "pluck-out-the-sinew" religion. Originally they came from Yicileye, a transliteration in the Roman alphabet of the word Israel. They are Chinese Jews.

The handful of descendants of nomadic Jews who settled at Kaifeng centuries ago have abandoned the practices that once set them apart. The men no longer wear yarmulkes. They no longer study the Torah. They no longer adhere to strict dietary laws. They no longer circumcise their sons.

There are no rabbis, and the last synagogue collapsed some time in the mid-1800s from years of neglect and the ravages of the flooded Yellow River, whose banks lie only kilometres away.

The site became a garbage dump, which it remained until the Kaifeng No. 4 People's Hospital was built there after 1949. Today a Maoist quotation greets the visitor: "Cure the ill and save the dying to realize revolutionary humanism."

A Kaifeng travel-service guide says the first synagogue was built in 1163, facing west toward Jerusalem. From the outside it apparently resembled a Chinese temple.

Only recently have scholars published papers about China's Judaic history. Pan Guangdan, now dead, wrote in *Social Sciences in China* that Kaifeng Jews probably left the Middle East for Bombay about 270 BC. His research shows that having lived there for more than 1,000 years, they moved eastward along the silk route and entered China by the latter half of the eleventh century.

Visitors will find no Star of David in wanderings through the streets and narrow lanes of Kaifeng, a flat and dusty city of about 500,000 nestled in the eastern half of Henan province. Only three ancient and deteriorating steles lying in an open shed of the municipal museum — another is thought to be buried beneath the hospital — remain as testaments.

Most of the characters on the stone tablets have been eroded by time and weather, but they are said to record references to Nuwo (Eve) and Alaoluohan (Abraham). According to a resident who said he is Jewish, one of the inscriptions reads:

"Although Judaism and Confucianism agree on essential points and differ on secondary ones, yet the principles of the religion are simply to honor the Way of Heaven, venerate ancestors, emphasize relations between the ruler and his ministers, show filial obedience to parents, live in harmony with wife and children, preserve the distinction between superiors and inferiors and have good relations with friends. These principles are not foreign to the five relationships of Confucianism."

Even a communal identity as pronounced as that of Jews was bound to weaken under the ethnocentrism of the Middle Kingdom. Assimilation was aided by years of isolation, intermarriage, famine and flood.

Ji Yaqin was married to a direct descendant of one of the seven Jewish clans originally permitted to settle at Kaifeng, then the imperial capital, by a northern Song emperor. The Jews presented the emperor with cotton cloth; in turn, he gave them Chinese family names.

In her eighties, grey-haired and hobbling on bound feet, Ji related this in her tiny courtyard home at 21 Teaching Scriptures Lane, the only outward mark of what was once a vibrant Jewish community that counted silk manufacturers, merchants and goldsmiths among its members.

Ji's husband was of the Zhao clan, which claimed as one of its own a famous general of the Qing dynasty.

"Their forebears came a long way from the west. There were no trains then. Many people died, but also many children were born along the way."

Her husband told her of some of the Judaic customs — circumcision and abstention from eating pork. Even by the time of his birth, however, circumcision had been abandoned.

"How many descendants remain is difficult to say. They're scattered everywhere," Ji said. "Even several generations ago, the Jewish men married Chinese women, like me."

HAIKOU — The operating room in the newly whitewashed two-storey clinic is grim and dirty, with much of the rudimentary equipment rusting in the moist air drifting through the open windows. Drugs are stored in a battered, aging and rusting refrigerator.

Nurses move through the building in long white gowns, surgical masks and knee-high rubber boots, an eerie contrast to the near-pastoral sub-tropical setting.

This is the Xiuying Leprosarium, the largest of nine colonies for victims of leprosy on Hainan, off China's south coast. The patients here have been stricken with a disease that is as much feared as it is misunderstood.

Eighty-four patients are still in the progressive stages of the disease, but another 204 who have recovered remain. Many prefer to do so because they have been ostracized from their communities.

"I was driven away," says Wu Menghua, at 80 the oldest patient in the Xiuying colony, recalling the time when she contracted leprosy. "I had no one to support me."

She is bitter about the memory, pulling up her pant leg to reveal the metal prosthesis that replaced the leg she lost to the disease. "If I had been treated in time, I might have been able to keep my leg," she says.

Leprosy attacks the skin, flesh and nerves, causing ulcers and mutilation. Most of China's lepers live in the southern coastal regions where the bacillus thrives on the high heat and humidity.

According to Dr. Ma Haide, the Chinese name of U.S.-born Dr. George Hatem, the earliest surviving description of leprosy in China is the medical classic *He Jing* of the warring-states period (403-221 BC).

Today, at the Xiuying Leprosarium, traditional Chinese medicines and acupuncture are combined with the antibiotic rifampin and sulfone drugs to try to arrest the disease. Province-wide surveys continue in order to detect new cases.

Reconstructive surgery for deformities and plastic surgery to deal with infections and burns, which occur because victims' nerves are damaged and they can't feel pain, are also performed on a small scale. The youngest patient here is 13.

Cured lepers live in five-metre-square mud-and-wattle homes with thatched roofs and work in the fields or the lumber yard, or at the brick kiln. In 1982, the average per capita income for recovered patients was about $26. The state provides some additional subsidies.

Patients who want to marry must be sterilized first, even if they are fully recovered. The arguments given are that any chil-

A Dai minority-nationality woodworker prepares a beam in Manjinbao, a village just outside Jinghong, the capital of Xishiangbanna district, abutting Laos and Burma.

dren would be unfairly stigmatized, and that there is no guarantee that genetic problems can be avoided.

Whatever the cause of the malady, China is trying to wipe it out. The second national leprosy conference, held in Guangdong 14 months ago, set as its target the year 2000.

TAISHAN — For the vast majority of the 200,000 people of Chinese descent living in Canada, the delta riceland surrounding this county seat in the southern province of Guangdong is the ancestral home.

The laborers who for one dollar a day built part of what later became the Canadian Pacific Railway, the miners in the Fraser River gold rush, the young men who later opened restaurants and family laundries — nearly all trace their origins to this county seat and the handful of adjacent rural districts.

Mostly single men of peasant stock, they left poverty, pestilence and bandits for an uncertain future across the Pacific.

The first group of 300 Chinese came to Victoria in 1858 on charters arranged by companies in San Francisco and Hong Kong. According to the recently published book *From China to Canada*, the Chinese population in what is now British Columbia reached between 6,000 and 7,000 by the early 1860s.

Some of these people had moved north from Oregon and California, where they had labored in gold-mine construction gangs and on railway projects. The 1885 Royal Commission on Chinese Immigration reported that 15,701 Chinese had entered Canada in the three and a half years leading up to June, 1844. Fully one-third were from Taishan and most of the rest from adjacent counties.

On a good day it takes two river-ferry crossings and a bumpy five-hour car trip to reach Taishan from Canton, the capital of Guangdong province. Although bustling with activity, generated by the estimated $30 million (U.S.) that flows in each year from overseas remittances, it is one of those sub-tropical places where the mildew and mold begin to grow on the Mediterranean-style arcades as soon as the cement dries.

Kang Pan, the director of the Taishan Overseas Chinese Affairs Office, says, laughing, that there are as many Taishanese living outside China — about 900,000 — as there are living in the county. His great-grandfather, grandfather and father all made the trek to the New World. Mr. Kang's father is buried in the United States, and a brother and a sister live there.

For Mr. Kang, the overseas connection is a proud one. The story of the first Chinese settlers in North America and their progeny is one of perseverance, courage and hard work. One nearby village alone, with a population of less than 1,000, boasts 25 clansmen living abroad who have earned doctorates.

"You see," Mr. Kang says, "many descendants of those who left are university professors, customs officials, engineers and even designers of rockets."

One of the Taishan descendants who made good is Vancouver-born Thomas Mah. After 35 years of banking in British Columbia he came out of retirement to open the Bank of Montreal's representative office in Peking.

Mr. Mah's grandfather, a merchant, and his father were born in Taishan and even today Mr. Mah, 57, retains the singsong dialect of his forebears. Swamped in the work of starting the Bank of Montreal office, Mr. Mah has not yet visited Taishan.

"I will at some time, though," he says. "It's like searching for your roots. . . . Like anyone, I guess, I'm interested in going back to see where my forefathers came from. That, I imagine, would be very interesting."

When he does go he will be welcomed with open arms. But it wasn't always so. Following the victory of the Communist forces in 1949, the overseas connection became dangerous, particularly during the Korean War and later during the Cultural Revolution, when foreign ties of any sort were violently opposed.

Huang Zaihua, now 84, was suspected of being a fifth columnist. At the age of 15, he left Taishan to join his father in Buffalo, New York, where he attended Public School Number Thirteen and Hutchinson High School. Later he graduated from Columbia University. He remembers a visit to Toronto: "When I went there it was just a small town, like Buffalo, but I think it's bigger now."

He returned to Taishan to teach English and set up a technical school. Thirty years later his foreign-tainted past caught up with him.

"For six years they put me to hard labor," he says in impeccable if halting English, which complements his dapper dress

319

and neatly trimmed moustache. "They thought I was a spy. I wasn't. But what could I do?"

Today Mr. Huang lives simply, a revered old man who is president of the Overseas Chinese Association. "I'd like to visit America, but I don't think I'm strong enough," he says.

As the Chinese in Canada became merchants, shopkeepers and tailors, they formed clan associations. The major function of one of them was to collect the bones of deceased Taishanese and ship them to China for burial.

By the turn of the century some of the Chinese in British Columbia had begun moving eastward. By 1911 there were 200 Chinese living in the Maritimes.

A feeling that Chinese immigrants were displacing Canadian labor fuelled discriminatory measures including a head tax of $500 on Chinese immigrants.

Most of the men who arrived before 1900 were brought in on consignment and worked off their indebtedness for passage. More common later was the so-called chain migration, whereby some returned home to marry and then came back to Canada, while others simply arranged passage for their families and relatives.

The number of Chinese peaked at nearly 47,000 in 1931, only to drop to about 35,000 a decade later.

Direct migration from China to Canada dried up in 1949. It was not to be restored until 1974, following agreement on a family-reunification program reached a year earlier. Last year between 4,000 and 5,000 Chinese emigrated to Canada.

Tensions between Vietnam and China were a regular feature for *Globe and Mail* journalists starting with John Fraser in 1978 who reported on the first border battles between the former Communist allies. In July, 1983, Oziewicz travelled to the inaptly named Friendship Pass on the Sino-Vietnam border and found that during the lulls between armed exchanges, it was "a generally placid setting". He even discovered that the bridge at the Friendship Pass had been used for a recent prisoner exchange. However, the railway line that used to link the two countries was now overgrown and when there weren't actual armed incidents (235 in one five-month period during 1983), both sides bombarded each other with massive barrages of abusive propaganda.

Su Yun, one of the nine Zen Buddhist elders at the Shaolin monastery, Henan province.

The pressing social issues during Oziewicz's tour of duty in China were birth control and law reform, both of which were weighed down with frightening problems, seemingly negating any possibility of comprehensive reform. Faced with the prospect that the Chinese population will pass 1.2 billion by the century's end, the government started requiring women with two or more children be sterilized. A little later, the one-child family became the official ideal and the government backed up its intent with harsh economic penalties for those who wanted larger families. China, as officials reported to Oziewicz, is paying a heavy price for Chairman Mao's neglect of this issue for 20 years.

For a nation that had few codified laws, China surprised many observers with a new-found commitment to law reform. Partly this arose out of economic necessity as hundreds of foreign firms vied with one another to enter into contractual relations with various institutions in the People's Republic. A whole set of commercial laws had to be created. Also, the Chinese leadership made bold statements about the need for a rule of law in order to prevent a recurrence of the "lawless" Cultural Revolution. As Bryan Johnson reported earlier, the trial of the Gang of Four was, among other things, to symbolize the new rule of law, and numerous Chinese officials were mystified at the negative reaction it aroused outside their borders. Nevertheless, the government persisted in its attempts to improve the country's legal framework and it was even prepared to consult with outside experts. Oziewicz talked to one and he had a complicated tale to tell.

PEKING — On almost every front, China is bursting with developments. The speed and frequency with which some things are taking place make it difficult to take them all in, let alone analyze them.

Hundreds of new publications, from science-fiction magazines to fashion catalogues, are swamping the post offices where they are sold. Though limited in scope and freedom of expression, new plays and films are enjoying an efflorescence seldom seen before. In sports, Chinese teams are travelling the world. Some do well; others, not so well. But at least they're out there.

Much catching up must be done in science and education and, within constraints, much is being accomplished. In industrial and technological expansion, seldom does a day go by without the announcement of some achievement.

It would be easy for a more cynical Westerner to belittle the importance of these developments, but that there are changes taking place is not questionable. Whether they endure is another matter, one which in large part depends on the securing of a legal code that would limit government by might or whim.

Jerome Cohen, part-time academic, full-time lawyer, has been studying Chinese law for more than 20 years. "I started to study Chinese on August 15, 1960, at 9 a.m. Now, at that time, people who were kind thought I was having a nervous breakdown. . . . Certainly law didn't seem to have much relevance to understanding China. Some of my colleagues thought it was misplaced: 'Law has no place given the Chinese tradition and the Chinese Communist Party's attitudes and the Nationalist Party's attitudes. What are you trying to do?' "

He didn't answer the question right away. But he did go on to become professor of law at Harvard Law School, director of East Asian Legal Studies and assistant dean. Today he toils for a New York law firm, advising mostly business clients on commerce in China. Along the way, he's become perhaps the most knowledgeable Westerner on the Chinese legal system and the current era of law reform.

Mr. Cohen has studied the blooming of interest in law in the fifties following the Communist victory. And he watched from afar its withering in the sixties and seventies.

"The current era of law reform — you may even balk at the phrase — interest and activity is certainly not the first, even in the People's Republic, involving a world-wide search now for what the best legal reforms might be."

In this, the demands made upon the tiny number of people talented in legal matters has been enormous in the past three years.

"When you think of the centuries taken by most countries to develop a legal system and the difficulties law reformers face, the first thing to recognize is the immense labor of an intellectual as well as political and economic nature, etcetera, that a relatively small number of people have been engaged in since the third plenum of the central committee in '78.

"And they've made some real progress."

He enumerates some of the developments: the criminal code,

A street vendor (left) and some of his cohorts in Jiaji, Hainan Island.

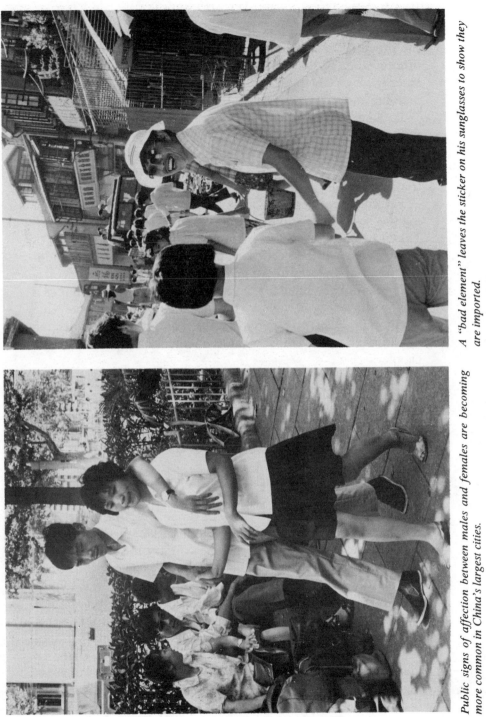

Public signs of affection between males and females are becoming more common in China's largest cities.

A "bad element" leaves the sticker on his sunglasses to show they are imported.

the code of criminal procedure, reorganization of the court law, the procurators law and local government law. Work has also proceeded on civil-economic laws, dealing with taxes on foreign enterprises, principles of joint-ventures, patents, corporate banking and so on.

To some extent, these civil-economic laws have a distinct utilitarian aim. In opening its doors to the West and seeking outside investment, China had to provide predictability for buyers and sellers. Otherwise, how do you run a highly industrialized economy?

The challenge is to somehow make it all work. Even assuming the best of intentions, there are some very real constraints. Take just one, for example. How do you train the millions of lawyers that will be needed when there are only several hundred thousand places for all higher education each year?

Once a fully codified law is in place, the real test is whether it will be allowed to become a victim of the political process. In a totalitarian society, the party and the police have a predilection for unilaterally deciding what is in the best interests of the people.

For some, the current period of law reform is a charade.

"Will the leadership appreciate the legal system even when it feels the pinch?" Mr. Cohen asks rhetorically.

"So far, we have mixed results on that. And we may have to refine our generalizations, depending on what field we're talking about."

All statistics in China boggle the outsider and none more than the vast size of the rural peasantry. Every *Globe and Mail* correspondent posted to Peking has had to live with the singular fact that 80 per cent of the population lives in the countryside, and in Oziewicz's time that meant eight hundred million people. Each correspondent knows that the majority of his time is spent in the cities and it was only recently that it has been possible to branch out and get a surer feel of the source of both China's endurance as a nation and the occasion of its greatest problems. In a final series of articles before he handed over the bureau to Allen Abel, Oziewicz tackled the issue forthrightly, trying to set the lot of the rural peasant against the broad background of the dramatic changes in policy that promised to affect the future of China profoundly.

PEKING — Stooped over a hoe in a dusty field or knee-deep in paddy-muck, the Chinese peasant represents an apparently timeless picture of tranquillity. But behind the image, an economic and social transformation is effecting an upheaval in the lives of eight hundred million peasants.

With rural reforms conceived and set in motion four and a half years ago by leader Deng Xiaoping, farmers are breaking away from the restrictions of collective agriculture in favor of family farming.

Free at last from the yoke of Maoist policies on rural development, they are being told that individual initiative is the key to enriching themselves, their families and, in consequence, the country as a whole.

Most peasants have experienced an unprecedented rise in their standard of living as the changes have accelerated. Per-capita cash income has more than doubled, to 270 yuan (peasants also have grain, vegetables and meat they produce themselves). The equivalent of $200 (Canadian) a year may not seem remarkable in the affluent West, but it is in rural China, where there are still pockets of dire poverty and unspeakable privation.

What's more, the per-capita figure multiplies to more than $1,000 for a family, and with this swift rise the peasants are clamoring for more durable goods, from bicycles to radios, television sets and washing machines. Ninety per cent of the nine million television sets in rural China have been purchased since the new policies came into effect.

Another indication of the new consumerism is that peasants are using their increased savings — they hold about two-thirds of the country's money supply — to buy farm machinery and build new and better housing.

The ranks of the *wanyuanhu* (households with an annual income of 10,000 yuan) are increasing, with the attendant problems of such success: the envy of neighbors and the backlash from Party and government cadres still steeped in Maoist fundamentalism, to whom "rich peasant" remains a term of abuse.

If the income figures are impressive, so are the gains in production. Agricultural output value grew at an annual rate of 7.5 per cent in the four-year period 1979-82, compared with 3.2 per cent in the 26 years from 1953, when the first Five Year Plan began. The 1982 grain harvest was a record 353 million tons.

Even that does not tell the full story, because unfettering the industriousness of the peasant and permitting private enterprise has generated sideline enterprises and crop diversification while spurring food processing, textiles and other light industries. Under the liberalized regulations, China has more than 44,000 free markets (comparatively free of state price controls) where peasants can sell their surplus farm produce and crafts.

"It is there for everyone to see," a *China Daily* commentator said of the boom. "The peasants are producing more from their land, and not only from their land. Their productivity has increased, they have more marketable commodities and higher incomes, and are, in general, much better off."

The change in the approach to rural development began after the important Communist Party plenary session in December, 1978, which consolidated the strategies of Deng Xiaoping.

"It was finally realized that the good intention of getting everyone to move ahead at the same pace — which is the essence of egalitarianism — cannot but result in nobody moving at all except at the slowest pace," the *China Daily* declared this spring in a three-part series on agricultural reform.

The grain output for 1978 was nearly three times that of 1949, when Mao Tsetung triumphantly stood at the rostrum at Tiananmen Square to proclaim the founding of the People's Republic of China. Yet, with a population increase of three hundred million (partly because of Mao's stubborn rejection of Malthusian concepts), people were eating no better. Some were worse off. The national per-capita income in 1978 was still only 70 yuan, and nearly one quarter of the country's commune members earned less than 50 yuan a year.

"In 20 years," a specialist lamented, "the communes failed to give their members much more than a bare subsistence in 80 per cent of the five-million-odd production teams. . . . It was clear that the peasant had to be given a break."

The state doubled long-term low-interest loans, agreeing to raise the prices it paid farmers by 20 per cent and 50 per cent for produce above quotas. Private plots and livestock raising were encouraged. A cottage industry and country fairs, once derided as remnants of capitalism, were allowed to flourish.

These changes, though significant, were nothing compared

Unemployment stands at twenty million, but expensive consumer goods are attractive to young people.

with the policies that came in their wake, policies that are re-shaping the lives and livelihoods of one quarter of the world's population.

The first was the discarding of the work-point system in favor of *zeren zhi* (responsibility system), whereby peasants sign con-tracts with production brigades to deliver a fixed amount of whatever the household produces. They can keep the surplus or sell it, either to the state at premium prices or at free markets. If they do not reach the quota, the difference must come from their pockets.

More than 90 per cent of China's production brigades have scrapped collective labor for the new system, which represents a triumph for material incentive. "Those who work harder and manage better now earn more," said one official, who in an earlier era would have been relegated to cleaning latrines for such an observation. "And hence the peasants' enthusiasm and rural prosperity."

The other change is the deliberate withering of the people's communes as Mao envisaged them when they were created in 1958. In last year's revision of the constitution, the 55,000 communes were stripped of their administrative functions and left only with their economic roles. Political power has reverted to the *xiang* (traditional rural township), which was abolished when farmers were collectivized.

The most liberating aspect of this development is that there is less meddling by bureaucrats in farm production. Peasants now generally determine what crops are best suited for their land, and how much and what kind of fertilizer to apply.

Despite the enthusiasm the reforms have generated, worrying trends have appeared.

Some intransigent local officials, discontented because their careers are in jeopardy and critical of the new policies as a be-trayal of Maoism, have been harassing farmers who are becom-ing relatively well off. To counter the obstinacy and obstruc-tion, the state council finally had to issue a decree ordering that judicial organs protect peasants whose tractors, trucks and other equipment were being seized by leftist zealots.

In some places, envious poorer peasants inspired by Robin Hoods are enforcing their own brand of Communism by steal-ing from the enterprising rich. The fact is, one third of China's eight hundred million peasants still have annual incomes below the figure Peking regards as the subsistence level.

Agronomists are also sounding the alarm about disappearing farmland. China has to feed one quarter of the world's population on less than seven per cent of the world's cultivated land. Less than 11 per cent of its territory (it is slightly smaller than Canada) is arable, and this is being eroded precisely as a result of increased wealth. Farmers who are doing well want to build bigger and better houses, as well as buildings for sideline enterprises.

Another serious — perhaps the most serious — contradiction has to do with population. What China does not need is more people, but the reforms give an immediate and direct financial advantage to any family that can increase its labor power.

Most Chinese are eating better today than they were four and a half years ago. But how many more people can the land feed? And what innovations will see them through the end of the century, when by the most conservative estimates their number will reach more than 1.2 billion?

Allen Abel with basketball player Mu Tiezhu, who is seven and a half feet tall.

CHAPTER ELEVEN: 1983 to the present

ALLEN ABEL

The Globe and Mail's eleventh correspondent posted to Peking is Allen Abel, 33, who went to China straight from one of the most popular sports columns ever written in Canada. Born in Brooklyn, Mr. Abel studied astrophysics at Rensselaer Polytechnical Institute in Troy, New York. Eschewing an obvious career in science, he started working with small New York State newspapers, eventually ending up at *The Globe* in 1977. In 1980 he won a National Newspaper Award for a series of articles from the Soviet Union.

Part of Abel's reputation as an astute observer of life and as a distinctive stylist is based on his finely honed sense of irony. This has served him well in the China that he discovered, starting in September, 1983. It is a China where the Deng Xiaoping leadership is well entrenched and hand-picked colleagues were busily experimenting with the cumbersome machinery of the state bureaucracy and central planning.

Abel found himself viewing more than his fair share of contradictions: a widening of the overtures to the outside world at the same time as a new campaign was mounted to combat "Western spiritual pollution"; stricter adherence to new laws on many levels at the same time as hundreds — perhaps thousands — of "well-known hooligans" were publicly executed after perfunctory trials; a growing foreign-policy frustration with the United States' relationship with Taiwan at the same time as President Ronald Reagan staged a highly successful visit to the People's Republic; further measures to rescue the body politic of China from the capricious whims of one-man rule even while yet another re-evaluation of Chairman Mao informed the Chinese masses that, all in all, the Great Helmsman was a good comrade after all.

For Abel, the taste of irony came early in his posting, when he witnessed the official opening of a fancy "Western-style" restaurant with a famous French name.

PEKING — Maxim's de Pekin, China's first belle-epoque beanery, opened its lacquered and gilded doors last night to the accompaniment of glasses tinkling and cheeks being moistly kissed.

Through the portal poured a tidal wave of the bourgeois decadence that one million Red Army fighters gave their lives to expel. It was a melange of haute cuisine and high snobbery reminiscent of the foreign concessions of the thirties. On this glittering night in the People's Republic, there were no hot dogs or Chinese allowed.

In a salon roofed by mirrors and bordered by impressionist murals, fashion designer Pierre Cardin inaugurated the facsimile of his famous Paris restaurant by reviewing troops of Chinese waiters who were fitted out with tuxedos, bow ties and a few words of French.

Outside, on a midtown boulevard that might fittingly be renamed Capitalist Road, hundreds of bedazzled comrades stared silently at the scene, blinded by the luminescence of the guests. Uniformed police and a prix-fixe tariff of 130 yuan — about $75, or two months' salary for some workers — kept the masses at bay.

But Mr. Cardin sang the Red China Blues and claimed that he would lose money on the operation, which is to be accompanied by a string of boutiques that will proffer cut-rate Paris originals to any Chinese Don Juan or damsel brave enough to be seen in them.

Said the couturier, to accusations that Maxim's might be a bit pricy for the middle kingdom: "It is not expensive! This isn't a restaurant, it's a factory."

Most of the opening-night clientele, like all of the restaurant's fixtures, carpets, furniture, lighting and artwork, had been flown in from Europe and the Americas — the bejewelled beneficiaries of what the state council calls "China's long-term, unchangeable, strategic principle to persist in the policy of opening to the outside world".

Only the waiters and the hostesses were home-grown, the

latter shimmering visions of satin, feathers and makeup, adornments that, a few short years ago, would have been enough to arouse angry condemnation on any Peking street.

(The new correspondent of *The Globe and Mail* wore an astonished expression and an Yves Saint-Laurent belt.)

It was not until 1981 that the Communist Party acknowledged that "the appreciation of beauty is not a bourgeois element", opening the path to foreign instrusions that would, after all, be visible mainly to foreign eyes.

The opening last spring of the Jianguo Hotel, a replica of the Holiday Inn in Palo Alto, California, was a first step toward high-tech tourism. Maxim's de Pekin, drowning in diamonds and Pouilly-Fuisse, is a quantum leap.

To the self-employed merchants who share Chingwenmen Avenue with Maxim's, the opening was further verification that the rigid, isolationist policies of the Maoists are as stale as yesterday's *gratin dauphinois* (scalloped potatoes). The site is, by day, a teeming corner of the old Legation Quarter, across the street from the stately Xinqiao Hotel and a billboard that shows a running tally of the casualties in Peking's unceasing war of autos, bicycles and pedestrians. In August, 47 died.

Claiming one small square of sidewalk yesterday was old Mrs. Wang and her trusty bathroom scale. The price of a weighing is two fen — a Canadian copper. For every 4,000 customers she hangs in the balance, Mrs. Wang can eat one lunch at Maxim's.

But Mrs. Wang said she wouldn't want to: "I'm not a bad cook myself," she said. Her plans for Monday dinner: "Steamed rice or wheat cakes, and maybe a few vegetables."

A cobbler who sells his sole on the same corner was equally unimpressed. "To tell you the truth," he said, "I'd rather eat Chinese food than that French stuff."

The shoemaker may get a chance to change his mind. A bargain-basement annex to Mr. Cardin's chowhouse called, naturally, Minim's, will open in a few months with omelets, quiche and other necessities priced at only a yuan or two.

Although the Chinese traditionally have shown a preference for things garlic over things Gallic, a passion for the Continental seems to be gathering momentum. This was evident last evening on the Capitalist Road, when Mr. Cardin's limousine

drove up and its occupant was met by one of his Chinese waiters who beamed and said, in perfect Parisian, "Ah, bonsoir,
madame."

As for contradictions, in the space of three months Abel reported
on the extraordinary ideological decline of the famous model
commune at Dazhai — the commune Chairman Mao personally
declared to be the "pace-setter" for all of China — as well as some
after-thought revisions to the official propaganda line on the role
of Chairman Mao himself. The legacy of Mao continues to be a
highly volatile inheritance for the Communist leadership, and the
conflicting use made of his memory and his deeds is perhaps the
most trenchant tribute of all to his role in Chinese history.

DAZHAI — The words echo from the pages of an old magazine:
Chairman Mao is our great savior, he is dearest to all of us. We
act on whatever he says. When Chairman Mao put forth the
principle of self-reliance, we fought heaven and earth with our
bare hands. . . .

It is a report from the members of Dazhai Brigade, supposedly written in 1969 by "the poor and lower-middle peasants" of a
tiny, backward, luckless village elevated to the status of a shrine
when the savior spoke five high-toned words. "In agriculture,
learn from Dazhai," Mao Tsetung said in 1964. Stripped forci-
bly of choice and conscience, the nation complied.

For 15 years, until it was admitted that the productivity of
these poor people was a deceit concocted by the village leaders,
and that the People's Liberation Army, not men's hands, had
moved heaven and earth, pilgrims came by the thousands,
marching the 40 kilometres from the nearest railhead behind
red banners and portraits of the dearest deity. Hotels were built,
songs sung, plays presented, tracts quoted, conferences held.

The peasants of Dazhai (pronounced "dodge-eye") were
displayed to visitors in purposefully patched jackets, hustled all
across China to speak at Learn-from-Dazhai meetings, lauded
in high places. The mastermind of the sham was made a member of the Politburo: he attended sessions wrapped in a laborer's
turban. The few hundred householders of an ugly plateau in
Shaanxi Province emerged from their whitewashed cave dwell-
ings as toilers one day, heroes the next.

In Dazhai today, in a round-roofed compartment carved from Tiger Head Mountain, sits Song Liying, 53, the wife of a stooped, deaf man who was one of the village leaders in 1963. That year, after a flash flood stripped Dazhai valley of its top-soil and the villagers faced famine, the peasants created new, fertile fields from the devastation by hauling rocks and digging terraces. Mao's call commemorated this act; the fantacisim of the Cultural Revolution perverted it.

"We didn't ask to be praised," Song says. Above her on the wall are old photographs of Mao and a framed portrait — half-hidden by a new Panda-brand television — of the late Premier Chou Enlai.

"In general," she continues, "the movement to Learn-from-Dazhai was the call put out by Chairman Mao and Premier Chou. When all the reports of our production started coming out, we knew something wasn't right, but we were just poor peasants. Some of the reports were quite false; others were influenced by ultra-leftism. . . .

"I went to meetings in Hunan and Shandong provinces. They made me get up and talk, but I didn't know anything."

Neither did the rest of China. Not until 1980, with Mao dead and a new group in power, was it revealed in *The People's Daily* that the grain production of Dazhai had been exaggerated by three hundred million pounds. No one was blameless. Deng Xiaoping, the commander now assiduously dismantling the communes, was the key speaker of the 1975 Learn-from-Dazhai conference. According to a report of the session he "was greeted by outbursts of stormy applause".

So was the turbaned fictionalist Chen Yonggui, the brigade leader who concocted the statistics. Chen today is a minor cadre at a farm near Peking. His son has been charged with multiple rape and his daughter is said to have committed suicide.

Once, long before the chairman's call, others in the hamlet considered self-destruction the only escape. An old peasant named Liang, who entertained Chou three times in his family's cave, tells of being reduced to beggary at the age of seven, of neighbors too poor to give the most meagre of alms, of people "who would go up on top of a ridge, take the cloth they used to bind the women's feet, use it as a blindfold, and jump off."

On those ridges now, while other counties suffer a severe

337

drought, there are irrigation tanks feeding elaborate sprinkler systems that water the terraces of Dazhai, the legacy of the army engineers who manufactured the miracle. Productivity is said by village Communist Party officials to be high by provincial standards, though short of the levels invented by Chen and his cohorts.

The announced policy of the Dengists, as reported in the Shaanxi provincial newspaper, is straightforward. The basic intention of the Central Committee is to make the peasants rich as quickly as possible. The means to this end is the "responsibility system", under which each family sells an agreed amount of produce to the state and reserves the surplus to peddle for profit. The current standard of wealth is $1,000 a year.

But Dazhai did not embrace the new arrangement until 1982, leaving suspicions that leftism still has its allies in these hills. There are some vestiges of the old allegiance. On a wall of the deserted conference centre remains the painted slogan: "Carry Forward the Red Banner of Mao Tsetung Thought."

"We owe our better life to the Party and Chairman Mao," Liang says.

"Things got better here year by year under their leadership. When Dazhai became so famous after Chairman Mao issued his call, we were happy. So many people came to see us, they covered the hills. We knew there were lies, that some things that were said about Dazhai weren't true — that is a fact, I cannot argue with that. But we are not embarrassed now. What happened to Dazhai was not decided by ordinary people like us."

The village's new Party secretary, Zhao Shuheng, blames the Cultural Revolution, a scapegoat that no longer can kick back.

Per-capita income in Dazhai in 1983 was only $240, barely one quarter of the national goal. In rural China, richness is a relative thing. A herd of penned deer on Tiger Head Mountain is shorn of antlers twice a year; the dried product, pulverized as a medicine for sluggishness, brings in $360 a pound, to be distributed among the 20 shareholders in the enterprise and the county treasury. From that treasury last month came $3,000 to buy television sets for all 126 households of Dazhai.

In Song's domicile, the new gizmo flickers; her brother says they turn it off only when the network leaves the air. The lady of the house is peeling a Macintosh apple. Asked what she

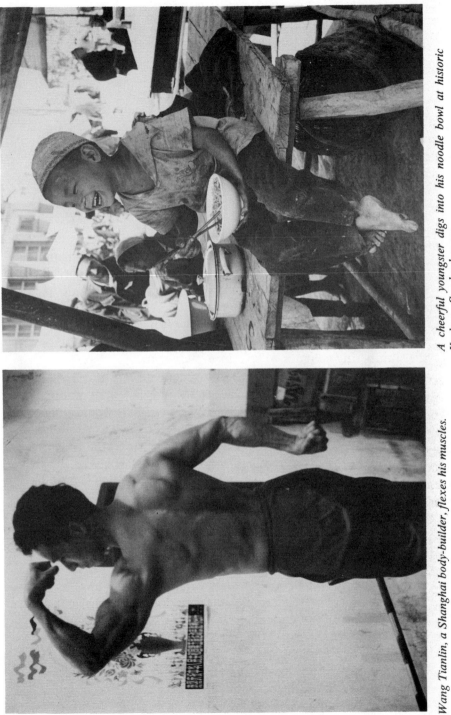

Wang Tianlin, a Shanghai body-builder, flexes his muscles.

A cheerful youngster digs into his noodle bowl at historic Kashgar Sunday bazaar.

thinks China has learned from Dazhai, Song looks up from her juicy work. "I guess," she says, "we learned that nobody's perfect."

I am lost in dreams, untrammelled dreams of the land of hibiscus glowing in the morning sun. Mao Tsetung in "A Reply to A Friend," 1981.

PEKING — The Great Helmsman is 90 years old today, a waxen mummy lying peacefully in an exhibition hall while lesser men strive to recast his enormous legacy to suit their immediate needs.

Once the deified ruler of more adherents, willing or otherwise, than any other lord in history, Mao Tsetung on this chilly anniversary is enjoying something of a mild renaissance, revivified as a soldier, philosopher and poet, his later, demonic excesses conveniently dismissed.

Meanwhile, his successors tiptoe through a political minefield fearful of touching off the explosion that might awaken the slumbering colossus.

"Without Mao Tsetung," an announcer intones during the amnesic film biography of the late chairman that went on public display last week, "the Chinese revolution would have groped in the dark for many years. . . . Here was a man who left his home town, his wife and children to serve the revolution, whose brothers were killed, whose wife was executed. . . . He was a human being who laughed, who wrote poetry, a fine calligrapher . . . a man who made mistakes, yes, but whose merits far outweighed his demerits."

Forty-eight years after he gained command of the Chinese Communist Party at the Zunyi Conference, seven years after his death, Mao has returned with a flourish to the headlines and movie houses, and a nation wonders what to make of it.

Across the country, seminars and meetings are being held to discuss, according to one report from Mao's native province of Hunan, "how to develop Mao Tsetung's theories under the new historical conditions".

Yet the new conditions — relative stability and prosperity, with a minimum of fanatic political display — are seen by the current leadership to have come about as a result of throwing

"The best little ballpark in Peking" is a diamond that knows neither pine tar nor tobacco juice.

most of Mao's economic and political theories into the garbage can.

What is left, then, is Mao the Genius of the Peasants' Revolution, architect of People's War — "when the enemy attacks, we retreat" — and lesser, more benign incarnations of the man.

There is Mao the Artist — three new editions of his collected penmanship will be issued today. Mao the Patron of Minorities. Mao the Statesman whose courtship of Richard Nixon, according to one scene in the film biography, was the first step in opening Communist China to the Western world. That it was Mao who had slammed the door in the first place is given no mention at all.

In fact, the 80-minute film, designed to hammer the prevailing assessment of Mao into young comrades who were born long after his "mistakes of later years" spawned a decade of violence and misery — ends for all practical purposes in 1959, except for that brief glimpse of the Chairman with Mr. Nixon 13 years later.

The Great Leap Forward, the Great Proletarian Cultural Revolution and other catastrophes are nonexistent. Mao at 90, it seems, has been dead for 30 years.

"A film about Mao's own life would be more difficult to make and would also be much longer," one of the screenwriters, Gao Weijin, tells a Peking newspaper. "It is true that the Cultural Revolution is not shown in pictures, but we do say in the narration that the errors he made in the latter stages of his life caused great damage to the cause of the Party and the people."

Still, pictures outweigh words and so the cameras roll, with full pages of snapshots of the Chairman in all the newspapers in recent days. Here is Mao trying on funny hats proffered by beaming ethnics; here is Mao lolling, belly-up, in the foamy surf; here and there, discreetly in the background but unmistakeable, is Deng Xiaoping, smiling at the master's shoulder, his years of disgrace invisible, as if the new, littler helmsman had had the imperial blessing all along.

The most effective new depiction of the late Chairman — more striking than the newspaper treatises or the stultified biography — is another film entitled *Crossing the Chi* (purple) *River Four Times*, a dramatization of a deftly executed portion of the Long March that kept Mao's Red Army one step ahead of

Chiang Kaishek's annihilation campaign in the early months of 1935.

The director cast a veteran actor named Gu Yue as the young, slim Mao, and the likeness is uncanny — a perfect double, down to the mole on the chin, but without the Great Helmsman's squeaky voice. When the audience glimpses Gu for the first time, it gasps as one, as if in the presence of a ghost.

In this motion picture, the transformation of Mao from the senile progenitor of the Ten Years of Chaos to a figure of mythic dimensions is made complete. This is a new, late-model Mao — China's George Washington — donating his shoes to a barefoot trooper, marshalling his starving, frost-bitten men, outwitting the smug, contemptuous Chiang, whose every appearance on the screen brings forth hoots of delighted, villainous glee from all corners of the darkened auditorium.

But this is the work of cinematic illusion and the real Mao is a body in a glass case. ("The remains," says a spokesman for the Propaganda Department of the Central Committee of the Chinese Communist Party, "are very well preserved.")

This morning, he will be visited by several hundred high-ranking cadres, Deng and his allies among them, the first official callers at a reworked mausoleum that, as long rumored, takes even the physical remnants of the chairman down a deeply suggestive peg.

Added to the tomb in Tienanmen Square have been the artifacts — but not the already scattered ashes — of three other venerated revolutionaries — Premier Chou Enlai, Marshal Zhu De, and Vice-Premier Liu Xiaoqi.

But there are limits to the revisionism. Liu, long vilified, has just recently been rehabilitated (posthumously), but Lin Biao, the "close comrade at arms" who once described Maoist philosophy as "a spiritual atom bomb of infinite power" and then was supposedly blown to smithereens by a conventional rocket at the Chairman's behest, appears in neither the movies nor the monument, erased from life and death.

The rotund ex-chairman Hua Guofeng, once Lin's successor in the intended succession, is said by party spokesmen "to be suffering from sickness", though they will not confirm reports appearing in foreign journals that claim Hua has attempted suicide and failed.

Jiang Qing, Mao's third wife — by some reckonings his

343

fourth — remains in prison. Asked if Jiang is aware of the activities planned for her late husband's birthday, Gao Liang of the Propaganda Department says with a sly smile, "She gets all the daily papers."

Compared with the gargantuan rallies once staged to honor the Chairman's deed and thought, the ninetieth anniversary will pass with a modicum of notice. A massed youth chorus of 10,000 voices is to convene at the Workers' Stadium on Thursday and there are to be less tuneful convocations of various study groups and academicians.

Mao Anqing, a surviving son of the Great Helmsman once reported to be mentally ill, has resurfaced to write a tribute to his dad in a literary journal; another son by Mao's second wife — a woman later executed by Chiang's forces — was killed by the "imperialist U.S. aggressors and their running dogs" in the Korean War.

Four postage stamps will be issued at Shaoshan, the Chairman's home village, and the biographical film will be shown tonight on national television, but no parades of adulation are expected.

As John Lennon and Paul McCartney prophesied 15 years ago, "If you go carrying pictures of Chairman Mao, you ain't gonna make it with anyone anyhow."

Sleeping now in yellowed contentment, wrapped in a crimson flag, the chairman is oblivious to the gentle commotion that the turning of the calendar provokes. Even so, the man from the Propaganda Department promises that it will be another 10 years before such notice is taken again. It is the Chinese custom, he advises, to honor anniversaries in multiples of 10, not a contrivance to fit current political purposes.

Meanwhile, a billion subjects surge onward. Their helmsman is gone to the land of hibiscus and no living man knows when he'll be back.

One doesn't have to be a prophet to safely predict that the fate of the British Crown colony of Hong Kong will be one of the most dramatic stories from China for the rest of the nineteen-eighties. The moment the Chinese government announced it intended to re-establish its sovereignty over the island of Hong Kong and the adjacent parcels of mainland ruled over by the British, the political agenda for the Chinese and British governments, not to mention the people of Hong Kong themselves, abruptly changed. The key date is 1997 when the first of what the Chinese call "the unequal treaties" expires, but the denouement is expected to come much sooner.

In a series of articles, Abel looked at some of the smaller players in the unfolding drama, starting with a Sunday match at the exclusive Hong Kong Cricket Club and ending with a visit to the little restaurant of a feisty small-time Chinese entrepreneur.

HONG KONG — A bright Sunday morning at the Hong Kong Cricket Club finds the defenders of the empire 45 for five and sinking fast. This is a simply awful score, but it gets worse. Now a young officer named Ian strides to the bat, gesticulates feebly at an off-spin delivery and is bowled out, first ball. In a distant corner of the verdant scene, an old retainer adjusts the scoreboard: 45 for six.

"Oh dear, at this rate we'll be all out before lunch," a woman named Margaret says from the gallery, where she has been sipping tea and eating digestive biscuits. "Tell me, Ian, did you even see it?"

"That's the sad part," says the failed batsman, skulking toward the clubhouse. "I did."

And these are the weekend woes of Hong Kong's Britons while five million Chinese colonials await 1997. On a close-clipped oval on a plateau called Wongnaichung Gap, two teams of imperialists bat about a red-rimmed ball in unsoiled whites, forming themselves into teams of Nomads and Vagabonds and Wanderers, testimony to their itinerant status in a land soon to be surrendered by the Crown.

Opposing the British forces this particular morning is a group of expatriates who call themselves the Optimists. One could search long and hard through Hong Kong these days to find 12 Chinese who warranted the appellation.

"We're under no illusions," a currency broker named Neil Smith is saying, sitting under a fringed umbrella near the club's cerulean swimming pool. "They don't like us here and we know it. No nation likes to be ruled by foreigners, least of all the Chinese, whose lords and masters all through history have always been the same color as themselves.

345

"It will be easy for us to get out. We've got a long history of scuttling. It's like my mum was just saying, this is nice, isn't it? Sittin' on a rock 8,000 miles from home while everyone back in England is freezing. We know we're on borrowed time here and that this place exists only at China's convenience."

The Smiths of North Yorkshire have been resident in the colony for three years, long enough, Mr. Smith says, for him to come to understand the gathering fears of the outpost's five million Chinese. Taken in the Opium War of 1842, lost to the Japanese at Christmas, 1941, at horrible cost to British and Canadian defenders, Hong Kong is to revert to China 14 years from now, though there are those who doubt that public order can be maintained that long.

"Last week, when the typhoon signal went up," Mr. Smith says, "I think we got a taste of what might happen — people shoving and punching in bus queues, the panic buying of food — and that was only for a rainstorm. When the currency (the Hong Kong dollar) fell below 9.50 to the U.S. dollar a few weeks ago, the same kind of things were happening at the banks and in the markets, and I was close to telling my family to pack up and go back to England. There's going to be a backlash against Gweilos here, I'm sure of that."

The Gweilos are what the Cantonese call the ruling round-eyes of the colony, a governor and councillors appointed by Whitehall and almost unaccountable to the broad masses. A recent attempt to install democracy, the direct election of some members of district boards, has been exposed as a rather hollow exercise. According to a report prepared by one of Hong Kong's two English-language television stations, only two per cent of the population voted in the elections and only six per cent had even bothered to register.

When several of the newly elected members were asked on camera to state the duties and objectives of their jobs, they answered: "It slips my mind," or "I really don't know."

In Hong Kong now, as always, money wields the real power, and when the dollar staggers, as it did drunkenly before government intervention fixed its ratio last week at 7.80 to the U.S. dollar, the colony teeters with it. Mr. Smith, the currency broker, says that several of his Chinese colleagues have already moved their savings off-shore and "arranged for foreign passports".

"There was no reason for the Hong Kong dollar to crash on the basis of economic data alone," the broker says.

Hong Kong has come out of the recession better than most of the rest of the world, but there is a difference here. In Britain or Canada or the United States, the ordinary man in the street is far removed from what his currency is doing. But here, every taxi driver and every *amah* can tell you what the value of the dollar is down to the decimal point. There are five million gamblers in this city and at the moment they don't like the odds.

Neither, it would seem, do the British forces, who are not about to try to keep the colony by force. China holds not only an inexhaustible, if outmoded, army, but the key to nearly all the food and water that fuels the mercantile maelstrom of Hong Kong. More closely akin to colonial quirks such as Gibraltar or the Panama Canal Zone than to the Falklands, Hong Kong is a fly in the world's most sensitive ointment, a "problem left over from history" that embarrasses a Chinese leadership that sees itself as the rightful leader of all the newly independent nations of the Third World.

The last thing the Peking government wanted to hear was Prime Minister Margaret Thatcher allude, as she did recently, to the fact that had it not been for the Communist giant poised over it, Hong Kong would have been granted independence long ago and would have become another "Singapore". And the surmising by one Hong Kong newspaper last week that Mrs. Thatcher might use Hong Kong as a Falklands-style rallying point to cover the embarrassment of her scandalized Cabinet brought no joy either. It threw cold water on the rest of the local press, which, in the absence of anything substantial, had declared the latest round of Sino-British negotiations to be proceeding with uncommon amity, all on the basis of a smile flashed by one of the Britons at the Peking airport.

But even the patriots of the Hong Kong Cricket Club will brook no talk of mounting the guns at Boundary Street and holding out for England. In the grandstand beside the manicured oval where the Forces are losing thickets of wickets, the wife of one naval officer is asked if there has been talk in military circles of mounting one last stand for Queen and Empire.

"Oh, no, I couldn't say that," the woman says. "At least I

couldn't say it in public." As she chuckles, a houseboy comes silently shuffling over with a tray of tea.

HONG KONG — In a little shop on the north side of Boundary Street, a bustling lane that marks the extremity of British territories no longer new, a man named Andy Yu sits surrounded by tanks of tropical fish and waits for his deliverance.

Some time on a summer's day in 1997 — or sooner, should either British resignation or Chinese impatience prevail — the People's Republic will take possession of this colony and make of Andy Yu and his guppies and his goldfish what he already believes them to be: Chinese from top to tailfin.

The merchant is one of Hong Kong's five million, a population already given over, 14 years before the deadline, to varying degrees of apprehension, eagerness and outright fear.

"Some people are very afraid," Mr. Yu says. He is seated on a folding chair, the fish tanks stacked above him to the ceiling of the tiny store. "But me, I say why be afraid? I'm just one of the little people of Hong Kong. I don't think that there's anything that I should be afraid of. It's the people who have a lot of money who are really scared.

"I'm Chinese, right? If they come in and tell me I can't sell pet fish any more, that's fine with me. I'm sure they'll arrange for something else for me to do. Too many people around here think that their country is just some little island called Hong Kong. But they're wrong — our country is all of China."

These are the brave words of a capitalist and patriot at a muggy noon on the line of demarcation. It is 123 years this week since the Qing imperial government, its gilded palace put to the torch by British and French invaders, signed the convention of Peking, ceding to Britain all lands south of what now is called Boundary Street. Later, in 1898, China leased to Britain for 99 years still more land, the New Territories, in a treaty whose approaching expiry has rekindled, here and in the government chambers of London and Peking, some of the flames of the Manchu palace that burned in 1860.

While British and Chinese officials resumed their periodic, secret, sometimes acrimonious and apparently stalemated negotations in Peking this week, the colony barged boisterously on.

It lurched through the imprisonment on fraud charges of one

of its most prominent real-estate wheeler-dealers, a gargantuan display of fireworks that lured a million viewers to the docks of the peerless Fragrant Harbor, and the pegging of the local currency to the tail of the U.S. dollar after a period of instability that saw the Hong Kong unit lose 20 per cent of its free-market value within a few days. A force-8 typhoon came through on Friday to add to the festivity.

But now, at lunch time, things are quieter — too quiet, in fact, in the Gong Gum Restaurant on the south side of Boundary Street, directly across from Mr. Yu's aquarium. For a time, as the 1997 issue metamorphosed from a mere spectre into the hard shell of reality, it was thought that China's designs on the colony might end at this unexceptional avenue, leaving the island and the rest of the Hong Kong peninsula to continue under British administration.

That was a mere fantasy; *The People's Daily* now speaks of "the Chinese government's firm resolve to recover the entire Hong Kong area and its irrevocable decision to resume and exercise its sovereignty over Hong Kong."

These are not comforting words to the ears of Lam Man Kit, whose little restaurant is devoid of occupants save himself, his mother, a yawning waitress and a reporter who is refusing an offer of a plate of indeterminate victuals. Mr. Lam, it turns out, is not at all worried about 1997. Like many other Hong Kong residents, he plans to be long gone before the treaty expires.

"Don't misunderstand me," Mr. Lam, a 30-year-old whose family has been in Hong Kong for three generations, says. "I like Hong Kong. I grew up there. But nothing is clear any more. The newspapers and the television are not clear. They tell us don't worry. Everything will be all right. Calm your heart. But still we worry. Every time there is any bad news, my mother goes out and buys all the rice she can.

"People here like to enjoy life. They like to go to the horse races, though I can boast to you that I am not one of those people. But then we think about how China rules its own citizens, and that people there are not able to enjoy life. So, in two or more years, we are going to the People's Republic of Dominicana."

Mr. Lam and his mother will not be the only ones who quit the territory. Already, two travel agents have been jailed for offering bribes to U.S. immigration officials in exchange for entry visas that would then be sold to a desperate public. At an appliance store in a brand-new shopping district along the Kowloon waterfront, a salesman reports that "half the people who come in here buy a lot of stuff and say ship it to Australia".

No such commands issue from Andy Yu. The shopkeeper says he hopes to continue in business but is ready to do the bidding of the "responsible comrades" of Peking. In the fish store, Mr. Yu explains that he was in fact born in the People's Republic, in a small village in Guangdong Province, but that his family "walked out" when he was two months old, in 1953.

"My mother told me that they did not like the government of China at that time," Mr. Yu says, "and so my father made the decision to come to Hong Kong. But now my father is dead and my mother is an old, old woman and it is I who make the decisions. There are many things I do not like about Hong Kong. The people here think of money first, which is all right, but they also think of money second and money third. To me, other things are also important, such as freedom and my country. I say, let China come."

Come it will in 1997, by which time Mr. Lam may have learned the correct name of his prospective homeland — the Dominican Republic on the Caribbean island of Hispaniola. His sister already is there, enjoying what Mr. Lam calls "a calm and happy life." Though nothing could be calmer than this deserted restaurant, the exodus will not be stalled.

"My sister," Mr. Lam says, "had some love problems in Hong Kong and was very sad here. She moved to the People's Republic of Dominicana and fell in love with a native. Now she wants to marry him, and she says that she earns good money and that we should come and join her and open a little supermarket. So we will go, because I think that when the Chinese come, the people of Hong Kong must give up many happinesses."

In 1979, the Chinese government decided to attempt a bold experiment. Risking both the possibility of defections and an unsettling of the fragile domestic accord, it permitted and subsidized thousands of its brightest students to study in North America, Europe and Australasia. Like previous Chinese reform-minded adminis-

An actor performs in the Monkey King drama for inmates of the Peking prison.

trations, Communist and non-Communist, the government wanted results fast and in its drive to modernize the ancient land, it was prepared to assimilate the problems such a large-scale and unprecedented initiative promised. A new sight was seen on many Western campuses as the Chinese students actually began to show up. Four years later, in an astute act of enterprise reporting, Abel started interviewing some of the students who had studied in the West and had returned home. The picture that emerged was, as is usual in China, not entirely clear.

PEKING — "On my first night in America," the former student said, "I could not sleep. I stood by the window all night, looking down, waiting for someone to point a gun and shoot me. . . ."

It is the voice of a young man recently returned from the outside world, one of the thousands of Chinese permitted by a progressive government to study in a foreign land, to be immersed in foreign ideas. Sent abroad as the privileged vanguard of their homeland's modernization, the students return — most of them — to a country whose leadership seems to strain their knowledge from the rest of their experience and then return them to the closed society whose isolation has been one cause of its own backwardness.

"We were in Los Angeles and I asked my teacher to drive through the slums of Watts. I had heard that the blacks were always shooting each other down there. I said: 'I want to hear the sound of gunfire.' Finally, he agreed to take me. I said: 'Stop the car. I want to get out and look around.' He said: 'Are you crazy,' and kept driving as fast as he could."

Like the other young men and women interviewed privately for these articles — an application to meet returned students on an official basis was rejected by the ministry of foreign affairs — the adventurer who yearned to hear the crackle of ghetto gunfire was eager to share his experiences on the condition that no mention be made of his name, home town, place of employment, position, the university attended or even his course of study.

The need for secrecy embarrassed some, frustrated others. It inspired in one young man, asked if he found the West to be freer than his Communist motherland, the reply: "Yes, yes, the straight answer is yes. But it's more complicated than that. We ourselves would often ask that question and try to analyze it. What is freedom? We were all brought up in China and have learned to adapt ourselves to the Chinese situation. What is freedom? You can go to New York and, yes, you are free, but you are restricted by fear."

"I guess I was one of the first to go abroad," said a fellow who studied in Canada in the mid-1970s, when the People's Republic still was in the grip of the white-boned demon Jiang Qing and her heinous Gang of Four.

"What did I know about Canada? Well, Dr. Norman Bethune, of course, because of Chairman Mao's essay, and we had learned in school about Indians and immigrants, and we knew that Canada was an agricultural country because they were already selling wheat to China at that time.

"But we didn't get much preparation. All I remember is that they brought us to Peking for a month of training and the ones who were going to Canada got an extra 100 yuan to buy a heavy coat and some boots. There really wasn't any political training but they took us down to Henan Province to see the great Red Flag Canal and to meet some peasants so we would get to know our own country before we went abroad. They were clever enough not to say that the West was very, very bad — they knew that we were going to be able to see for ourselves."

Another student recalled the selection process in his home city: "I was in one of the first groups to go overseas after the Cultural Revolution. Some people from the ministry of education came to our school and announced that there would be a written test and that the ones who scored the highest would be going abroad, to England and other places.

"They said you had to be under 21 to take the test and so, the first time, only five people showed up to try it. That wouldn't do. So then they invited everyone and that's how I got my chance. I was rather innocent and naive. I figured, even if I failed, it was no big deal because I would still be a university student in China and that was pretty good in itself.

"The first test was very strict and decided purely on merit, mostly translations and English comprehension. After that, it got more complicated as more and more people wanted to go. I heard about people like the mayor's son trying to pull strings to go overseas. Another girl passed but failed the physical test — they checked your liver and things like that — and she went running around all the hospitals, trying to find someone who would say that she was all right.

"They didn't tell us anything about the West. I remember arriving in London and the person who met us said we'd have to take the underground into the city. He handed us some money and dashed through the stile and headed down the escalator and we were just left standing there with this strange money in our hands, confronted by this baffling ticket machine, not having the faintest idea what to do."

The establishment of formal diplomatic relations with the United States expanded the educational horizon enormously. Mesmerized by the sudden turnabout by a government that for three decades had been the sworn enemy of American imperialism, U.S. institutions opened their portals to Chinese scholars, offering fellowships and grants-in-aid. On Chinese campuses and in government offices, the rush for places began.

One man, already established in a government department, remembered the day it was announced that staffers would be eligible to compete for places at a university in the U.S. Midwest: "They asked who would like to take this exam. Everyone in the office signed up. I said: 'That's just great. Now who's going to administer the test?'

"There were many reasons why people wanted to go. Some were very serious about their studies and thought it would make them better at their job when they returned. Some were seeking purely material things. They wanted to see the richness we had heard about.

"But I found it much the same way in the States. Some were in college to get a good education and others were just there for the parties — this puzzled us very much. Myself, I could handle it both ways. I studied hard but every day at 3 o'clock everything shut down for 'General Hospital'."

Every *Globe and Mail* correspondent posted to China has been struck by the conflicting demands placed by the Communist authorities on "the intellectuals". The word itself covers just about everyone who has ever got beyond middle school. Alternately oppressed and pampered, they can be the cruelly treated butt of a national propaganda campaign or the venerated front-runners of a newly proclaimed national revival. Few Chinese citizens better typify the ups and downs of the intellectual's plight than the veteran poet Ai Qing, who found himself reviled during the Cultural Revolution after a lifetime of commitment to the forces of radical change in China. In the post-Mao era, he was rehabilitated with much fanfare, only to find himself being used as a standard-bearer in the latest propaganda campaign, this one being an effort to combat "spiritual pollution".

There are people who think you don't need "inspiration" to write poetry. They are probably people who advocate artificial insemination, but they are unlikely to be poets. — Ai Qing.

PEKING — The old man mounting the barricades of art is the half-blind poet who calls himself Ai Qing. At 73, his vision wrecked by 16 years of enforced rustication — his punishment for earlier crimes of creativity — the prince of Chinese poetry is on the winning team now, defending the People's Republic from the alienated, humanitarian, individualistic school of thought that the leaders label "spiritual pollution".

Bombing no barracks, invading no islands, China turns inward and launches an assault on the minds of its own citizens. In the press and on radio and television, the battle rages, a struggle against "bourgeois ideology, which promotes the principle of benefiting oneself at the expense of others . . . and other decadent ideas". Included in the latest official list of pernicious abstractions are works that deal with "human nature and love".

Ai Qing (pronounced "eye ching") once wrote a poem to love — "to your lips that kissed me; to your face, warm and soft, the color of earth" — but that was 50 years ago, the blandishments of a child given away by his parents to the wet-nurse who suckled him. Now, the New China supplies not only nourishment for the body, but demarcates the limits to which the brain may be fed. Deng Xiaoping calls it "appropriate stipulations with regard to what bourgeois ideas should be prevented from spreading".

An earlier campaign against those who thought incorrectly — or thought at all — came to be known as the Cultural Revo-

355

lution, but Ai Qing, who was made to clean latrines on a farm in distant Xinjiang, vows these mad excesses will not be repeated. Neither, he says, will there be a reprise of the betrayal of the "Hundred Flowers" movement of the late 1950s, when Mao Tsetung encouraged artists to express themselves freely and then punished those who took him at his word.

"I was recently in the south of China," the poet is saying, called to a "free exchange of views" with foreign journalists on behalf of the Chinese Writers' Association, of which he is vice-president. "I was told that down there, more than 20,000 kinds of plants are grown. So you can see that we have many, many flowers blooming in China. But some of them are plastic flowers, some of them are false flowers, and some of them smell very badly and make your nose run."

"In this campaign," Ai Qing is asked, "will any writers be arrested?"

"No one will be arrested," he answers. "We will offer comradely advice. Can I order someone to stop thinking? At most, we will say to a writer, 'This is not healthy.' Whether he accepts the advice or not is his problem."

"But Mao had writers arrested," a reporter persists.

"My friend," replies the prince of poetry, "Mao is dead."

For 20 years, from his banishment in 1959 as a "rightist" to his rehabilitation in 1978, the readers who had admired Ai Qing's hymns of the proletariat thought he, too, had gone to the grave. (Ai Qing's real name is Xiang Haisheng; he changed it while living in France in 1930, when a hotel concierge confused him with Chiang Kaishek.) Throughout his confinement, broken only by two trips to Peking to see surgeons about the cataracts on his eyes, he continued writing — "a man never stops thinking" — but these poems were never published. When his work re-emerged in a Shanghai newspaper after the long silence, he received hundreds of letters from people who had given up on him; he wrote to them, "I have managed to survive, like a walnut lost in some small corner."

The rehabilitation was complete; after two decades in the cultural and geographic desert, Ai Qing was permitted to make a tour of universities in the United States. In New York, in the "electric canvases" of the Museum of Modern Art, he found:

The epitome of materialism
Some will enter the halls of heaven
Some will drop into the pits of hell
And the goddess of Liberty
Is no more than a likeness
Standing alone
On an island out in the harbor
Gazing on vacantly, watching this great city.

Preferable, in the poet's view, was Iowa City on the fertile prairies:

A corn-popping town. . . .
like a village maiden
soft spoken and hard-working
who rarely gets to go to Chicago
even though it's not very far.

This is the world as seen by Mao and his successors: the noble peasantry, mutely laboring; the wicked city, seething with intellect and incontinence. Part of the current campaign against "spiritual pollution" is a struggle to keep out of China the most virulent of the "capitalist germs" that might be in the same cargo hold as the grain and gear and greenbacks the country desperately needs. These "germs" include pornography, punk music, bizarre fashion, the material things that, in Deng's words, "degrade the standards of social conduct and corrupt the people".

But the campaign targets more than dirty books and Mohawk haircuts; it reaches now into the recesses of conscience and leaves it for the state, not the artist, to decide which works contribute to "socialist spiritual civilization" and which ones "preach bourgeois free democracy, individual emancipation and individual struggle".

One of the veterans empowered to draw the line is the old poet with one eye that sees. (Another is the younger poet He Jingzhi, who says the campaign is "a bath to cleanse the spirit".) The war against "spiritual pollution" is to occupy the proletariat while a three-year process of "rectification" is under-

357

gone by members of the Communist Party. *The People's Daily* and various theoretical journals speak these days of little else.

"Pollution," says Ai Qing, drawing on a cigarette and a metaphor, "is all right in small quantities. If the air in a room is generally clean and someone lights up, well, he does not frighten you. But it may be that so many people are smoking, it affects your breathing. And there may be some people who have never smoked before, and so it affects them greatly. In society, those who smoke and those who must breathe the smoke are victims just the same.

"This pollution generally comes from outside the country, but this does not mean that we will abandon our open-door policy. The door is already open, and we hope that there is fresh air coming in, but it is inevitable that some dirty air will come in as well. So we must differentiate between clean air and pollution.

"We don't want to exclude the influence of foreign literature from our culture. While growing up, I myself was influenced by foreign things. I read Shelley and Byron, books about romanticism, books about symbolism, Pushkin and Hugo, and I can say I benefited a lot from those books. But in recent years some people have translated in an unselected way, and I've been told of books that are pornographic.

"I myself have read books about sex, and they haven't done any harm to me, but I know that young people are reading these things and they are at an impressionable age. There have been many cases of rapes and killings in China; well, the purpose of art is to reflect life, but rapes and killings are only a small part of life. Some of the young people may have read about these things and followed the example. China has punished some criminals very heavily, and people have shouted 'China is so inhuman.' But what is human about rape and murder?"

So far, no writers have been known to give their lives in the cause of bourgeois abstraction. More typical was the recent case of the modernist Peking artists who were denied permission to display their works; at the same time, an exhibition of Picasso oils and graphics was being shown at the Peking Art Museum, on loan from the French government in the name of international friendship.

But the campaign seems to be heating up. In the Guangxi Autonomous Region in the far south, the propaganda department of the local Party committee has ordered a thorough search of all bookshops and magazine stalls, having found that "the atmosphere is polluted and the souls of young people are poisoned". The Party called for the "criticism and education" of people found to be selling impure materials, and said that "extra-heavy punishments must be meted out in particularly bad cases".

In Shanghai, a crackdown on stage performances has begun after the discovery that local organs were diligent in collecting taxes from theatres and music halls "without bothering about the contents of the performances". The Party found that "even some Chinese novels of gallantry published in Hong Kong, which are not allowed into China, have been adapted and rearranged for performances on the stage".

Closer to the evil and as yet unliberated Hong Kong, a stage show in a Canton hotel was closed by the Public Security Bureau after two singers "intentionally revealed their thighs" during a performance. Fines and "unspecified sanctions" were imposed on the performers and the hotel's compliant management. The importation and copying of Hong Kong and Taiwanese "yellow music" is a booming underground industry.

It had been thought that China, so assiduously welcoming foreign things, might not trace this route again. Five years ago, having finally been freed from the dusty wasteland that had been his prison for so long, Ai Qing wrote "To Welcome So Bewitching a Spring":

She is here, really here
You can smell her fragrance,
You can feel her warmth. . . .

It was the spring of China's open door, but now it has been decided that some Chinese have become too rapturously bewitched. The result is a campaign against invisible enemies, waged in newspaper exhortations and "criticism" sessions. The old poet, called to the battlements, has walked both sides of the wall; he says, "I fear nothing any more. I was in exile for 20 years. I do not have that long to live again."

He brandishes the cigarette and exhales the wisdom of the exile. "Nobody can decide what goes on inside the mind," Ai Qing says. But in the eighties, China keeps trying.

There is no neat conclusion to an account of a still-functioning newspaper bureau. In the fall of 1984, Abel is still in Peking. Contradictions are expected to continue, as will the fascination in the West for the Chinese way of doing things. Earlier in the year, President Reagan made his important first trip to the People's Republic.

"Tousled by the storm winds of a nation he once derided for its reliance on 'the idiocy of Karl Marx'," reported Abel, "President Ronald Reagan stood bareheaded yesterday under the Communist flag and a band of liberation fighters played the 'Star-Spangled Banner'. Behind him, on an intemperate and weirdly scripted afternoon, sprawled the Great Hall of the People and beyond that, in the fields and factories of China, lay, as always, the billion untapped customers of the 50 huckstering states."

In exploring the ironies accompanying President Reagan, Abel approached one of the ubiquitous army sentries guarding the foreigners' compound, and asked him if he ever thought he'd see the day when Tiananmen Square would be "wrapped in red, white and blue to greet the New American Right".

"In China," replied the soldier, "anything is possible."

WHERE ARE THEY NOW?

Frederick Nossal:
Mr. Nossal moved to Hong Kong after eight months in Peking in 1959-60 when the Chinese government refused to renew his visa. He wrote a book about his China experiences called *Dateline — Peking*. After working in Toronto with *The Globe and Mail*, he returned to Hong Kong as a correspondent for the Toronto *Telegram*.

Mr. Nossal died in the autumn of 1979 in Belgrade, where he was attending a meeting as an information officer for the World Bank. He was 51.

Charles Taylor:
After leaving Peking, Mr. Taylor, now 50, spent a month in a Hong Kong hotel writing the first draft of *Reporter in Red China*. He spent another month in Vietnam before joining *The Globe and Mail*'s editorial board. He covered the Arab-Israeli Six-Day War and opened the paper's Nairobi bureau in 1967.

Today, Mr. Taylor helps to run the E. P. Taylor operations, whose jewel is Windfields Farm, a world-renowned thorough-bred-racing-breeding complex. Former chairman of the Writer's Union of Canada, he continues to write. He is the author of *Radical Tories — the Conservative Tradition in Canada*.

David Oancia:
Mr. Oancia, now 54, left China for Spain. Returning to Canada, he joined *The Montreal Star* as a writer. He later served as director of journalism at Concordia University in Montreal and director of the University of King's College School of Journalism in Halifax.

For about a year he was publicity director for the University of New Brunswick. He lives in Fredericton, where he has returned to writing full-time.

Colin McCullough:

Mr. McCullough, 54, publisher of *The Victoria Times*, is the author of the book *Stranger in China*. He was *The Globe*'s London columnist in 1972-73, and later was named assistant publisher.

Norman Webster:

Mr. Webster, 43, *The Globe and Mail*'s editor-in-chief since August, 1983, worked for a year at the *Winnipeg Free Press* following his tour of duty in China. He also wrote four books for schools entitled *Discovering Today's China*. When he returned to *The Globe* he was Queen's Park columnist from 1974 to 1978. He was appointed assistant editor in 1981 following two and a half years as the newspaper's London correspondent.

John Burns:

Mr. Burns, 40, left *The Globe and Mail* following his Peking posting to join *The New York Times*. He was a *Times* correspondent in South Africa before being appointed Moscow bureau chief. His new posting brings him back to Peking as head of the *Times* bureau there.

Ross Munro:

Mr. Munro, 43, joined *Time* magazine in Hong Kong following his stint as *The Globe and Mail*'s Peking correspondent. Mr. Munro remained in Hong Kong, covering Southeast Asia for *Time*, until the summer of 1983 when he was reassigned to the magazine's Washington bureau.

John Fraser:

After returning from China, Mr. Fraser, 40, wrote *The Chinese: Portrait of a People*, which was chosen as a Book-of-the-Month Club main selection for January, 1980. For two years he wrote a national column and was then appointed *The Globe*'s National Editor. In July, 1984, he and his family moved to London where he is *The Globe*'s European correspondent.

Bryan Johnson:

Mr. Johnson, 35, returned from Peking to *The Globe and Mail*'s Toronto office where he is a feature writer and sports columnist. He maintains an avid interest in Southeast Asia, where he occasionally travels on assignment.

Stanley Oziewicz:

Mr. Oziewicz, 32, is now *The Globe and Mail*'s religion reporter. He lives in Toronto. In January, 1984, he covered the North American visit of Chinese Premier Zhao Ziyang, who was the first premier of a Communist country to address a joint session of the Senate and House of Commons.

Allen Abel:

While he was living in China, Mr. Abel's book *But I Loved It Plenty Well,* was published. His Peking posting has given him the opportunity to write about Pope John Paul II's visits to South Korea and Papua New Guinea. He is 34.